Through My Eyes and Into Your Heart

Yvonne Betts *With* Gary Betts

DORRANCE
PUBLISHING CO
EST. 1920
PITTSBURGH, PENNSYLVANIA 15238

Dorrance Publishing Co
585 Alpha Drive
Suite 103
Pittsburgh, PA 15238
Visit our website at *www.dorrancebookstore.com*

ISBN: 978-1-6853-7066-4
eISBN: 978-1-6853-7913-1

Through My Eyes and Into Your Heart

DEDICATION TO
THE SECOND BOOK

With much love, I would like to thank my wife, Yvonne for making the ultimate sacrifice so that this book could be written. She knew that she must die so that her spirit could help me in writing my first two books. When she was stricken with liver cancer, she did not fight it. She died with dignity on March 2, 2010, less than a month after it was first diagnosed. Then she crossed over into Heaven. Ten months later, two novels were completed. Yvonne's bravery and her insight will not be forgotten.

Gary Betts

DEDICATION TO THE FIRST BOOK

Three years ago, Colleen Cook began to teach us about the spirit world. Since then, under Colleen's guidance, both of us have evolved into a partnership of Yvonne's spirit and Gary that was able to write our first three books. Colleen is not only our friend and confidant, but she is also the driving force behind our books. This one being the first. Without her, our books would not exist. We have a deep affection for Colleen, with a love that even death will not end.

Yvonne and Gary Betts

Table Of Contents

FOREWORD

One of the questions that has dogged human civilization from their very roots is God. Do we look like him? Will he destroy us if we sin too much and then send our souls to hell? Then we get more questions. What does Heaven really look like? And how do spirits really act?

Religions going back to beginning of ancient cultures, have attempted to guide people with answers to these questions. But they have incorrectly used the fear of God to keep their people in line. "You will burn in hell for eternity if you sin." "You will be cast into eternal torture if you do not attend church." "You will..." Well, you get the picture.

God is not like that. He loves all of us and would not harm a hair on our heads. There is no hell. There is no devil. But there is a Heaven that is home to God and all the spirits. This book will show humanity for the first time what Heaven is really like. How spirits really behave.

This is done through the eyes of Yvonne Betts who was chosen by those in Heaven to write this novel. Her body died on March 2, 2010, and her spirit crossed over into Heaven shortly after. Yvonne will take you on a tour of the real Heaven. She will tell you everything she has seen, heard, and felt in her Heavenly experiences through me, her husband.

Put on your seat belt, throw out all your Earthly ideas and laws. You are in for the trip of a lifetime. This is the real Heaven as seen through the eyes of a real spirit.

Gary Betts

CHAPTER ONE

Life After Death

When Yvonne's heart finally stopped in Room 402B, sixth floor, Tower D at Victoria Hospital in London, Ontario on Tuesday night, March 2, 2010, her spirit was released. She now looked like a grey whiff of smoke. Yvonne climbed down unto the floor and gave her body of forty-seven years one last look. It was sad to see her body that way, but she had a good idea where she was headed. And that made her happy. She looked around the dark room lit only by a small light over the bed of her sleeping room mate.

Then she saw a grey translucent curtain that penetrated the darkness. On the other side were shadows. The curtain gradually disappeared revealing her mother, Jean, and Yvonne's seven spirit guides. They appeared in human forms to give Yvonne some comfort. Jean appeared as the proper English lady she once had been. She was pushing eighty years, but still had a face that hinted at nobility. The lady was close to six feet tall, a slim build, and had short grey hair. This woman still had a certain charm about her.

Jean smiled and lovingly said in an English accent, "Welcome home, dear."

She walked up to her daughter and revealed, "You must cross over now."

Jean and the spirit guides then changed over to their natural forms looking like fog over a warm pond or just a whiff of smoke. And Yvonne, too.

Spirits did not speak in any language. They communicated by silently exchanging thoughts.

Yvonne nervously asked, "You mean Heaven?"

Jean explained, "Some call it Heaven, the Other Side, God's

Place. But it's all the same. Yes, dear, that's where you are going."

Jean led Yvonne toward a shimmering hole in the room's wall. It was square, six feet by six feet. And it was black. But when they walked through it, they instantaneously entered a bright silent place. Everything was white and it was flooded by bright white lights. The first thing that caught Yvonne's attention were silver orbs darting all over. Some went in wide arcs. Others moved at ninety-degree angles. They were very fast, but there was no way to tell how fast because there was no time or space here. These silver spheres were high-level spirits. They were of different sizes, with the larger ones at higher-ranking levels.

Yvonne saw that there was nothing familiar to her. To her physical life, that is. No trees, no rocks, no water, no food, no furniture. And to her dismay, no board games to play with her mother. Heaven was not a world or even space. It existed beyond God's Universe in a different dimension for eternity as a home for the spirits.

There were small lights buzzing around Yvonne. She smiled as her memory of Heaven was starting to return. These lights were blinking on and off like fireflies, and were about the same size. Except these creatures dazzled with reds, greens, blues, yellows. Some playfully nudged Yvonne as they welcomed her back home. These were spirits that had chosen to become the mischievous little imps that lived in many worlds. They were called by various names, depending on the world. On Earth, for example, they were known by such names as a fairy or a leprechaun.

Yvonne walked around with her mother. They passed several spirits who always greeted her in friendly ways through thought. They passed a creature that had three legs, purple skin, large white wings growing out of its back, and wearing a long white gown.

"Yvonne asked, "What's that, Mom?"

Jean replied with a laugh, "That's an angel. They take on the shape of the world they come from. There are countless worlds in God's Universe, and you can visit them all. Your memories of this Place will return in a few moments."

Jean then stopped and seemed to be listening to something. Then she disclosed, "I've got to get going. I've got a hearing to attend."

"A hearing where God judges you?" Yvonne questioned.

"God does not judge any soul. And the angels can judge souls on only two different occasions," Jean pointed out.

Jean carried on, "Your spirit guides will stay with you until you feel more comfortable. Just walk at your own pace and look around. There's no pressure. Not right now, anyway. I love you."

Then Jean was gone.

Yvonne continued to wander around with her spirit guides in tow she came upon a spirit in front of a porthole. She quizzed the spirit, "Are you going some place?"

The spirit, also a female, responded, "I'm between lives on a planet called Obliiv. I've been debating what I want my new life to be like and what lessons I want to learn. So, I'm visiting a world where there is no animal life, just vegetation. It's a nice place to go to relieve stress."

Yvonne confided, "I've just returned from a life on Earth and somethings still seem new to me."

"That's what happens when a life ends on a planet. It's hard to let go of your old physical life and embrace your real life in God's Place."

"Is that another name for Heaven?"

"No. Heaven is another name for God's Place. That's what God named all of this when he created it."

"Can I ask just one more question, if you have the time?"

The spirit laughed and pointed out, "There is no time in God's Place. That's the hardest thing for a former physical life to understand. Ask away."

"We actually have the freedom to plan our lives on other worlds?"

"God has given us enormous freedom. We alone can decide what world to go to, what lessons to learn, the form we will take. Even our mother. It's a wonderful experience."

Yvonne thanked the spirit who then stepped through the porthole.

Yvonne walked some more, and she could feel her knowledge of Heaven returning to her. That's when she realized that Heaven was her true home where she truly belonged.

One of her spirit guides approached Yvonne, "We sense that you have finally come to terms with your life in God's Place. Is this true?"

She happily replied, "Yes, it's true. I feel really at home now and I don't need your assistance anymore."

"Thank you. We have another spirit that we must accompany to Earth for his new life there. But if you need more help..."

Yvonne interrupted, "I know. All I have to do is ask and another spirit or angel will immediately appear."

CHAPTER TWO

Visiting Other Worlds

Yvonne was starting to grow accustomed to her new sur-roundings, but Heaven was not really new to her. She was beginning to remember when her soul had joyfully roamed her home as she and her kindred mate prepared for one of their many lives together on Earth. And she realized that her mate would join her very soon to start the process all over again. Except that their next life will be far different than all the others. Gary was already gathering the souls of each child that will become theirs in their new existence on Earth. It will be an unusually large family with each member displaying special talents that will change the world.

With her spirit guides gone, Yvonne became curious and asked for help

Helen, another spirit guide appeared. Yvonne asked her, "I'm curious. Can I visit other worlds?"

Helen smiled and replied, "Of course you can. Do you have one in mind? Maybe Earth?"

Yvonne divulged, "No. I want to visit some place new."

"As you wish," Helen remarked. "Follow me."

She led Yvonne a short distance and stopped. Helen had a single thought, "Melbe."

There was no wall, but the familiar shimmering hole ap-peared again out of nothing. It was six feet by six feet and black in the middle.

"How can that be?" Yvonne questioned. "A hole can't exist where there's nothing."

Helen patiently answered, "Yvonne, you are still thinking like a physical being. You will very soon come to think like a spirit, and all this will make sense."

Helen carried on, pointing toward the hole, "This is a porthole that can carry us instantly to any world in God's Universe. Some worlds are inhabited, others are not. But we can visit them all."

"Melbe?"

"We have designated each world with a name that we can pronounce. Even though spirits can talk to the people of other worlds through thought, the names they have given their planets are impossible to pronounce and remember. Even with thought.

"This planet that I have chosen is in a galaxy near the edge of God's Universe. It travels around a star about the size of Earth's star. But I don't want to give too much away."

Yvonne followed Helen through the porthole onto the green soil of Melbe. Yvonne almost jumped back through the porthole when she saw the inhabitants of this world. They were pink in colour. They walked on two legs and had two arms, but their heads were between the legs. The face was featureless, except for a single round hole. They wore clothes that bore a metallic shine but were as loose as cloth. Their garments were of different colours and shapes.

Helen laughed, "Don't worry, Yvonne. They can't see us or the porthole. And just remember that each one of those bodies has a spirit. A spirit just like you."

Yvonne began to relax. They visited this part of Melbe during the day, but the light from their star was filtering through the atmosphere as orange. Plants grew on the green dirt, but they varied in colour. Yvonne walked over to a large tree. But the trunk was red and felt like smooth metal. Instead of leaves, long thin red spikes hung from the branches.

Helen led Yvonne over to a nearby river if you wanted to call it that. The liquid was orange and thick. It slowly flowed down its course. And this liquid contained life. Yvonne could see a physical being pulling a creature out of the river with a spear. The green creature was as big as a person's head as it struggled in a fruitless effort to survive. It was round and had four tentacles. The only feature it had was a large round hole.

Helen led Yvonne back to Heaven through the porthole.

* * *

"How will I remember the names of all these worlds?" Yvonne asked.

"Spirits, without physical bodies to hold us back, have superior intellect," Helen revealed. "Far beyond any being in God's Universe. The names and descriptions of each world are in your memory and will come to you anytime you wish."

After her Helen left, Yvonne remembered a conversation back on Earth between her human husband, Gary and her spirit daughter, Shirley.

"Are beings from other worlds here?" Gary had asked.

Shirley had replied, "Oh, yeah, they're here and they live among humans."

"Why? To help us?"

"No. It's because they fear humans."

"Why?"

"I don't know. Why don't you ask them after your spirit is released?" Shirley had shot back.

Yvonne reasoned, "I don't have wait. I can find out now why other more-advanced worlds fear humans."

Yvonne mentally went through the catalogue of other worlds and their descriptions. She chose a very advanced civilization that the spirits called Obliiv, remembering the other spirit she had talked to had lived lives on this planet. This world was capable of travel throughout many galaxies, and they closely resembled humans. Plus, they lived very close by in a galaxy that the humans called Andromeda.

Yvonne simply wished to go to Obliiv, and the shimmering porthole appeared. She crossed over into Obliiv in darkness.

She could see nothing but heard sounds coming from the other side of some mountains. She flew over the mountains to find what appeared to be a well-lit military base. Armed guards patrolled the perimeter. There were huge buildings bigger than anything she has ever seen. You could fit a city into one of them. They were a plain silver colour with no doors or windows. She also saw towers that would take her breath away if she had a breath. They were a least three times taller that the former World Trade Centre. They also had the same plain silver colour with no doors or windows.

She went down into the base to get a closer look at the guards. They were covered from the top of their heads to the bottom of their feet in a dark covering where only their heads, arms and legs could be defined. There was no fence or laser beams, but when Yvonne crossed the perimeter, a loud alarm sounded. She heard a voice over a loudspeaker in a strange language. But she was able to hear the thoughts of one of the guards.

He was young and excited. "A spirit has entered."

"Remember your training! No thoughts!" an older guard commanded.

Then the thoughts disappeared. Yvonne attempted to retreat but was forced back by some energy field at the perimeter. She could see a giant black machine rolling her way. It was as big as an arena with a huge black hole in front. She saw different colour sparks inside this hole. That's when she was unexpectedly pulled straight up, over the mountains, into the porthole and back home.

* * *

Helen was waiting for her. "Yvonne, Yvonne. Before you visit other worlds, you must read any warning that is given at the bottom of each description. Obliiv is extremely advanced. They can even detect spirits. They hope to capture one someday."

"How did you know I was there?" Yvonne wanted to know.

Helen divulged, "Angels. There are so many of them and they are very powerful. Angels look after each spirit and sometimes look after physical beings around the Universe. One saw that you were in trouble and simply brought you back to safety."

But Yvonne was determined to return to Obliiv to find out why they feared humans. Why would such an advanced civilization fear a crude race like humans?

Yvonne returned to Obliiv to find answers. This time, it was during the day when she crossed over. She was in a forest. The trees were huge – up to two hundred feet tall – and appeared to have wooden trunks. The leaves were green, but in different shapes. There were no maples or oaks. Just weird patterns – almost like snowflakes. Walking through the woodland, Yvonne found a stream with clear water babbling down its course.

"This looks so much like Earth," Yvonne thought to herself.

But she had to find a town occupied by civilians to find answers. Yvonne flew away from the mountains, this time. The rugged mountains were about twenty thousand feet tall and were beautiful. The peaks were crowned with white glaciers.

She finally came upon a sprawling city. At first glance, it looked like Toronto. Skyscrapers at the centre, with suburbs around the outer edges. But that's where the similarity ended. Yvonne settled down to land in a residential area.

The houses were small square structures about the size of a bungalow, and they stretched for miles. The homes were all the same, made from a grey stone-like material. There were doors, but no windows. Yvonne could see beings entering and leaving them. Streets and sidewalks were absent. The ground, instead, was covered with a rough coating that looked like cement but was softer. She could see beings sink an inch or two into it as they walked. There were no vehicles and no vegetation whatsoever. Not even a single weed.

As Yvonne walked, she came upon what looked like a train, but it was not a train. There were no tracks. There wasn't even a visible route for it to follow. On the side was a script which seemed to resemble a combination of the ancient Greek alphabet and the old Russian alphabet. There were no doors or windows, but when it stopped to pick up a group of people, doors appeared and slid open.

Yvonne rushed to get on board into total darkness. When the doors closed, however, lights sprung to life. The train accelerated very quickly with an extremely smooth ride. There were windows after all, but they were not visible from the outside. Yvonne looked out, but everything was just a mindless blur. The train had to be travelling at the speed of a jet plane through a populated area.

The train quickly decelerated at the next stop. As with the rapid acceleration, there was no effect on the passengers at all. Yvonne got off here. She watched as the train silently sped off toward the towering skyscrapers.

She appeared to be in a commercial area. Beings were scurrying about. They looked very similar to humans, although a bit smaller in height. All of them were bald, with large eyes. A mouth with no lips and two holes where the nose should have been, almost appeared to have been carved out of their faces. The heads were top-heavy with sunken cheeks. Their skin was ash-grey in colour, with short arms and legs. And none of them smiled.

They wore drab clothes, mainly white and grey. Some black. There were no colours at all. As a matter of fact, Yvonne couldn't remember seeing any colours since she entered the city. If it wasn't for the blue sky and golden sunshine, this would have been a very dull place, indeed. One odd thing was that no one wore hats. With bald heads, one would think hats would be mandatory in the intense rays from their star.

The buildings here were a larger version of the residential houses. Again, there were doors, but no windows that could be seen from the outside. These beings rushed around – leaving buildings, entering buildings. It was a chaotic scene. Yvonne tried to communicate with them, but only got a disarray of thoughts. It was impossible to contact a single individual, so she walked back to the suburbs.

It was starting to get dark, and Yvonne was ready to give up when she heard single thoughts coming from a nearby house. They weren't directed at her, but she was curious. She followed the thoughts to a door and just walked through it. It was dark inside, except for a dim light coming from the basement. She went down the stairs and found two beings. They were laying on long chairs with just their heads propped up. There were armrests on the sides. The light was coming from a candle on a small table between them.

One of them jumped up and shouted in a strange language Yvonne could not understand. The other one sat up and appeared to ask a question. The first being said something and then started to communicate with Yvonne thought. There are no language barriers with thought.

"Where are you from, spirit?" the being asked.

"Heaven," Yvonne replied.

"Heaven? Ah, yes, I know about that. I mean the world where you once resided."

"Earth."

"Earth! Our enemy." The being gave a little chuckle and smiled.

"You know about Earth?"

"Only from the mindless propaganda that comes from the government."

"Your race is so powerful, yet you fear a minor world like Earth. Why?"

"Let me tell you a story."

* * *

Intelligent life on Obliiv had been established several thousands of generations before that of Earth. Early in their civilization, these beings, through a series of books, had become exposed to the spirit world. As a result, their early religions had disappeared being replaced by spirits on their planet. They had understood that each physical body had a spirit, while other souls had roamed the planet without bodies. They had befriended the spirits. Beings practising clairvoyance had become famous and wealthy. The people had even got a glimpse into the other side where most spirits had lived, and God had ruled.

But the development of intelligent life had brought warfare. They had been fighting other people for things like land, water, and freedom. But one leader had found out the true reason for wars. His name had been Siel.

Seil was the leader of the largest nation in Obliiv. And it was the only democracy.

One evening in the capital city of Biv, Seil gave a speech to the party faithful that would help to change the course of their history. The speech was given in the huge all-purpose building that every city had. In those days, glass was very important in the design of buildings. But it was a super-glass capable of withstanding any natural windstorms, plus the very occasional meteor or asteroid that struck Obliiv. Buildings and even residential places were simply metal frames with glass.

Seil stood alone on a large round platform in the middle of the building. The building was also round with seats around the platform on the floor and then gently rising almost to the glass ceiling. Two hundred thousand people were there that night. Each seat had a perfect view of the stage. And, despite the lack of any microphone, each person heard every syllable that Seil uttered. Lights flooded the platform from a dark place in the ceiling. As was the custom, Seil slowly turned in a tight circle so that he would face every person in that room.

Obliivians looked exactly like they do today, except for the clothes. Seil was dressed in a bright red top and purple pants.

His shoes were yellow. The beings watching him were dressed in similar colourful clothes. Some smiled when Seil took the stage.

"My fellow citizens," Seil declared as he smashed his right fist into his left palm, "we must end the blood bath that has been going on in Obliiv for what seems like an eternity. Why do we fight? Most people do not like to admit it, but it's because they look different. They are not of our race. But the reality of the situation is that we all are of one single race on this planet. We all are Obliivians!"

Seil was unable to finish his speech because the crowd rose in a deafening roar. They had seen enough of war.

After his speech, Seil summonsed his ministers to his office in the government building. His office was extremely large with the usual glass walls and ceilings. Except this glass was only one way. One could see out, but not in. A special permit was required for this glass. The feeling among the people was that there should be nothing to hide. A huge screen stood in the middle with four sides. It was about twenty feet by twenty feet and was turned off. There was no desk, just a group of long comfortable chairs that his ministers laid on with only their heads propped up. But Seil did not sit down.

Seil remarked, "My speech came across better than what I had thought. Apparently, over 80 percent of our citizens watched. And others from outside nations. Anybody got the poll numbers yet?"

Taf, the Minister of Interior Relations answered, "They've just been released from YZG." He scanned the palm of his hand which had just lit up. "91.672 percent of our citizens agree with you, Seil."

Polling was done instantly when citizens just touched their screens with their votes. The votes were rapidly classified as to a scientific predetermined manner and tabulated to all sorts of results. From the beginning to when the outcome was released, this operation took less time than it did to eat a meal.

"That's what I've been waiting for," Seil announced.

Seil pointed at Jel, the Minister of Peace. "I want you to pull all our troops back within our borders. All space and air vessels will return to base. Water vessels will return to the closest base."

Jel pointed out, "You're taking a big chance here, Seil. We're giving up land, space and water that took generations to conquer."

"I know," Seil replied. "But peace does come at a cost."

He turned to his Minister of External Values, "Send your diplomats to each nation we are at war with. Offer them peace on our planet. If one should be killed, send another. If you run out of diplomats, go yourself."

Months had passed. Jel was now meeting with Seil in his office.

Jel had dire news. "Countries all around us are attacking our borders and bombing our cities. We are just in a purely defensive mode. The head of our troops wants permission to launch offensives all along our border. The air and space chief wants permission to strike cities in enemy nations and to destroy enemy space vessels that have just been deployed."

Seil responded, "I knew this wouldn't be easy. Just stay in defence."

Jel pointed out, "Your term will be up in two years. You will lose if this keeps up."

"I know."

Seil did, in fact, lose that election to a pro-war candidate. Being the seasoned politician that he was, however, Seil had one last trick up his sleeve.

He was back at the same platform as before in the same huge building as before, just five days before his departure. However, there was just a scant ten thousand loyal followers in the largely empty building. Two hundred guards from a unit loyal to Seil were posted around the stage. They wore brown helmets and brown full-body size light armour that could stop any small weapon. Their light boots were also brown. The helmets were complete with a small monitor and satellite positioning.

Seil thundered, "The enemy has crossed our border in three spots. We must deploy our troops immediately to save our nation. Therefore, I am declaring that all rights will be temporarily rescinded until the danger has passed. That includes the newly elected government.

That night back at his office, Seil met with his full cabinet.

He challenged, "As we speak, the leaders of the troops, and the entire space and air command are being arrested and locked up in a secure area by troops loyal to me. Any military personal who openly oppose me, will be shot. I will be declared the Great One in a few months. Who's with me on this?"

Three of the twenty-one ministers stood up in support of Seil.

"That's too bad," he noted. "I had been expecting much more."

Seil pulled a small weapon from his yellow jacket. It was a highly polished metal tube, four inches long and an inch in diameter. There was a hole at one end.

"This weapon was just developed by engineers with our troops," Seil revealed. "It hasn't been made public yet. All I have to do is point it and squeezed it with some force. The target will be disintegrated with no trace."

All the ministers stood up in alarm. Seil pushed a button. As the ministers approached him, several troops entered the room. They all watched as Seil eliminated all the dissenting ministers, one by one. Then the troops left.

Seil pointed out, "You are the only ones I can trust. Mea, you will be the new Minister of Peace. Steou, you will be the new Minister of the Interior. And Jaulk, you will be the new Minister of the Police."

Seil continued, "I want each one of you to go through the ministries under your control and remove all personnel opposed to me. The troops units loyal to me will help."

Then Seil marched up to each minister. "Mea, you will brutally keep the military in line and continue with the peace process."

"Steou, you will flood the citizens with propaganda and ways to keep them happy."

"And Jaulk, you will use the police to eliminate any opposition to me – inside and outside of our country."

All three ministers nodded and silently left.

Jaulk did his job extremely well. He produced thousands of highly trained police, armed with the latest weapons from the military. Except they would not use them as the military would have. In a fair battle.

The dictator of Obliiv's second largest country would not listen to Seil's peace plans. He wore plain black and white clothes as all his people had. They were a very solemn and downtrodden population. The dictator was Ni and kept himself locked up in a huge building with no windows or doors. Except, there were windows from the inside. And when someone who had been approved wanted in or out, a door would appear and slide open.

Jaulk's police had an informant inside Ni's building. He cooperated with the police on a promise for a high-ranking government position in the new order. The police waited outside when the informant opened a door. He had previously disconnected all security devices. He was the chief of security, after all.

A battle had begun a few miles away. Mea's troops had just invaded and were in a pattern to hold back the enemy from saving Ni.

The police pulled a massive weapon up to the open door. It was half the size of the building. It was black with a hole in the middle. Brightly coloured sparks danced around in the black hole. They fired and a bright-blue light flashed inside. The building shook and then collapsed on itself. Any thing inside was vaporized.

The commander of the police called headquarters. "The objective has been destroyed. Ni is dead."

The commander turned to his informant and quietly said, "We don't trust traitors." The informant was then vaporized with the same weapon Seil used.

Mea was in the room when the commander's message arrived. "Send in the troops from behind the enemy army. Bomb every base from the space vehicles and use the air vehicles to support our troops."

The enemy forces had no idea what hit them. They were in disarray. All their air vehicles were destroyed. The ones in space surrendered before a shot was fired. Ni's military surrendered with two days, but the carnage had just started.

Seil wanted to make an example out of them for the rest of the nations. All the enemy leaders were vaporized one-by-one live on international broadcasting for all monitors to pick up. This was a new weapon and something the people of Obliiv had never seen. And it frightened them. They started with the national leaders, then the municipal leaders, then the military leaders, and some military subordinates just to stretch it out. They did offer a way out, however.

Seil attended several executions and even killed many himself. But he also played politics.

Several times, he had made the same speech to the live monitors. "I am a compassionate leader of our planet, Obliiv. I just want peace in our lifetime."

Then an enemy soldier appeared on the screen.

Seil continued, "Here we have Abt, the third in command of the enemy army."

He turned to Abt and continued, "I will spare your life, if you pledge your allegiance to me."

The soldier nervously replied, "I pledge allegiance to you, Great One."

They embraced and the soldier was lead away. Seil turned to the camera and smiled. "See how easy that was? I'm asking that all other people in the world outside of our peaceful alliance, please demand that your government surrender to us to avoid anymore bloodshed. You will be treated fairly and with respect."

Off camera, Seil followed the same pattern. He took aside the person whose life he had just spared and quietly vaporized him.

After watching weeks of the public executions, the remainder of the independent nations surrendered to Seil one by one. But as they surrendered, the leaders of the fallen nations were quietly put to death. Once Seil became the Great One of the entire planet, he gave another speech in the new capital city of Obliiv, Biv. The scene of Seil's most popular speeches.

He took his place on the stage surrounded by two hundred thousand of the same people who had originally elected Seil to office. They were delighted to see that the wars had ended. They were delighted to see that their country had conquered the world. They were delighted to see that the Great One was Seil. But that feeling would not last the night.

Seil declared in a harsh voice, "From this moment forward, all citizens of Obliiv will be called Obliivians. Not everyone will qualify to be citizens. To become a citizen, a person must pledge allegiance to the Great One, be a member of the Great One's party, and be wealthy. All others can earn their citizenship by serving in the military for twenty-five years or serving the Great One's party for twenty-five years."

Silence hung in the air before voices of discontent murmured throughout the building.

Seil continued, "All of you have lost your freedom, except for citizens. There will never be elections again..."

Angry voices tried to drown him out.

Seil shouted above the uproar, "The Great One will be the leader for life. Only the Great One will pick his successor. Women will become..."

But that was it. The furious crowd turned into a mob. They rushed the stage, but Seil disappeared. Expecting violence, his image was just a hologram. There was no security present as thousands of people were trampled to death. Others tore down the stage. The sane ones looked for exits.

The Great One ruled with an iron fist, putting to death without trial all opposition. Or those that may become opposition. He liked the way Ni had ruled his people and he made all his subjects follow the same patterns. The glass buildings and homes were ripped down and replaced with solid grey material. No doors or windows could be seen from the outside. The people had to discard their colourful clothes for grey and white ones. Black could be an option.

As the Great One finally laid on his bed dying at a ripe old age, he summonsed Jaulk and the supreme commander of the military to his side.

He turned to the commander, "I want you to develop space vehicles capable of exploration in the universe. There are other races out there that we can study and learn from."

He turned to Jaulk, "You will become the Great One after my death. Please honour my order for space exploration.

Both nodded as Seil's heart finally stopped.

Years later, the young Minister of the newly formed Universe Exploration Ministry (UEM) met with an ageing Jaulk in the Great One's office. His office was smaller than Seil's old office and had only one small window. There were only two of the standard long chairs. Original publications, much older than Jaulk, sat on a shelf. They were titled, Spirits Among Obliivians and The Spirit World Beyond Obliiv. Like most people on his planet, he had been a true believer in spirits since childhood. He even had a famous clairvoyant giving him personal readings and advice.

Jaulk said, "I hope you have good news for me. My time is short before my spirit leaves for its true home."

The young Minister was named Obist. Both beings were wearing black and white clothes that had become standard among all the people.

He smiled and replied, "I do. We have developed a new space vehicle that can travel at great speeds over many generations. It will carry twenty citizens, who have been specially trained for long missions. And here is the best part. Because of the extremely high speeds, the people on the craft will age very little."

Jaulk smiled, "That's what I wanted to hear. But if the vehicle can travel at such high speeds, will it not run into planets or asteroids?"

"No. Space is largely empty of objects. Each star is generations away from the nearest star. But we do have an advanced warning system that can detect objects in danger of a collision. It will have the choice of either destroying that object or altering course."

"I don't like the sound of destroying objects. Remember, these vehicles are exploration and scientific missions. Not to destroy and conquer."

"I agree with you, 100 percent. The warning system will not destroy any object where it detects life. And it can detect life as small as an insect from several generations away."

"Are you going to manufacture more space vehicles and train more citizens?"

"We are training several hundred volunteers at this moment. This vehicle is going to a series of stars close to us. If it works out, we have plans to make several hundred more. Because of the great distances involved, however, we can only explore our own galaxy."

"That's too bad. I would have liked to eventually explore other galaxies."

"With what I'm about to tell you, I hope you don't think that I'm trying to be God here, because I would never think of doing such a foolish and shameful thing. My engineers have stated to work on a porthole similar to those the spirits use in God's Place."

"We just want to explore. God would not take offence to

that. And if he did, I'm sure he would let us know."

"Thank you, but this device will not be ready for several generations."

Jaulk explained, "My time is near to cross over. When that happens, I want you to have my position as the Great One. That way, I would be assured to keep alive Seil's dream of space exploration. I know that is your passion. And remember to have your replacement able to carry on our vision."

Obist simply nodded and walked out of the room.

The space craft left for a series of stars that were the closest to Obliiv. It was round, about one hundred feet in diameter and about two stories tall. It was a shiny-metallic colour with no doors or windows visible. There was script around the sides, giving the make, model, and fleet number of the craft. Bright lights circled the vehicle to avoid collisions with other air and space vehicles.

As with all their space craft, it simply went straight up. About a mile off the ground, it rapidly accelerated through the atmosphere. There was no friction because the space vehicle was designed to carve a tunnel ahead of it. Once in space, the craft quickly attained its top speed. To onlookers, it was virtually invisible.

It took less than half of a generation to get to the midway point with the star. There were no problems at all. Jaulk's spirit had been released long before this moment.

Obist, the present Great One, gave his first speech in the Great Hall of the capital city of Biv. The Great Hall was the newest marvel of Obliivian engineering. It was round with no doors or windows visible from within and without. It comfortably held five hundred thousand citizens.

Each seat was spacious, but not in the design of the regular Obliivian chair. These seats had the bottom and back parts the same length. The back could be moved from straight up to reclining to a 45-degree angle. It was comfortably padded. There was lots of leg room with small tables between each seat. A monitor was placed on each table where patrons could check on the menu and then order from it by simply touching the screen. Within seconds, a hole appeared beside the monitor. The order popped up before the hole closed.

Lighting in the hall was dim, but not too dim where you couldn't see your food and drink. Plus, bright lights were an option from the ceiling, walls, and the floor level. Every seat had a perfect view of the attraction. In the nose-bleed sections, invisible glass was able to bring each performance as close as the seats on the floor. Sound was heard the same throughout the Hall. And it was self-adjusting so that you could hear an orator shout in comfort, but still hear a pin drop on a carpet floor.

Once the performance was over, brighter lights immediately turned on. And behind each level of seats all around the circumference, doors slid open to well-lit passageways. Each passage had its own elevators to whisk people down to a spacious lobby. People had the choice of staying in numerous bars to discuss the show or head home on the long Population Carriers. They entered the lobby and then left with its passengers through a sliding door before snaking off around the city.

There was no security at this event. Obliiv was going through good times. There was plenty of everything for everyone – for both citizens and non-citizens. And the rules for becoming a citizen had been relaxed. The Great One was able to appear in public with no danger whatsoever.

The Great One materialized onto the large round stage to the thundering applause of the crowd. This technology was not available to the masses. It rotated so that the Great One would not have to physically do it himself. The stage was white but beams of light drenched it in colour. The Great One stood out. Despite the fact that everyone on Obliiv must wear white and grey clothes, the Great One was decked out in a yellow shirt, a red jacket with the front open, blue pants, and orange shoes. He was, after all, above the law. He was the law.

He raised his arms to silence his audience. The room fell silent while the Great One just stared at those around him. Then he broke the stillness.

"My subjects," he began, "my space vehicle has performed flawlessly."

The people broke out in applause.

The Great One waited for it to settle down before carrying on, "I'm here to announce that I have ordered several hundred more space vehicles to be built over several generations. I have also ordered that each new generation of these vehicles must be a great improvement over the earlier ones. The crew of my vehicles will explore new worlds in our galaxy. The scientists in my vehicles will bring home new knowledge. In the future, with a new porthole under development, my vehicles will travel to distant galaxies in an instant."

The Great One heard the crowd murmur in horror and disbelief. Their voices were starting to rise.

He cut them off. "I know what you're thinking. How could anyone, even the Great One, try to copy one of God's creations from the home of our spirits. If God was not pleased, do you think I would be standing here now? No, I wouldn't. He would have made my spirit cross over to the other side. But the fact that I am here is proof that God is pleased. I even consulted the best clairvoyants we have to talk to the spirits. They all agreed that I am on the right path. The path of exploration, science and peace!"

The Great One held up his arms in victory. The crowd was relieved. Their deafening applause reverberated throughout the Hall.

Obist had hoped that the porthole would have been ready before the departure of his spirit, but that was not to be. His worldly body was laid to rest after over eighty years ruling as the Great One. He had outlived two of his successors. But the third was the charm. Scito took over as the Great One. She was young and she was counting on the porthole to be her legacy.

On Obliiv, males and females were equal in all respects, except war. That was solely a male profession.

Early in her career as the Great One, Scito's dream came true. A functioning porthole was completed. Unlike her predecessors, Scito kept this invention a secret. She remembered how the crowd had reacted when Obist had announced the mere development of the porthole. The fact that a porthole was now a reality, may cause rebellion and anarchy. The people did not want anyone meddling in God's affairs and encroaching on the spirit world. Spirits were sacred to the Obliivians.

The Minister of the Universe Exploration Ministry stood in the Great One's office. It was the same office that Obist had used. She saw no need to make any changes.

"You understand that the porthole must be kept a secret?" Scito questioned.

"I do, but we must be realistic. Millions have worked on this project over generations. Word is bound to be leaked out," the young Minister replied.

"How far can we send my vehicles?"

"Our porthole..."

The Great One gave him a dirty look.

"Your porthole is not even close to God's, but we can reach probably thirty galaxies in the blink of an eye. Over the generations, we have already visited most habitable planets in our own galaxy. That why we'll start with a large galaxy close to ours. Our telescopes in deep space have picked up a blue planet travelling around a small star. There maybe life on this one, but there is no sign that the life is advanced. Maybe primitive at best. We have our eye on several other planets in that galaxy, but this is a good place to start.

"When is the first craft going to use it?"

"Today."

"Keep me up to date."

The Minister nodded and silently left. He went straight to the launch site using a small air vehicle.

The porthole was on a very large military base on the other side of the mountains in an uninhabited area. Armed guards patrolled the perimeter. They all wore the battle-issue uniform. It was a black cloth which covered their entire body, including the head. It could protect the soldier from any small-weapon fire. The helmet was a communication centre that allowed exchange of voices. The helmet also housed a small screen that could be switched to anything from the soldier's immediate area to the battlefield. The perimeter was also protected by a force field that sounded an alarm when it was touched.

Several large hangers, where space and air vehicles were repaired and stored, dotted the base. Small launch pads were in the centre of the base. Since all vehicles went straight up, the area was very compact. A few extremely tall towers were scattered around the base. They had the colour of plain silver with no doors or windows visible. Each one was about one thousand feet in diameter and stood about three thousand feet tall. These structures were where the fuel for space and air vehicles was manufactured.

But there was one huge building that dominated the entire base – the porthole. The structure was about five miles long, two miles wide, and two thousand feet tall. It was black, made of different material than any other building. There no windows in this building at all. Three doors that a person could enter could be seen along each side. Two large doors were visible at each end. They measured about two thousand feet wide and one hundred feet tall.

Inside was well-lit from the ceiling and walls. In the middle was the porthole. It measured the same as the end doors and could be used from both sides. Its bottom rested on the floor, with a smooth velvet-like material extending from the floor to the ceiling and walls. The porthole was black inside and was always left operating, using the energy from a nearby tower. If it was turned off, it would take weeks to restart it.

When the Minister arrived, an advanced model of the space

craft was inside the building, moving up to the porthole. It was the same as the earlier models, except more technologically advanced and bigger. This one was five hundred feet in diameter and two stories tall.

Wala was in charge of the flight. He had a crew of forty citizens. There were scientists, but no military personnel. Inside the craft was very spartan. Wala was the only one to have the typical-Obliivian long chair. The others sat in chairs similar to those in the Great Hall. The engineers over the generations had constructed air and space craft that created a tunnel ahead of each craft. As a result, the crew inside felt no pressure at. They could walk during the launch with no problems.

The control centre for the craft was a dimly lit circle, gold in colour, about fifty feet in diameter. The dome ceiling was about ten feet high. Wala sat in the rear of the room. Around the circumference were five monitors, with a crew member watching each one. This was the total flight crew. There were no controls or gauges; the vehicle flew itself. The internal brain of the vehicle, however, followed the orders of Wala. And Wala only. If the artificial brain sensed that Wala was dead or not fit to command, it would allow the number-two member to become the new flight leader. And so on, down the line.

Below and behind the control centre were five other rooms. The biggest was a square medical structure, bright white in colour, under the control centre. Even the floor was white. It contained three gurneys, with a monitor and a large silver-coloured tray beside each one. On the table were instruments designed to probe inside living subjects and catalogue the findings. Also on the trays were very small tracking devices that could be implanted inside living beings, which would monitor their movements to gain a better understanding of other races.

Behind this room were two smaller rooms. One was a where the crew slept in shifts. There were twenty beds in close proximity to each other. Each was shaped like a large seat, because

Obliivians slept sitting up. All crew members slept here, even Wala.

Next to the sleeping quarters was where the crew ate and relaxed. There were ten of the typical long Obliivian chairs. Like the Great Hall, a table and a monitor stood beside each chair. The crew member decided what he wanted to eat and drink from the menu and then make his choices by touching the screen. His food would appear through a hole on the within seconds. Crew time in this room, however, was limited.

Above these rooms and behind the control centre were the other two rooms. One was the only place on the vehicle where a door and window existed, but they could not be seen from the outside. It was yellow in colour. When the door was opened by a crew member, stairs slid out that would conform to the height needed for the crew to leave safely. In trays mounted on the wall were weapons. Two highly polished metal tubes four inches long. Seil had used similar ones to disintegrate his enemies.

Next to this room was a dark structure with black walls. Four small pads, glowing with energy, were on the floor. On the ceiling above each pad was another one, radiating light. They were spaced far enough apart, so that different sized beings could be kept captive and sleeping in the force field. There was only one door that connected just these two areas. Away from the pads, however, was an elevator that stopped outside the medical room. The elevator from the control centre was beside it.

Wala casually ordered the brain, "Enter the porthole."

The space vehicle silently powered up and soundlessly entered the porthole. On the other side, the craft was now slowly orbiting around the blue planet. The porthole disappeared.

Wala asked, "What is the composition of the atmosphere?"

A crew member replied, "It has more oxygen that we are used to, but that should not be a problem. The atmosphere, however, is thinner than ours, Wala."

Wala asked the brain, "Is this planet's atmosphere safe for Obliivian citizens to enter?"

It replied in a male voice, "Yes. There is no danger."

"What about inhabitants?" Wala questioned."

The brain replied, "There is a small primitive civilization near a sea just north of the continent of their origin. Other less-advanced beings live around the globe. This race has minor numbers, but they are larger and more-muscular than the Obliivians."

"Take us down to the civilization," Wala ordered.

The space vehicle entered the atmosphere at a high speed. Despite its speed and angle of descent, no one on the craft felt any strain and were able to function normally. Even walking.

The craft slowed as it neared a large town built near a river. The area around the town was a hot desert, except along the riverbanks. The land here was cultivated, growing grains, fruit, and vegetables. There was an irrigation system consisting of canals and small dams. The houses in the town were made from mud that had been dried in the form of bricks.

The people had bronze skin and were muscular. The woman had long black hair, while the men had medium-length black hair. Both sexes wore coverings only for their mid-sections and walked on bare feet.

The beings saw the Obliivian craft come soundlessly rushing toward them out of the blue sky. They pointed at it and were very excited. As it got closer, fear ran through the small population. They all ran into their houses.

The space vehicle landed a short distance outside the village. The door opened and the stairs ran down to the ground. The flight crew remained in the control centre, while two scientists exited the craft. They crept toward the village holding the small weapons. As they reached the village, a dozen male beings slowly gathered in their path. They were holding clubs, ancient knives, and spears.

The scientists stopped and started to back away. The beings

took this movement as fear and charged the scientists. One of the scientists fired his weapon at a nearby plow and it disintegrated. That stopped the men in their tracks. One of the scientists approached the group and dropped his weapon. He then slowly extended his right arm and smiled. The being that appeared to be the leader looked confused. He looked at the extended hand and raised his momentarily, only to back away.

The scientist then picked up his weapon and backed up to his colleague. "We've got to give them something to gain their trust. Maybe some food or a tool they could use."

"I agree," came the reply.

Both entered their vehicle. The door closed and the stairs retracted.

Meanwhile, in the control centre, a crew member shouted, "The weapons have powered up, Wala!"

Wala demanded to know, "What's going on!"

The vehicle brain replied, "I have detected an advanced alien space craft west of our location in the middle of a hemisphere on the other side of a very large sea. It has just landed."

"Where is it from?"

"It's not Obliivian and I have not yet developed an archive on space craft from other worlds. I could start one now if we intercepted this craft."

"No. I don't want to start a battle with someone who may be friendly. Is everyone inside?"

A crew member answered, "Yes."

"Fly over to it and we'll try to make contact," Wala said.

The Obliivian space craft lifted straight up until it was clear of the village and then it headed west at an extremely high speed.

The brain remarked, "The alien craft has detected us and has lifted off."

Wala asked, "Can we make contact?"

A crew member replied, "I've been trying on several channels, but there has been no response."

"The alien craft has entered space," the brain pointed out. "It is much slower than me. Do you want to pursue?"

"Wala responded, "No. Just take us back through the port-hole."

The weapons powered down and the vehicle sped back toward the porthole. As they approached, it reappeared.

After getting an update from Wala, the Minister of the Universe Exploration Ministry reported to the Great One's office.

The Minister revealed, "Your space vehicle successfully went through the porthole to the closest large galaxy. It visited a planet with primitive life and made contact with them. The scientists want to gain their trust by giving them food or tools. We don't know if our food will be toxic to them so I favour giving them tools that can advance their race at a moderate rate."

The Great One agreed, "We must advance exploration and scientific study. Have the scientists carry out their idea with the tools. It just might work."

"We are not alone in space," the Minister disclosed. "The crew detected a space vehicle of unknown origin on the same planet. It was not as advanced as yours, so its home planet is probably in that galaxy."

The Great One observed, "I never thought for one moment that we were the only ones out there. The only thing that we have to be concerned about is the power other worlds have and what their intentions are."

The Great One continued, "I want other space craft out there to explore the other planets."

"Your insight is always revealing, Great One. We have several of the next-generation space craft that will shortly be ready for use. Each one is bigger, more powerful, and more technologically advanced. Plus, they have better weapons – for defensive purposes only."

"Make sure it stays that way. I don't want to start invasions of other worlds. We have enough problems of our own. Keep me informed, but I will not be around for a while. I'm attending an economic conference for the states."

When Scito died, she was replaced by another Great One interested in space exploration. When that person died, he was replaced by another. And so it went for hundreds of generations. The scientific observation was particularly valuable because scientists reaped the benefit of new interpretations of old laws, verification of former suppositions, new reasoning powers, and the discovery of the unknown. As a result, Obliiv became a better place to live. Obliivians were a happy and content people. That ended, however, with a terrible tragedy in the reign of Blotios.

Like all the many Great Ones before him, Blotios had his own personal clairvoyant who was consulted daily. She was illegal, but who would question the Great One? Her name was Sette.

On one such reading, Sette predicted, "I see a large family of powerful spirits being sent to a planet called Earth by God to unite the entire planet."

The Great One was angry, "Enough! Send in the Minister of UEM (Universe Exploration Ministry)!"

An agitated Blotios met the Minister in the Great One's office.

Blotios declared, "Our God has decided to help another world over Obliiv. I will not stand for it! It's a world called Earth. Tell me about it."

The minister pulled a small graphic modulator from his pocket and ordered, "Give us a quick study of the planet Earth."

The modulator responded in a male voice, "We have been to this planet many times over the generations to explore and for scientific study. It is a minor planet with very little in the way space vehicles. They have not even left their solar system. Different factions of their race are usually at war with each other, keeping the people at a technological disadvantage."

"What's going on?" the Minister asked the Great One.

The Great One replied, "I've learned that God is sending powerful spirits to Earth to unite their race."

"You must remember, Great One, that God did the same thing for us hundreds of generations ago and we have thrived ever since."

The Great One calmed down and uttered, "Of course. I jumped to conclusions here without thinking. Will the unification of these people be a problem for us?"

The Minister cautiously responded, "It could be. We have discovered many advanced races in that galaxy, but they are all weaker than us. And we have formed peaceful agreements with them."

The Minister then questioned his modulator, "Will a united Earth be a problem for Obliiv?"

It revealed, "Earth is a special case. If not for its constant warfare, that race would have been extremely advanced. Despite the wars, the people on Earth have developed powerful weapons to threaten each other. If that race was to unite as Obliiv did, they would be able to focus in only one direction as a united race. They would very quickly develop weapons and space vehicles to rival yours. And being the violent race that they are, the people on Earth would become a threat to you."

The Great One cried out, "How could God do this to us? We have been faithful servants for generations!"

Then he ordered, "Call all my ministers to my office. NOW!"

The Great One was in a bad mood, so all forty-three of his ministers were falling all over each other to get there fast. Some had to charter high-speed air vehicles to arrive on time. The small office, the same one that belonged to Scito, was crammed.

The Great One announced, "God has betrayed our people by uniting Earth and making it a threat to Obliiv. I am not going to tolerate this. I have broken off our relationship with God. Spirits will no longer be tolerated."

He turned to the Minister of Internal Relations, "You will find a method where spirits can be detected and disposed of. All the ministers responsible for air, space and troops will help you. And you will round up all known clairvoyants and psychics and put them to death."

The Minister nodded his obedience, but added, "The people will rise up against anything done to God and the spirits."

"That's where the Ministers of the Troops and the Police will come in." The Great One pointed at them and went on, "You will destroy any uprising, any protest, even any meeting that goes against my orders."

The Minister of Space Values asked, "Do you think it's wise that we go against God in this manner?"

The Great One pulled out a weapon from his pocket and disintegrated the minister on the spot. "Anybody else want to disagree with me."

There was just silence.

The Great One finally turned to the Minister of the Universe Exploration Ministry. "I want you to gather as many space vehicles as possible. They are to cross over to Earth and destroy the entire race. Troops will then land on the planet to finish the job. We are going to nip this threat in the bud."

"Will we still be able to explore and carry on scientific studies with the other worlds." the Minister of UEM wanted to know.

The Great One answered, "Of course you can, until they become a threat to Obliiv. This will serve as a reminder to the other worlds of our might."

God heard Blotios's plan to destroy the human race and he would not allow that to happen, but he would not intervene himself. Instead, he sent ten angels to Obliiv. They all had lived on the planet as spirits and looked like Obliivians. Except for the wings, of course. All ten descended on the planet and landed in pairs at different locations.

Two angels flew down to the front of Obliiv Broadcasting,

which was the only company to supply the entire planet with programs for the monitors. Two armed police were outside guarding the place.

When they saw the angels, one shouted, "They don't pay me enough for this."

Both police ran away. After Blotios's attack on the spirit world, they feared retaliation from God.

One angel pointed at the building. The door appeared and slid open. They walked in and surprised the office staff who stood frozen in fear. They took the elevator to the third floor and took over the set where political debates were broadcast to the public. And waited.

When the military learned about the arrival of the angels, they sent in five hundred heavily armed troops and two large weapons that could take down the building. The troops surrounded the building. Then twelve specially trained soldiers tried to open the front door, but it would not appear.

The commander ordered, "Cut off the power to the building."

He tried to call inside the structure with his modulator, but he got no answer.

The commander turned to the sub-commander, "I don't like this. No one answered my call. The angels could have killed them all. Fire the Striker at low power to just open up a wall so that the troops can enter the building."

They turned the Striker at the structure and pushed the fire button, but nothing happened.

"What's wrong!" the commander demanded to know.

"I have no idea. It's always in perfect operating order," the sub-commander replied.

"I have a bad feeling. Try the Disintegrator."

"That could take out most of the building."

"Then why did we bring it? DO IT!"

The weapon was pointed at the building and it, too, failed to function.

The commander went to a nearby soldier and took his small weapon. To the alarm of the soldier, the commander pointed it at him and squeezed. To the relief of everyone around, the weapon did not work.

The commander lamented, "The angels have disabled all our weapons."

He called headquarters to give them the bad news.

The same scenario occurred at four broadcast stations around the planet. These stations were able to broadcast verbal programs only.

When the all the angels had secured their targets, they broadcast the same message over the airways. Despite the fact that power had been cut off to all five structures.

"We are angels in the service of God. He has commanded us to warn the Obliivian race against any attack on Earth. God will not allow you to do so. If you even try, God will send in hundreds of angels to punish all those responsible. And that includes the Great One. You are no match for the power of God "

The angels then returned everything to normal and flew away. With their white wings and white gowns, they looked like doves in flight.

Blotios, the current Great One, had heard the message with his personal secretary.

Blotios mused, "I should have expected this. The angels were right; we are no match for God. He could destroy our world in the blink of an eye."

He took out his modulator and called the Minister of the UEM. "You heard the speech? Call off the attack on Earth. We are no match for God. Just one thing, though. I want military personnel to fly my space vehicles to Earth. No scientists. I want them to monitor what's happening on that planet. Especially the development of new weapons and space craft."

After he ended the call, the Minister of Police arrived, "What do we do about the crack down on spirits and the people?"

The Great One ordered, "Keep that in force. God didn't mention them at all. All spirits will be hunted. All clairvoyants and psychics will be put to death. And having the people living in fear of me will help out considerably."

Commander Bu, an air and space military officer, was in charge of one of many Obliivian missions to Earth. His orders were clear. His flight crew was made up entirely of military personnel and included ten troops as passengers in the other sections. Just in case. Space vehicles from other worlds, under agreements with Obliiv, were still operating scientific studies on Earth. Those days for Obliiv, however, were over.

Bu's space vehicle was the latest model. It was of the same basic design as the others, but was bigger, faster, and more powerful.

They were cruising in Earth's upper atmosphere, when a crew member dryly remarked, "A fresh nuclear signature has been detected on the North American continent."

Bu commanded the vehicle's brain, "Take us in at high speed for a look."

The Space vehicle sped toward its target and abruptly stopped over a military base. No one on the craft felt any discomfort.

The vehicle brain revealed, "This is an American military base. Nuclear materials have not been detected here before. It is extremely well guarded. More than just a normal base should be."

The commander considered, "A base that has never had nuclear material before. And now it has. Are they developing a new nuclear weapon? A different nuclear weapon?"

A crew member revealed, "Weapons have just been activated."

The commander calmly asked, "What's going on?"

The brain responded, "Two fighter jets are rapidly approaching us."

"I want to see what's going on here." The commander ordered, "Lead the jets far away from this sight. Then come back here."

The commander added, "Keep your speed at a lower level so you don't lose them."

The space craft moved away in an easterly direction. The jets closely followed. After thirty minutes, the space craft accelerated straight up at a ninety-degree angle. Then it turned at another ninety-degree angle and headed west at a high speed. The jet pilots lost sight of it in a second. The craft was back over the base in five minutes.

The commander had announced, "You people in the back – wake up. You have your first mission at a heavily armed..."

The brain had interrupted, "Two large helicopters are headed our way. Do you want them destroyed so that you can complete your mission?"

The commander had answered, "Of course not. There must be something top secret being built there for all this action."

The brain had observed, "Two more fighter jets are approaching us. One has just fired a missile. It has exploded on the outer rim. No damage. Do you want me to return fire?"

The commander had ordered, "No. Let's get out of here."

The spaceship had accelerated straight up at an incredible speed. Radar had lost it in less than a minute.

The commander had mused to himself, "But I'll be back."

* * *

The clairvoyant concluded his story by saying, "Gone are the days of exploration and scientific discovery. We are now monitoring the situation on Earth, with special interest in the military. Humans are no match for us right now, but who knows what the future might hold?"

"Do you know?" Yvonne questioned.

"Yes, I know, and you know, too. Peace," the Obliivian answered.

Yvonne inquired, "Why don't you just tell everyone the truth? The future only holds peace."

The being laughed. "You are so naive. I would be executed for practising clairvoyance."

Yvonne nodded in agreement and flew back to the porthole and Heaven. She had her answer.

* * *

Yvonne now had a taste for travel. She wanted to travel to a place more like Earth, but peaceful. She picked out a world in the Milky Way, but on the other side of the galaxy from Earth. With just a thought, Yvonne made the porthole appear. She crossed over to a place where its people were still in the early stages of development. The area where Yvonne stood was hot and humid. Lush trees and bushes and plants grew everywhere. The trees grew to about seventy-five to one hundred feet, but their branches extended out about two hundred feet. The leaves were up to five square feet, with shredded edges.

In places, where branches from several trees meshed together, the blue sky was not visible. Darkness filled the jungle floor day and night. But, oddly, plants, bushes and young trees flourished in the gloom. The plants were of countless varieties with flowers varying from a simple white cone with a large hole on the top to a single multicoloured flower that glowed in the darkness.

The location teemed with wildlife. There was a snake-like creature about twenty feet long, but it walked on several legs that were no more than six inches long. Through one of the clearings in the jungle canopy, Yvonne actually saw a large bird with a wingspan of thirty feet and a beak full of razor-sharp teeth curved inward, pluck a large hairy beast with only two limbs from the top of a giant tree. Yvonne walked a short distance and found a fast-flowing river about a mile wide. Despite the fact that it was cutting into the banks making the water muddy, life flourished here, too. Large, two-hundred-pound fish, with fins but no gills, could simply walk out of the water on small legs to hunt six-inch insects that crawled on the floor.

This was interesting, but Yvonne wanted to find people. She took to the air above the trees and finally found a settlement. Tree stumps surrounded the village. There were eight large huts with wooden sides and large tree leaves for the roof. There was a fire in the middle of the village where they were cooking the catch of the day. These people were totally naked. The men were hairy creatures, while the women were almost hairless. They had very dark skin with two legs and two arms. The area around their jaws was very large, but the forehead was smaller.

Yvonne was about to go down to interact with these beings when a large disc appeared from high above the village. It silently approached the settlement and stopped, hovering above the tree stumps. There was no fire or even heat. The people rushed toward the vehicle, laughing. The craft was one thousand feet in diameter and about four stories tall. It was a shiny-metallic colour with no doors or windows visible. There was script around its sides that matched the script which Yvonne saw on the train in Obliiv. Bright lights circled around the craft. A door slid open, stairs descended to the ground and two beings walked out to the cheers of the primitive inhabitants. They were definitely from Obliiv.

Yvonne watched as the two Obliivians, with bald heads and short stature, walked up the other people, smiling. The life forms from the primitive race were double the height of their visitors. One Obliivian extended his hand, which was firmly gripped by the tribe's leader with the skin between the thumb and index finger of both hands coming together. Then the leader's four fingers crossed over the back of the Obliivian's hand.

Primitive women brought the visitors food and drink, which was consumed on the spot. Then two Obliivians went back inside the space craft and brought out a plow. Yvonne could hear their thoughts, but they heard hers, too. One of the Obliivians pointed in her direction and Yvonne quickly left. She found her porthole and crossed over into Heaven.

CHAPTER THREE

Preparing For Another Life

God had given spirits much freedom. They can decide just to stay in Heaven. They can decide just to visit other worlds. Or they can decide to live physical lives on other worlds. To go and live on other worlds is not easy. All life, capable of thought, harbours spirits on God's worlds. From a life form on one world to a fish on another to a human on Earth. They all have spirits most of which will return to Heaven once the host body dies.

Having decided to return to a physical world, Yvonne took the first step in the process – a review of the catalogue of the planets. Every planet in God's Universe was listed with a name given to each one by an angel. A description of every world was included. An impossible task? For physical life forms, yes – but not for a spirit which is intelligent energy. And there was no time in Heaven.

After mentally going through the catalogue, Yvonne selected three worlds. Earth, Ghourryt, and Ob.

She already knew Earth after spending several lifetimes there, but she must visit the other two and then make a decision on which one she will start a new physical life.

Before Yvonne was able to go anywhere, however, an angel appeared. He had the form of a human because that's where Yvonne had spent her last life. He had short black hair with black skin. The white wings and the white gown were also present.

He smiled and remarked, "I see that you have made your choices for your next physical life."

Then he warned, "Just keep in mind that you are a kindred spirit with Gary's spirit who still lives on Earth. Any decision you make for yourself will also be for him."

Yvonne replied, "I realize that."

The angel added, "Very well. When you decide on a world, I'll assign a spirit guide to help you."

Then he was gone.

The black porthole appeared, and she stepped through it onto Ghourryt. The planet was several hundred galaxies away from Earth. Its star was close to the same size as the Sun, but she could see right away that there was a problem. Ghourryt was the fourth plant orbiting the star. Beyond Ghourryt, however, there were no other planets. No gas giants to protect the inner planets from collisions with such things like comets.

She flew around the planet, which was twice the size of Earth. The equator was filled with lush jungles and then more temperate forests to the north and south. There were no ice caps, however. No cities could be seen; just primitive towns and villages. The one thing she had been expecting, craters, were not to be found.

She spotted a large village well to the south of the equator. The people had ash-white skins, long white hair, and black eyes. Except for minor features, they were all the same. They had two legs and two large toes facing to the rear on each foot. The two arms worked at the back of each person, not to the front as with humans. And there was a reason for this. These life forms had heads where the mouth one eye faced to the rear of the body. The stomach and chest were at the rear, while the backbone was at the front. Their rectum was below the stomach and when they sat down, the face always looked forward.

All the primitive houses and buildings were roughly made out of wood. The fields outside the village were cultivated, using many life forms to do the work. They did not have tools such as ploughs. The people wore animal skin just to cover the mid-section and walked barefoot.

Yvonne then heard a loud boom high above in the sky. A large meteor was streaking down to the planet, trailing fire, and smoke. She saw it crash into a nearby forest in a very big explosion. Dust was carried up several miles into the atmosphere. The light from the star was blotted out. The people, however, paid no attention to it, until hot dust and debris slammed into their village and beyond.

All the people died, but there was never any panic among them. She could see their spirits being released and the spirit guides showing them the way to Heaven. There was no dark side here.

Then Yvonne saw a comet enter the atmosphere and crash several hundred miles away. It was like a large atomic bomb going off. The shock wave quickly passed through her. She looked up into a clear portion of the sky and there were several trails from objects about to smash into the planet.

Yvonne went to the crash site of the first meteor to see why there were no craters to be found on the planet's surface. She found a deep crater about two miles in diameter. The plants, however, were actively growing in the crater. She could actually see them move and grow. It appeared that weeds and bushes were the first to start to sprout. Then the fast-growing trees were next, to be followed by the slower growing trees. Evolution had developed so that vegetation was able to quickly grow back after meteor strikes.

Yvonne had a funny feeling about the people. She returned to the village to see all the people walking around. And she could sense that there were souls inside each life form. Either the old souls had returned or, more likely, new ones had come astonishingly quickly. Almost like they were on standby in Heaven. Some were washing themselves or their children. Others were cleaning up the debris or gathering weapons for the next hunt.

She looked at the fields beyond the village. People were already cultivating their crops which were already returning to life. These life forms were going about their routine tasks like nothing had happened. Like evolution had turned death from multiple comet and meteor strikes back into life that was almost instantaneously rejuvenated. Yvonne could not live in a society where death was treated in such a cavalier attitude. She returned to Heaven as another meteor crashed onto the planet's surface.

Once inside God's Place, another porthole appeared in front of Yvonne. She stepped through it and crossed over onto Ob to check out her second choice. This planet was in the Milky Way. Like the last world she visited, Yvonne was looking for a race similar to humans but in a different environment. The race on Ob, however, were extremely similar to humans. When Yvonne gets back to Heaven, she made a mental note to ask if there is a connection between the two.

Ob itself was a warm world. It was orbiting a star bigger than the Sun and it was the second planet from that star. It was a world smaller than Earth with a thin atmosphere. The equator was the hottest with temperatures from 120 to 140 degrees Fahrenheit. It was nothing more than a desert. The temperature gradually cooled north and south of the equator. The two poles were the only places on the planet where life could comfortably exist. The temperature at the poles was in the range of 70 to 110 degrees Fahrenheit.

The people who lived at the poles looked like humans, but they had much larger noses. They were bronze in colour with black hair – long for both sexes.

The people in the south were technologically advanced with vehicles that could fly in the air and on land. But not space. They wore clothes that covered most of the body. There were three main cities and several towns. The buildings and houses were made from a concrete-like material that could withstand, to a degree, the earthquakes that plagued them. Due to deforestation, mud slides were common in the rain. And these people had polluted all of their water and must now put drinking water through an expensive purification process.

The people at the north were far behind the south. They still depended on animals to get them around, but they lived in

Heaven compared to the south. These people actually worshipped the land and the trees. They cultivated only open fields and meadows. They killed wildlife for food only when the crops failed and built primitive shelters out of stone. Their water, however, was polluted in populated areas due to untreated waste. But for the most part, the water was clean.

Yvonne first went to the largest city in the south and tried to contact the people who were scurrying about. She had no luck. Then she saw a huge building. For an earthquake-prone area, this building was high – 120 stories. It was spread out, howwever, over the bottom fifty stories. She went inside through a wall and checked out each floor. Then she heard something interesting on the top floor.

A group of five well-dressed men and women were sitting in a large office. There was a sizable imitation-wood desk with four imitation-wood chairs in front of it. The king-size chair behind the desk was covered with imitation leather.

The man behind the desk was the president of the south country. The four others were his entire cabinet. "We've been on this planet, which is not that big, for several millennia, but only now have we discovered a new country in the north. Is that about right, General?" the president asked.

The general was actually in charge of the police force. There was no need for a military on this planet. "Yes, sir, that's right. But you've got to remember that we thought there was nothing beyond the bad lands. And only recently have we developed an aircraft that could travel that far."

The general added, "And we only stumbled onto it by accident when the pilots were trying to set a new distance record by flying over both poles."

The development minister revealed, "Mr. President, from the photographs that the pilots took of this new land, I believe we should invade it and take it over. The people there are primitive and still use animals as a mode of transportation. It will be easy to conquer them."

The minister of religion challenged, "So, we discover a new country, and your first response is to invade it."

"They have material that we are desperate for," the development minister shot back. "There are trees that we could use for building again. There is teeming wildlife that we could domesticate and use for food. There is land that we could cultivate for crops and have our over-population settle there. And we certainly could use their fresh water."

The environment minister suggested, "So, you want to strip that country of their trees, pollute their water, use their land for our own selfish purposes. Let's not go down that road. We don't want to do to them what we did to ourselves. We are only now realizing the damage we have done to our own environment."

The president offered, "And that's why you have such a high-profile position."

The president turned to the general. "Before we get all worked up over nothing, is it possible for us to get enough police up there to take it over, General."

The general replied, "Not at this moment. No. But maybe in a couple of years. We have to divert funds to the police force for long-range transport aircraft and..."

The minister of development interrupted, "Why can't we just use land vehicles? We have plenty of them."

The general gave her a dirty look and said, "It's obvious that you haven't been to the bad lands. There is no water, and the temperatures are so high that it's like entering an oven. A trip like that would be suicide."

"As I was saying," the general continued, "we also need to hire more police and to train them in military action. And develop new weapons for warfare. Something we have had no need for in the past."

The president stood up and ordered, "All right, General, carry out your plan for an invasion. There's an election in three years. I want the invasion completed in one and a half years."

The general stood up and complained, "That's an impossible timetable!"

"And take whatever money you need from the environment ministry," the president directed.

The environment minister asked, "What about our long-term plan to clean up our own country?"

The president revealed, "That use to be our number-one priority because we had no choice. But now we do. Our environment is not on the priority list at all. Taking over the north will solve all our problems."

The president added, "By the way, you're out of a job. I'm going to appoint someone who will do exactly what I tell them with no complaints."

Yvonne had seen enough. A big power invading a primitive country for its resources. It sounded all too familiar to her as she reviewed her lives on Earth. If she chose Ob, Yvonne would have gone through the whole dirty mess again. At least on Earth, such invasions rarely happen now. She returned to Heaven and made Earth the destination of the next life for herself and Gary.

* * *

Now Yvonne must contact the spirit guide that has been assigned to her. To do this, she walked over to a plain white pillar that has just appeared nearby. The pillar was round, but it had a circumference that never ended. She looked up the pillar and it disappeared into the mist, never to end. This pillar represented the never-ending expanse of God's Universe and those beyond. There was no end and there will never be an end.

It served as a reminder to those spirits who have chosen to start a new life on another world just how small they really were in comparison to the Universe. Call it a reality check so that they will humbly live out their physical lives and not with swollen egos.

After pondering the meaning of the pillar, Yvonne touched it. The pillar disappeared leaving a spirit guide that was assigned to lead her through the process. The spirit guide appeared in the same form as all the other spirits – just a whiff of smoke. Because Yvonne has requested to start a new life on Earth, this spirit guide was chosen because she had live lives on Earth for several millennia.

The spirit guide greeted her, "Hello, Yvonne. My name is Shelly. I have been chosen to help you and Gary through our system so that you two may start another new life on Earth."

Yvonne asked, "Before we get started, I would like to know if there is a connection between the planets Earth and Ob?"

"That is a question that an angel should answer," Shelly replied. "But it is my understanding that there are physical connections between many planets."

Yvonne said, "Thank you. I have been through this process many times, but I'm worried this time that the Test maybe required. We have never been through the Test before."

The spirit guide revealed, "You especially have the right to be concerned because you want to go back with your kindred spirit. An angel will sit in judgement on whether to allow you to return to Earth to star a new life. This is one of only two times that God will allow a spirit to be judged, I might add. I can't see any problem with you, but I think Gary will have to go through the Test because in his last life he had all but ruined two lives on Earth because he was too eager."

"If they won't allow Gary to go, then I won't go either," Yvonne declared.

The spirit guide remarked, "You know better than that. Once the process has started, it cannot be changed. You may have to go without Gary."

The spirit guide continued, "We have one thing in our favour. God is very fond of kindred spirits and has protected them from angels breaking them apart. He will allow it only in one circumstance – the Test. I have seen angels actually break apart kindred spirits because they considered one partner not worthy of starting a new life on other worlds. Angels, however, do this very rarely because of God's feelings."

"I realize that, but he is making amends for it on Earth as we speak, "Yvonne pointed out. "He not only completed his lessons early, but he has learned other lessons such as fatherhood, companionship, sharing and honesty. He will be a great man in the next life."

"I only hope you're right, Yvonne or you'll be going to Earth alone."

"Then I won't go."

"Yvonne, we've just been over this. Once a process starts, it cannot be changed," the guide reminded her.

But she added, "You do have an edge, though. I was chosen to aid you because I'm one the most experienced and probably the best spirit guide around. I could have been an angel by now if I had chosen that road. God willing, of course."

In Heaven, truth was demanded. And it's given and accepted without any feelings, just as the plain truth.

Shelly disclosed, "First I must go to Earth to talk to Gary's soul and get his side of the story, because he's the weak link in your request."

Yvonne asked, "How is that possible while he's still in his human form?"

"When his body goes to sleep. In researching this enquiry, I've learned that his soul quite often leaves the body during sleep."

* * *

As Shelly thought of Earth, a dark porthole appeared in front of her. She stepped through it and found herself on a dark street in Mexico City. Sometimes she was able to hit her target, and at other times not. But she had been to Earth many times and knew her way around. She flew north to Canada to a city in Southwestern Ontario called London. It was 1:00 A.M. local time.

London was a medium-sized city nestled in the lower Great Lakes. The historic Thames River flowed through it. It was a college town, home to two major learning and research centres. Fanshawe College and the University of Western Ontario. It's called the Forest City, but the city has allowed the destruction of many of its woodlands in recent years due to development. Progress, I guess.

She found Gary's house. It was a townhouse in a condominium complex in the south end. It was one of the biggest complexes in London. The historic London-Port Stanley railway was established in 1854, and is still active, lied just to the east. Between the railway and the townhouses was a naturalized ravine with a stream flowing through it. Trees from a majestic walnut to maples to even a pear and a cherry cover the ravine in a forested blanket

The ravine just happens to be behind Gary's unit. The house was a brown-brick structure with light-brown siding, and three-floors. A basement door led to the rear patio. The front door led to the living room and kitchen.

Shelly could feel the future beginning to unfold in this house. A future of helping even more spirit children. A future where Yvonne would spend more time here than in Heaven. A future that looked beyond this house to starting an extraordinary family on the south side of Lake Erie. But also, a future that could soon be ended in Heaven.

She found Gary sleeping alone in the master bedroom. He occupied the bed that Yvonne had used before the death of her physical body. This room was nicest room in the house. Yvonne and Gary had decorated it only a few months before her death. There was a large window that looked out to the front. It was fairly clear. Yvonne had pulled it out and cleaned it a short time ago. The room was painted in an off-white colour. The brown wall-to-wall carpet was still thick and showed little wear. The double bed was covered with a soft white-satin bedspread that Gary had bought her as a comfort during her declining health. Gary was sleeping on the covers with two cats sleeping beside him. Princess, their lab-mix dog, was sleeping on the floor beside the bed. Since Yvonne's death, she often slept in Yvonne's room.

Shelly could sense a great sadness in this room, but also a great never-ending love. Keeping her spirit form – just a whiff of smoke – in the semi-dark room, she watched as Gary's spirit left his body. It was temporarily replaced by one of his spirit guides for safe keeping.

Gary's soul was about to leave. It was a ghostly image of his body. In his early sixties, he was six feet tall with grey hair and a grey moustache. He was pushing over 270 pounds, but, unknown to him, he was about to lose weight under Yvonne's guidance.

As Gary's soul left its body, Shelly cut him off.

"Where are you off to tonight?" Shelly quietly thought.

Gary was surprised. "Who are you?"

"I'm Shelly, a spirit-guide from God's Place."

"God's Place?"

"You call it Heaven."

Shelly carried on, "Your eternal mate, Yvonne has applied in God's... I mean Heaven for the two of you to return to Earth in your next life."

"We've talked about our next life many times," Gary divulged.

"Does she visit you very often?"

"Everyday," Gary answered.

Shelly continued, "I'm helping Yvonne with her request, and I need some information from you about the mistake you made at the start of your present life."

"Is that going to hurt our chances of staying together?" he worriedly asked.

"We have to wait and see. Now tell me what happened."

"Who's that, Dad?" Julie asked. She was Yvonne's and Gary's three-year-old spirit daughter. She looked like a ghostly image of her former body. A white girl with short blonde hair and a beautiful smile.

Another spirit daughter entered the room. She was a sixteen-year-old named Shirley. She was a tall black girl with long black hair, and very intelligent. "I'm sorry, Dad. I tried to keep her in her own room, but she was worried about you."

Gary lovingly remarked, "That's okay. This is Shelly. She's helping your mother and myself to get things straightened out in Heaven. You can ask Mom about it tomorrow."

He carried on, "Now, go back to bed, Julie. Everything's okay. Remember the children's shows tomorrow."

"You mean cartoons, right, Dad?" Julie corrected.

He responded, "That's right. Cartoons."

The girls left.

"They are beautiful girls," Shelly observed. "And you have nine others, I believe."

"Eleven children here and one in Heaven."

"You and Yvonne must be very proud."

"We are. In our next life together, all twelve of these children will be part of our family. A very special family."

"Yes, I've heard just how special your next family will be. It's going to really shake up things on Earth."

"Anyway, tell me about what happened when you started this life," Shelly requested.

Gary's spirit replied through his thoughts, "I have been to Earth hundreds of times, mostly with Yvonne. We are kindred spirits with love that will last forever. I know there's no time in Heaven, but things were just dragging on back then."

I had been looking forward to physical sex. Not to making love, but to the sexual act itself. I was to be born as William Shipley. Yvonne had approached me as we were almost ready to go. And she had looked nervous. I had been standing alone at the porthole.

"Bill, you should be spending time with your spirit guides and go over everything," Yvonne remarked. "Stuff like the lessons you have chosen to learn, the year of your conception, your moth..."

Bill interrupted, "I know what the protocols are. I've been through this a lot more times than you. And I don't appreciate you telling me what to do!"

Yvonne offered, "That doesn't sound like you, Bill. Over all our time together, you have never spoken to me like that. Are you forgetting our eternal love?"

Bill softened his tone. "Of course not, Yvonne. We will love each other for all of eternity. I'm sorry if I sounded gruff. Spirits do not talk with impatience like what I did. I don't know what's come over me. Maybe I should seek the advice of our angel."

He opened his mouth to call for their angel when Yvonne said something that she has long since regretted. "I wouldn't bother with that. Why don't you just talk with your spirit guides?"

"Okay," Bill agreed. He joined his seven guides and began to go over the plans of his next life. But then he threw up his hands and marched back to the porthole again.

Yvonne rushed to his side and asked, "What's wrong?"

Bill answered, "These guys are just going over the same old things, time after time. I just want to get going."

Yvonne pleaded, "Bill, you're too eager. Slow down so that you don't make any mistakes."

Bill replied, "I know what I'm doing. I've done this hundreds of times. It's just that I'm anxious to experience your physical love again."

"So am I."

"Okay, okay. Let's go," Bill had demanded.

In a soothing voice, Yvonne had asked, "Slow down. Do you remember the year of your conception?"

But that had been it. Bill had had enough. He had passed

through the porthole into the Earth dimension and had disappeared.

Gary continued, "But I screwed up the year of my conception from 1964 to 1946. I was born almost two decades before Yvonne."

Shelly conveyed, "So, Yvonne stopped you from contacting your angel which would probably have solved your problem. That could be the piece of the puzzle I've been looking for."

"I don't want that to come out in Heaven," Gary revealed. "I'm in trouble and I don't want Yvonne looked at in the same light. That would end both of us from going back to Earth forever."

"As you wish."

Shelly was about to leave and then questioned, "Where were you going before I stopped you?"

"The North Pole. I like going there, especially near the end of June. The sun is always overhead at that time," Gary replied.

Shelly disappeared and Gary returned to his body as his spirit guide was leaving it. No North Pole tonight.

* * *

Shelly stepped through the porthole into Heaven. Yvonne was waiting for her.

"How did you make out," Yvonne anxiously asked.

"Not too good," Shelly replied. "He's got nothing to offer to help out in a possible Test."

"What about you?" Shelly asked. "Are you hiding anything from me?"

Shelly's first and only concern at that moment was Gary. He's the one who would probably undergo the Test, while Yvonne was free and clear. She wanted to use the fact that Yvonne had discouraged Gary from calling their angel when they were about to start off on a new life.

Yvonne carefully went through her thoughts before answering, "There is one thing that I kept from you at Gary's insistence. He didn't want me to get into trouble."

Gary had been showing impatience. He had been getting careless because of his eagerness to get started. He had been standing alone at the porthole and I had approached him to calm him down. I was to be born as Yvonne Pepler and he was to be born as William Shipley.

"Bill, you should be spending time with your spirit guides and go over everything," Yvonne remarked. "Stuff like the lessons you have chosen to learn, the year of your conception, your moth..."

Bill interrupted, "I know what the protocols are. I've been through this a lot more times than you. And I don't appreciate you telling me what to do!"

Yvonne became very angry, an emotion she had seldom experienced as a spirit. Bill and Yvonne were bound together for eternity by love, but now she was feeling something far different. Something very dark.

"How dare you talk to me like that!" Yvonne shot back. "We've been together for hundreds of generations on Earth. We've had families, we had losses, we felt love and hate. But the one thing that we had through ALL our experiences together both here and on Earth was a respect for each other. And now you try to put me in my place by shouting at me? Where is the respect you once had for me? We're equals, Bill. We're equals!"

Bill softened his tone. "You're right, Yvonne. There is no way I should have talked to you like that. That was totally wrong and I'm sorry..."

"Sorry doesn't make it any better," Yvonne butted in.

Bill continued, "We will love each other forever. Spirits do not talk with impatience like what I did. And kindred spirits do not speak to their eternal mates like what I did. I don't know what's come over me, but something is terribly wrong. I'm going to speak to our angel and get to the bottom of this. Our new life on Earth has to wait until I find out what's going on."

Their spirit guides – fourteen in all – mingled together watching the argument.

Yvonne's Door Keeper stepped forward and warned, "Anger is not going to solve anything, Yvonne. You should just take a deep breath to calm..."

Yvonne turned angrily to her spirit guide, and he quietly stepped back.

Yvonne remarked, "So, you're just going to take it upon yourself and cancel our next life together."

Bill revealed, "Our next life together is not being cancelled. Just delayed."

"And can't you solve your own problems? Are you going to go crying to our angel every time something goes wrong? Maybe I fell in love with the wrong spirit."

In an effort to gain revenge, Yvonne had planned to take Bill to the very edge of madness and then to reel him back in. That would show him what it felt like to be put in one's place.

Bill opened his mouth to call for their angel when Yvonne said something that she has long since regretted. "Listen, Bill. You are NOT going to call our angel. And you are NOT going to delay our next life. Now go over to your spirit guides and get down to business!"

Bill meekly agreed, "Okay." Yvonne watched with satisfaction as he joined his seven spirit guides. She went over to hers.

Then Yvonne watched in alarm when Bill threw up his hands and marched back to the porthole again.

Realizing that she had gone too far, Yvonne rushed to his side and asked, "What's wrong?"

Bill answered, "These guys are just going over the same old things, time after time. I just want to get going."

Yvonne pleaded, "Bill, you're too eager. Slow down so that you don't make any mistakes."

Bill's spirit guides were concerned that something horrible was about to happen, but they were powerless to stop it.

Bill replied, "I know what I'm doing. I've done this hundreds of times. It's just that I'm anxious to experience your physical love again."

"So am I."

"Okay, okay. Let's go," Bill had demanded.

In a soothing voice, Yvonne had said, "Slow down. I'm going to call our angel."

But that had been it. Bill had had enough. Bill had passed through the porthole into the Earth dimension and had disappeared.

Yvonne carried on, "My Door Keeper told me that Bill had transposed the year of his conception from sixty-four to forty-six. He would be born as Gary Betts eighteen years before my birth."

"So, you're the real cause of this mess, eh Yvonne?" Shelly suggested. "If you had let Bill call your angel when he wanted, you two would have lived the next life on Earth the way it was supposed to be."

Shelly added, "And both of you hid the truth, although I'm sure that God would have known."

"Things are going from bad to worse," the spirit guide observed.

"Yvonne sadly admitted, "Yes, it was totally my fault. I'll admit the truth and let Gary off the hook."

"It's a little too late for that," Shelly cautioned. "If the true story came out about what really happened and that you two covered up the truth with lies, there will be hell to pay. I've seen this before. You and Gary would never be allowed to leave God's Place again and you two would be punished. Like cleaning up the mess after every parade for a top spirit for eternity."

Shelly continued, "I'll have to join in with your deception. Your real involvement in this will be kept between the three of us. May God forgive me for putting the task that he has given me over the truth."

* * *

As they were discussing the chances of a possible Test, both Yvonne and Shelly heard a voice in their heads, "The hearing will begin now to consider Yvonne's request. Enter the chamber at once."

A porthole appeared. This one would not go to another world but to the next level of Heaven. Aside from a spirit becoming an angel, this was the only time spirits were allowed to this level and above.

They crossed over into a huge white room called the chamber and took on their last physical forms dressed in white gowns and white slippers. Because this was a request to go to Earth, all the others who attended also took on their last human forms. The angel, however, had already taken on the appearance of a being from Earth. Everyone, except for the angel, would be standing throughout this experience.

Yvonne was a short white woman, pleasingly plump. Her long hair was premature grey for her forty-seven years of age. She had a natural clean beauty about her because she had never used makeup in her physical life. Her eyes were a haunting green colour.

Shelly was a dark girl of sixteen years. Her physical body had died at sixteen and spirits always remain at their death age until their next physical life. She had long black hair and a lovely charm of her youth. After living several lives on Earth, Shelly decided never to go back and concentrated instead on being a spirit guide. She eventually worked her way up to a Door Keeper, which was the head spirit guide looking after physical forms on other worlds. But now she stayed in Heaven guiding spirits who want to start lives on other worlds.

The angel sat on a white stool on a white stage, one hundred feet above the others. This was to show everyone the high stature that the angel had compared to the spirits below in the room. The angel's name was Gad. He came from a spirit that had resided on Earth for hundreds of lifetimes. He looked like all angels – flowing white gown and large white wings out of his back. His skin was a dark-Mediterranean colour with short black hair. He was called the Recorder. His job was to record everything for God to read at his leisure, and then to approve or deny Yvonne's request. Because the room was so bright, it was hard at times to get a clear dividing line between the stage and the angel.

Standing beside Yvonne and Shelly was the Tester, called Markous. It was his job to present the angel with all the facts, and to help Gad by suggesting approval of the request or the Test. He was short with a slim build and had very-pale white skin. His hair was cut close and was blonde in colour.

From the very beginning, he had chosen that he could best serve God by remaining in Heaven.

"What do we have here, Markous?" the angle asked in the usual silent-thought process.

Markous replied, "I have carefully gone over the facts, Gad. I recommend that Yvonne be approved."

"I have a problem with her mate, Gary, however," Markous added. "While crossing over to his last life on Earth, he made a crucial error that resulted in Yvonne and Gary not getting together for several years. Two children were not born as a result. For him, I recommend the Test."

"Can you offer proof?" Gad wanted to know.

"I can," Markous replied.

"This could have dire consequences, Markous," Gad offered. "God has prohibited the breaking apart of kindred spirits. These are rare and very special to God. They are the only spirits that will remain together for eternity. If I approve Yvonne and deny Gary, this kindred-spirit couple will be shattered. God will not be happy with that or with me."

Markous reasoned, "By God's instructions, angels cannot split kindred spirits unless the split comes in the Test. That is the only time God will agree to such a break."

"Yvonne's request has been approved," Gad ordered. "But I must ready myself to judge Gary's request, which has been put

forward by his mate, in the Test. This will not be an easy decision. And it could be a risky decision."

The angel disappeared and the three spirits walked back to
their level through the porthole.

When Yvonne and Shelly were recalled by Gad, they were
surprised to see two Door Keepers in attendance at the Test.

One was Yvonne's former Door Keeper. His name was Michael. He was an older white man with a rounded face and an
obvious big belly. He had short grey hair. This one was expected, but the second Door Keeper was the surprise.

This was a thin, clean-shaven white man with a full head of
black hair. He was thirty-five years. His name was Henry, and
he had a real attitude. He had mocked people he was supposed
to serve. He had laughed and had joked at authority, but he
had one thing going for him. He really cared about his clients
and always went the extra mile for them. Okay. That's two
things. He was Gary's Door Keeper.

Markous turned to Henry first. They were only two feet
apart.

"You are Gary's head spirit guide?" Markous asked.

Henry replied, "Yes, I am. And I do not appreciate being
taken from the person I am supposed to guide throughout his
life on Earth."

"Gary still has six spirit guides," Markous pointed out.

"That's right, but I'm in charge and I should be there at all
times," Henry shot back.

"You didn't have to come," Gad interrupted. "You do not
have to obey Markous. He is you're equal."

Henry revealed, "I have to obey when he says, 'I summon
you in the name of Gad.'"

Gad jumped to his feet and stared at Markous before he remarked, "How dare you use my name? You have crossed the
line this time."

Markous quickly and urgently replied, "This Test is in your
name, Gad. You are in charge and so I summonsed this spirit

guide in your name because he would not attend, otherwise. I want you to have all the available information to help you make your decision."

Gad sat back down and pointed his finger at Markous. "I reluctantly accept your argument, but this is not finished. You are only supposed to present the facts and not care about what decision I make. But you seem to be driven to block Gary from going into another life. In other words, to win. And in God's Place that is unacceptable. After this Test, you may be forced to seek another position."

Markous complained, "Gad, that is not the..."

"Carry on with the Test," Gad shouted.

Markous continued to question Henry, "Please tell us what happened when Gary was ready to leave God's Place for his present life on Earth."

Henry responded, "He was too eager to cross over, that's all. He left before his mate and used the wrong information. We all tried to slow him down, but he wouldn't listen."

"What was the wrong information he used and what were the consequences?"

"I'm not going to run down the man who my sole purpose is to help and guide. It's wrong for you to even ask me."

Gad looked at Henry with sympathy. "If not for Markous' deceit, you would not be here. But now that you are here, you must answer the questions."

Henry divulged, "Gary transposed the year of his conception from 1964 to 1946. He was born eighteen years too early to the wrong mother. He was supposed to be Bill, but was christened as Gary. Yvonne was conceived in 1962 as scheduled but was lost without Gary. He didn't meet his kindred spirit until she was near death."

Markous questioned, "What became of their children?"

"Obviously, they were never born," Henry revealed. "There were to be two – a boy and a girl."

"Thank you," Markous offered as he stepped away from the

witness. Henry immediately disappeared through the porthole.

Markous then approached the other Door Keeper and asked, "Michael, you were Yvonne's spirit guide during her last life on Earth?"

"Yes," came the reply.

"Tell us what happened just before Yvonne and Gary were preparing to leave to start their life on

Earth," Markous directed.

"At that time, Gary was not Gary. He was to be born as Bill before his mistake. After his mistake, he was born as Gary," Michael divulged.

Markous impatiently said, "Alright, alright. Just tell us what happened."

Michael carried on, "Bill had been through this many times before. He was a very experienced traveller. But this time, he was too eager. Yvonne and Henry tried to get him to slow down, but he wouldn't listen. When Yvonne asked him a question, Bill had enough and crossed over alone."

"Is this normal procedure?"

"There's nothing wrong with it. If all goes well, they will meet in the Earth dimension."

"Did all go well?"

"No. I saw right away that there was a problem. As I had told Yvonne, Bill had transposed the year of his conception from sixty-four to forty-six. He was born as Gary eighteen Earth-years before Yvonne. She was very distressed over the whole matter and wanted to change the year of her conception to match Gary's."

"Is that possible?"

"No. She cannot alter the plan for herself once it has begun. Bill's mistake would stand because he had done his by mistake. So, Yvonne crossed over to Earth without her kindred-spirit partner. Her first four decades were very difficult. We had to do a lot of work to eventually steer her toward Gary."

"Thank you," Markous mentioned as he backed away. Michael disappeared through the porthole.

"That's all the proof I will offer, Gad," Markous observed.

Gad declared, "It's your turn, Shelly."

"I would like Gary's spirit here, Gad," Shelly revealed.

"Why would you want to take such a drastic step?" Gad asked. "It's not that Gary's spirit will be punished for his indiscretion. The worst that can happen is to separate the two spirits from each other."

"For Yvonne and Gary, that is punishment. I just want to present you with all the proof necessary to make your decision. And I want to carry out God's will that kindred spirits will never be parted," Shelly replied.

Then she added, "And please note that I came to you instead of going behind you back."

In order to please God, Gad was looking for a way to allow Gary's spirit to return to Earth with Yvonne.

He looked at Markous and then lamented, "This is turning into a very difficult Test for me to determine. I can fondly remember happier and care-free days as a spirit. But this is the task that God has personally chosen for me, and I will not disappoint him. Let me think over your request, Shelly. But present any other proof now that you may have."

Shelly turned to Yvonne. "Tell us about Gary before your Earthly body died."

Yvonne replied, "He was an alcoholic, but as long as he stuck to beer, he was a happy one. And I made sure he didn't touch a drop of the hard stuff. We loved each other very much and truly found who we really were with Colleen's help. Colleen later turned into Gary's mentor. Despite financial troubles, Gary always gave me what I needed. Such as a safe vehicle to visit my mother. Or a cell phone in case I got into trouble away from home."

"How was he as your death approached?"

"Gary was there for me everyday, spending all day and night with me at home. And eleven hours a day at the hospital. As I grew weaker, he even fed me. Plus, he accompanied me to every test the doctors had ordered."

"Did he change after your death?"

"Yes. Gary had completed all the lessons that he had set out for himself before he turned forty. As we

gathered spirit children for our future family on Earth, he took on new lessons. He is now learning to be a good father and it shows in how he treats his spirit children. He is learning how to handle money so that we will not be burdened in our next life."

Yvonne added, "Gary will become a multimillionaire in his present life, but he will spend most of his fortune on a new hospital for child-burn victims."

Shelly backed away from Yvonne who stayed in the room.

Markous announced, "Gad, this proof offered by Shelly changes nothing. It's just second-hand from a minor spirit. I ask that you refuse Gary's request to go to Earth with Yvonne."

Shelly shot back, "You used second-hand proof from two spirit guides, Markous."

Markous explained, "Yes, I did, but they are very experienced with much knowledge."

Gad revealed, "You know, it's really nice that Gary plans to build a children's hospital, but Earth is just one world in God's entire Universe. It loses any significance in God's Place."

Shelly claimed, "But Yvonne and Gary are writing books that were sanctioned by the highest level of spirits and maybe even God. They didn't think of it as trivial."

Gad stated, "Despite the personal intervention of other spirits here, that still does not make the hospital or the books more than minor events in the scheme of heavenly matters. It maybe so on Earth, but not here."

Gad carried on, "Markous is right, Shelly. I'm going to rule that Gary..."

"Gad, have you forgotten about my request to have Gary attend this Test?" Shelly interrupted.

"No, but I was hoping that you had," Gad responded.

Gad questioned, "How do you suggest we get Gary's spirit here without his body dying?"

Shelly suggested, "Gary's spirit occasionally leaves his body. When this happens next time, you can order his spirit to attend this Test."

Of course, Markous objected, "Gary knows nothing about God's Place. How can we expect accurate proof from him?"

Shelly contended, "His body may be lacking in such knowledge, but his spirit is very experienced and knowledgeable. He knows his way around this Place."

Gad ruled, "We will hear from Gary."

This maybe difficult for humans to understand. Everyone in the room waited for Gary's spirit to leave his body. No one left. On Earth, it took over a month for Gary to have an out-of-body experience as he slept. But in Heaven, there was no time.

So, just a moment after his ruling, Gad ordered, "Gary come to me now."

Gary's spirit walked through the porthole. He was overweight and stood about six feet tall. Despite his sixty-three years, he was a muscular man. His round face had a day's growth of stubble on it. And his unkempt hair was grey in colour. He rapidly blinked his eyes and was confused. Then he saw Yvonne and rushed toward her, but Shelly stopped Gary in his tracks.

"This is not the time nor the place for such activity," Shelly observed.

Gad told Gary, "This is not the way we like to do things, but this is a special case. You are bewildered as most spirits are when they first return to this place from a physical life. But you must overcome how you now feel and answer all questions."

Gary silently nodded. Gad remarked, "Carry on, Shelly."

Shelly took her place in front of Gary and asked, "Tell us about yourself since Yvonne's death."

Gary combed his fingers though his hair in an attempt to get his bearings and then disclosed, "I'm an alcoholic and I will not stop drinking until the day I die. But I have learned a lesson from this experience and will not be a drunkard in my next life. Because of my father's drinking habit, I did not have my first drink until I was twenty-five. I did not start to drink heavily until I was forty-seven. I almost made it past this phase, but I was alone and forlorn. I sought alcohol as a friend. This will not happen again.

"I have also learned a lesson on how to be a good father. In my first sixty-three years, I have failed miserably in this area. But through my spirit children, I have learned to be an excellent and loving father. They all love me, and I love them. They will be my children in the next life. They will be happy and loved.

"I have learned the lesson in finances. The books that the spirits have allowed me to put my name on as an author, will make me a millionaire. Since Yvonne's death, I have become very careful in how I deal with money. The millions that I will make will not be wasted. Nor will the lessons that I have learned when it comes to my next life.

"I have also learned the lesson of taking a slower pace in life and in God's Place. I will never be in a rush to go anywhere or do anything. There is no time here. And on Earth, I will make the time.

"I have learned the lesson that my future family must be honoured and supported. Yvonne will be my future wife giving birth to twelve children, eleven of whom we now care for. All twelve of them and my future wife will change the Earth. And I am honoured to simply be a part of the family.

"And finally, I have learned very much from Colleen, whose spirit is held in very high esteem here. She taught me about the spirit world. Such as how to deal with spirits, how to embrace them, how to love them. She shared her special knowledge with both Yvonne and myself."

Gary added, "Gad, I made many mistakes in my present life and just before as a spirit. I swear to you and God that I will not make the same mistakes again. Through my prayers as a human, I have never lied to God."

Markous opened his mouth to speak when Gad put up his hand with the palm facing Markous.

Gad smiled and declared, "I have heard enough. Yvonne and Gary are given permission to start a new life together on Earth as kindred spirits as soon as Gary's spirit is released. God is pleased and I am pleased."

Gad carried on, "Gary you must go now, and you will remember nothing of this."

Gary left through the porthole without giving Yvonne a simple glance.

Markous hung his head in defeat.

Gad looked at him with sympathy. "Markous, there are no winners or losers in the Test. You will no longer be a Tester, but I will personally help you to find a task that is more suitable for your vast talents."

Yvonne and Shelly left the room through the porthole. They were now in the true form of spirits – just drifting smoke or a fog over some warm pond.

Shelly happily said, "We did it, Yvonne. You and Gary and your twelve children will be starting a new life on Earth."

Yvonne revealed, "I am so happy. My kindred spirit will not be taken from me after all. We are two spirits but will act as one for eternity. My new family will change the planet, Shelly. We will change the planet."

"I don't know how to thank you, Shelly."

"Knowing that your family will stay together is enough thanks for me."

Shelly disappeared and the pillar returned. Yvonne looked up at the pillar and silently thanked God.

God heard and said, "You're welcome."

God also rejoiced with Yvonne. He would not have interfered, but he was pleased that two souls will remain as kindred spirits to bring unity to Earth.

CHAPTER FOUR

The Dream Factory

After successfully completing the Test, a shadow appeared before Yvonne. Shadows are very rare in Heaven. A female angel spoke from the shadow. Yvonne, who could make out the shape and the wings, approached the shadow.

The angel ordered, "Stop! Do not come any closer or you will fail the dream course."

Yvonne stopped.

"You have been to the Dream Factory many times, but we will not allow you to remember the past ones," the angel continued. "Before going to a physical life on another world, each spirit must complete a course that will guide you in the dream process. This is important because every being that our spirits occupy will dream. I will meet you again when you have almost completed the course. Remember what I have just told you. It is very important."

The angel added, "A door has just appeared behind you, Yvonne. It leads to the Dream Factory. Enter and begin to learn your lessons in dreams."

The shadow and the angel disappeared. Yvonne turned and was surprised to see an old wooden door. The red paint was curling up and flaking off revealing old wood. There were three hinges and an old brass doorknob. As she approached it, the door slowly opened. The rusty hinges squeaked like a rat.

Yvonne walked inside. It was a very small room about the size of a bathroom. However, something was odd about this room. While Heaven was a brilliant white, the walls of this room were black. A small naked light bulb on the black ceiling provided a weak light. The door slammed shut behind her.

There was nothing else in this room until a porthole appeared in front of her, but this one was different. Instead of just blackness, colourful sparks jumped inside. She hesitated. It reminded her of the huge vehicle that was coming for her on the Obliiv world. Yvonne knew she had to do this to complete the process.

She crossed over alone into a blackness travelling faster than light. Travelling past a huge star, she quickly out paced its light until the star appeared to just blink out. She travelled into the black hole at the centre of the Milky Way. In the dense matter, she slowed to a crawl until she exploded out of the other side. She accelerated so fast that debris from the black hole followed her until it was reclaimed by the black hole. She was now in a different time and a different dimension. Feeling time gave her an odd sensation because there was no time in Heaven.

Her spirit travelled from one galaxy to another in a matter of seconds. The speed made her feel exhilarated. She slowed down in a galaxy and started to skip from one world to another. One world was super hot, with volcanoes exploding everywhere. The air smelled of sulphur, but giant red animals roamed in the lava flows, growling at the air. They had small heads with no teeth, standing on three legs. There were no arms and no eyes. She saw one swallow a hot boulder.

Then she was off to another world that was extremely cold. Its star was so far away that it seemed to be no larger than a golf ball. The planet was covered with ice and seemed to be lifeless. Then a creature broke through the thick ice. It was like a gigantic snake with tusks for teeth. The creature had sensed prey that Yvonne could not see. Then she saw it. It was an enormous white bird that tried to fly away, but the other creature caught it and dragged it down below the ice. When things settled down, Yvonne saw other animals that looked like white basketballs with six legs scurrying across the ice. Their mouths snapped at the frigid air as they ran.

Yvonne left the surface of this planet into the darkness of a starless void. Then she found herself in a room strapped to a bed. A large light above her bathed her body in bright light and the rest of the room was dark. She was in human form and could not move her arms and legs.

She was well blow six feet tall and overweight. She had long premature-grey hair and green eyes.

"This is impossible!" Yvonne shouted. "Spirits can't be strapped down."

A man in a white coat appeared at the side of her bed. His face was hidden by the darkness.

He calmly remarked in a soothing voice, "We can do what ever we want in dreams, Yvonne."

He pulled back and burst out laughing.

A small screen was lowered out of the darkness within six inches of her face. It showed a grey mass of flesh with blood dripping from it on top of a metal table. It was what was left of a baby boy that had been aborted. Hands that wore thick yellow rubber gloves picked up the lifeless body and threw it into a green plastic garbage can.

The baby's soul cried because he was alone, and he was afraid. He was painfully taken from a warm womb and thrust onto a cold metal table. His body died, but his soul could not understand any of this. He looked for his mother. He wanted his mother. He needed his mother.

But his heart was still beating. Yvonne could hear it, "Lub Dub, Lub Dub, Lub Dub..."

"Make it stop!" she screamed.

The heart beats stopped, and the screen went black.

With tears running down her cheeks, Yvonne closed her eyes tight. When they reopened, she found herself standing inside the Dream Factory. She was in the form of a spirit form again.

"That was an odd experience," she thought to herself.

She turned to leave, but the door wouldn't open. As a matter of fact, there was no door.

"You didn't think it was going to be that easy, did you Yvonne?" a male voice asked.

"What?" Yvonne timidly asked.

"What's wrong, Yvonne? You've been here many times."

"I can't remember."

"Ah, yes. You can't remember," the voice agreed. "Let's see if this will jog your memory."

* * *

Yvonne found herself in the past getting ready for a new life on Earth. She was both the Yvonne from this past moment and the Yvonne from the Dream Factory watching.

"How can I be in the past when there is no time in Heaven?" she asked.

"Anything is possible in a dream," a voice replied.

The one who will be born as Yvonne Pepler had pleaded with her mate, "Bill, you're too eager. Slow down so that you don't make any mistakes."

The spirit who was be born as Bill Shipley had replied, "I know what I'm doing. I've done this hundreds of times. It's just that I'm anxious to experience your physical love again."

"So am I."

"Okay, okay. Let's go," Bill had demanded.

In a soothing voice, Yvonne had asked, "Slow down. Do you remember the year of your conception?"

But that had been it. Bill had had enough. He had passed through the porthole into the Earth dimension

Yvonne's Door Keeper had approached her. This one had been a female and had been in charge of Yvonne's other spirit guides. "There's a problem, Yvonne."

"Oh, no," Yvonne had said.

"Bill is no longer Bill. In his rush, he transposed the year of his conception from sixty-four to forty-six. He's going to be almost eighteen years older than you."

"This cannot be real. We've never been apart for as long as I can remember."

"Except for the period from conception to childhood," the Door Keeper had corrected.

Yvonne had ignored the comment and had said, "I'll just change my year of conception so that we can be together,"

"You cannot alter your plan for yourself once it has begun. Bill did his by accident because he was so eager and so it will stand. Your mate will be conceived in 1946 and born in 1947. You must go now, Yvonne. You will be conceived and born in 1962."

She had reluctantly gone through the porthole without her kindred-spirit mate.

* * *

Yvonne was now back in the Dream Factory, heart broken.

"What are you trying to do to me? First my baby and then my spirit mate." Yvonne questioned.

"It's all about dreams here, Yvonne. You cannot function in a physical body on some world if you don't know all about dreams. We make dreams here. But first, how about a nightmare?" the voice declared.

Yvonne found herself in her Earthly body standing in the room where her Test had taken place. Gad, Markous and Shelly were all there. Gad, however, did not have any wings, but he did have a long white beard and wrinkles on his face.

"Here is the guilty sinner, God," Markous announced. "Yvonne has not prayed to you, she has not attended church, she murdered her baby, she took illegal drugs, she smoked cigarettes, and she had sex before she got married."

Shelly lamented, "There's nothing I can do for you, Yvonne. You are a guilty sinner. You will fry in hell for ever."

Her Earthly husband, Gary was also there. "I got you into a church once, but you wouldn't go back. And remember when I told you to go to hell? I meant it."

Yvonne shook her head in disbelief. "We're kindred spirits,

Gary."

"Not anymore, Yvonne. I've already got myself a pretty young lady," Gary said with a smile.

Then God's voiced thundered across the room. "You do not deserve a place in Heaven, Yvonne. You are going to burn for eternity in the fiery pits of hell."

"Can't I say anything in my defence," Yvonne pleaded.

God replied, "Yeah. You can say goodbye."

Yvonne then found herself in a hot cave where fires were burning everywhere. The only light came from them. It seemed to have been carved out of rock and smelled of and tasted like sulphur.

A man approached. He was about six feet tall with a slim muscular build. He wore a short black beard and had a tail and horns. This being was dressed in black with a red cape. He held a pitchfork.

"Hi, I'm the devil, but you can call me Satan."

He looked at a scroll and carried on, "I see that you're Yvonne. Not much in the way of sins, but we'll take any soul they throw at us. God must've been in a bad mood today."

The devil instructed, "Okay. Go down this long burning corridor to the second hole on the right. Go in there. Adolf will show you the ropes. You'll be breaking apart smouldering rocks for eternity. I'll check in later, but for now I've got an appointment with a guy called...uh, let's see...Barack."

* * *

Yvonne closed her eyes and screamed. When her eyes opened, she found herself in the parlour of an old house. A dull light came from three lamps and four lights on each wall. The walls were light brown in colour and the wooden floor was polished to a high gloss. Wood crackled in a large fireplace. A large bookcase covered most of one wall and was crammed with hard-cover books. A clock on the top shelf chimed twice –

it was 2:00 A.M. Old Victorian furniture stood around the room.

Then she saw a young man sleeping on the couch. He was about six feet tall with a slim build. The hair was cut in a short military style. He wore shorts and a T-shirt with a logo from the 2010 Winter Olympics in Vancouver.

A young female was sleeping on a nearby chair. She was a bit over five feet tall with long red hair. She wore tight shorts and a tight top, showing off her ample breasts.

Then two spirits entered the room, but they kept their former appearance in a ghostly way. One was a male close to six feet tall. He had grey hair that covered his ears and a huge moustache that blended in with long sideburns. He had shiny black boots that went up his legs to just below the knee. His pants were brown and a loose green long-sleeve shirt.

The other spirit was a woman who had long grey hair tied in a bun on top of her head. She wore a small cap on her head. A black dress that nearly touched the floor was covered with a stained white apron.

They crept up to the sleeping man, giggling.

The woman said in an audible whisper, "It's my turn, Nathan."

The man quietly corrected, "I don't think so, Molly. Remember that you entered the minds of the last couple that lived here. That was about, oh, I dunno, maybe almost a year ago."

"There's no tricking you is there, my love."

"Now, watch his face."

Yvonne could see the male spirit get very close to the man. The male spirit laughed out loud as the man sat bolt upright, screaming.

The woman jumped to her feet just as the two spirits were disappearing. She didn't see them.

"What's wrong!" the woman shouted.

"Oh, man, I just had the weirdest nightmare," the man replied. "There was this old guy right in my face. He was in my face laughing at me and had rotten teeth. He kept grabbing my balls. We've been here one night and the crap's started already."

The woman teased him. "The poor baby had a nightmare. Come to Mommy and you can put your head on Mommy's big tits."

They both laughed. And so did the spirits, just waiting for them to go asleep again.

Nathan hugged Molly and thought, "It's a good thing we didn't cross over all those years ago when our buggy went over the cliff. Look at all the merrymaking we would've missed."

* * *

The room suddenly went black, and Yvonne's spirit suddenly found herself in a dark damp place. She could sense rats running all over the place. As her sight gradually became accustomed to the darkness, she saw that she was in a cave – crowded with spirits. But these spirits were different. They were in the spirit form the same as Yvonne – a whiff of smoke. Instead of Yvonne whiteness, however, these were dark. She was in the dark side.

Somehow, these spirits didn't notice Yvonne. Probably because they were agitated from their leader's pep talk. He was Lord Chamberlain who sported a long black beard and unkempt long black hair. He wore a dirty white long-sleeve shirt and long black pants. His black leather boots were scuffed.

"You know what you have to do tonight," Chamberlain told the group through thoughts. "Look for children who are in danger of being murdered by their family. Then wait until the child is killed and then move in and take the child's spirit."

He continued, "We are getting dangerously low in the numbers we have taken. We can't count on too many adult spirits willing to join us anymore. Not like before. So, we depend on child spirits to keep our numbers climbing.

"But last night, all you got were three children. That's not worth the trouble of breaking them in. Although, I still enjoy seeing them tormented with their pleas for mercy, screaming and crying."

They all laughed at Chamberlain's little joke. He knew how to handle an audience.

He concluded, "You are going to travel to North America! South America! Europe! COME BACK WITH ONE HUN-DRED SOULS!"

They shouted and cheered as they flew off to their individual targets. Excitement at the prospect of capturing one hundred child souls dripped from their mouths like blood from a vampire bat.

Chamberlain stayed behind – he had sensed Yvonne.

He looked at her and asked, "What's your name, my dear?"

She shot back, "You cannot hurt me or try to take me captive."

"I wouldn't even try," he confided. "Older spirits are too much trouble to be bothered with. Too hard to break but breaking a child spirit is really easy."

He added, "But not too quick. I like to make them suffer."

"What brings a Heavenly spirit like you to a murky place like the Dark Side?

Yvonne replied, "I was sent here from the Dream Factory."

"Uh yes, the Dream Factory. I've heard about it, and I hope to never see it."

Chamberlain carried on, "Come with me. If you're studying dreams, this should interest you. I'm in the process of giving a five-year-old girl nightmares in the hope that she will one night be scared to death. I know it's an old-fashioned way of taking spirits, but I still enjoy the old ways from centuries ago."

He flew off to a quaint little village in upstate New York and Yvonne followed. It was 1:00 A.M., but no one stirred. The streets were quiet, lit by only ten streetlights. There was a grocery store, a bank, a restaurant and twenty houses. It was close to Christmas and the snow was already two feet deep.

Decorations hung from each streetlight.

Chamberlain targeted a small white frame house on Main Street. They entered a large bedroom that contained a king-size bed, two dressers and a closet. A man and a woman were sleeping on the bed with their only child sleeping between them. A young girl named Mandy. She had long brown hair, an angelic face, and a normal child's body. But her brain was not normal, thanks to the dark spirit.

Through his thoughts, Chamberlain revealed, "After several nightmares, the little girl won't sleep alone anymore. But that won't stop me. She is so fearful right now that there is terror in just going to sleep. The night that one of my nightmares scares her to death, I will take her soul to the Dark Side."

"Look into her mind and you'll be able to see the horror that she faces every night," he remarked.

In her dream, the girl was sleeping in her own bed when she heard her mother screaming. Despite the fact that she was terrified, the girl got up to investigate. She walked into her parents' room. The room was bathed in bright light. Her mother was laying on her bed while her father was fighting another man.

Her father was very slim and very fit. He was about six feet tall and had short black hair. He wore only green underwear.

The other man was taller and weighed over two hundred pounds. He was dressed in black pants, a black sweater, and black runners. A black hood covered his head with three holes for his mouth and eyes.

The man dragged her father over to a guillotine and forced him to kneel down behind it. He pushed a button, and the blade sliced the top of her father's head off. Blood spattered over the girl and his brains fell out. She could not move or scream – the girl was frozen with fear. But her father was not dead, so the man put her dad's neck on the block. The blade sheared off his head. It fell to the floor. Blood from the arteries in his neck sprayed all over Mandy and she absently licked the blood off her lips.

The eyes on her father's head suddenly opened and looked at the girl. With blood dripping from its mouth, it smiled and uttered, "Give Daddy a kiss, Mandy."

The little girl woke up screaming, startling her parents again. She would not sleep the rest of the night.

* * *

With the scream, Yvonne found herself back in Heaven standing beside the never-ending pillar. She was in the usual form of a spirit. A female angel stood in front of her, smiling. She had the usual white wings and white flowing gown. Because Yvonne was going to Earth, the angel was in the form of a human, with long golden hair.

The angel spoke, "That was quite a ride."

Yvonne replied, "Yes, it was. Is it really over now?"

The angel asked, "What do you think?"

Before Yvonne could answer, the angel wanted to know, "What have you learned."

"All dreams are made in God's Place, here at the Dream Factory," Yvonne answered. "The Dream Factory scrutinizes every being on every world and will send dreams for each individual to that being's spirit. Then the spirit will give those dreams to the person's brain."

Yvonne continued, "Nightmares come from spirits who have chosen not to come to cross over to Heaven and spirits from the Dark Side."

"When we last met, I asked you to remember something," the angel revealed. "Do you remember what that was?"

"What? Uh, no," Yvonne stuttered.

The angel disclosed "I told you that 'I will meet you again when you have ALMOST completed the course.'"

"It's not over?" Yvonne exclaimed.

* * *

Darkness then descended around Yvonne and the pillar turned into a rough stone wall. And the angel turned into Lord Chamberlain.

He stated, "Let's go, Yvonne. We've got children to catch before the sun comes up. I think we'll go to Paris tonight."

Yvonne confusedly replied, "What? Catch children?"

Another man, in what appeared to be a dark cave, asserted, "Lord Chamberlain, I told you Yvonne was starting to lose it. She's of little use to us now."

Lord Chamberlain responded, "How can she loose it? She's a spirit, pure energy. She has nothing to lose."

"And she has captured more child spirits than you can ever imagine," he added.

"Come on, Yvonne," Chamberlain remarked. "Ignore this guy. I'm the leader of the Dark Side and I'm the only one who really counts here."

"For now," the other spirit claimed.

"Are you challenging me?" Chamberlain wanted to know.

"Of course not. I'm not that stupid."

Chamberlain turned his attention to Yvonne. "Change over into a spirit and follow me."

Yvonne did as she was told and noticed something different about her spirit form. It was just a whiff of smoke as always, but this time it was black in colour. They flew over Paris with Chamberlain looking for a child who was in imminent danger from being killed by family members. He always thought that it was odd that children were in more danger from those that supposedly loved and protected them than from strangers.

"Oh, well. Their loss and my gain," he happily thought.

He swooped down to an apartment building which had a distant view of the Eiffel Tower. It was a ten-storey upscale white building. There was even a doorman. He went to an apartment on the third floor to find a man and woman arguing over money.

Their apartment was painted a powder-blue with thick white carpeting. The living room set was white leather, with light-brown end tables and a coffee table. The coffee table had a glass top. Three lamps shed a soft-white light throughout the room. Original oil paintings were on three walls, with the balcony on the fourth.

The woman was in her forties, with a thin build and a height of only five feet. Her brown hair was tied in a bun. The man also had a thin build, but he was close to six feet and had short black hair. He was clean shaven.

"I think we got here just in time, Yvonne."

Yvonne countered, "I can sense that another child in this building is in danger of being murdered. Can we capture them both?"

Chamberlain lamented, "No. For every child spirit that we bring to the Dark Side, there are ten others, regretfully, that return to Heaven. We can only do so much."

The two spirits continued to watch from the outside as the man marched into the kitchen. He returned with a butcher knife. The woman backed away, screaming. She defensively put up her hands, but he made a stabbing motion that slashed open both of her hands. She backed up against a wall. He drew close to her and stabbed her chest over and over. With blood dripping onto the white carpet, the woman lifelessly slid down the wall into a sitting position. A painting fell over her body and was cover with blood.

Yvonne felt strangely excited.

The man looked at the body for a few minutes and then he looked at the blood-stained knife.

"She's dead and I'm going to kill myself," he silently reasoned with himself. "The children will be left alone. I can't let that happen."

He walked into the children's room. His wife's spirit followed him, pleading for her children's lives. But he couldn't hear her. He walked up to his five-year-old daughter's bed. She woke up and saw him standing over her. She had a pretty face and long brown hair.

She smiled and asked, "Time to get up, papa?"

Tears flowed down his cheeks. "I love you, my darling."

She opened her mouth to reply when he raised the knife over her defenceless body and plunged it once through the thick covers over her body. She cried out in pain, but he didn't notice.

He walked over to his three-year-old daughter's bed. He didn't waste any time here. While she slept, he stabbed her once through the covers. She never woke up and never felt any pain.

As the spirits watched, the three-year-old's body was surrounded by her spirit guides. Seven of them. Her mother's spirit, sensing danger, rushed to her dead daughter. As the little girl's spirit rose from the body, the two evil spirits rushed in. Yvonne was the first to arrive and enveloped the girl's spirit into her own. The other spirits couldn't stop them. As the mother silently screamed in agony, the dark spirits happily flew away with the frightened spirit of the little girl.

When they arrived on the Dark Side, Chamberlain and Yvonne changed over into ghostly forms of their former bodies. They made the little girl also change over. The leader felt more satisfaction watching a body suffer instead of just a mere spirit.

Her body trembled with fear as tears streaked down her flawless dark face. She had long black hair.

Chamberlain took off her night gown to reveal the body of a typical three-year-old. He did not have sexual assault in mind. Oh, no. He had something else far worse than rape.

"Do you want to take her into the pit and do the honours, Yvonne," Chamberlain asked.

Yvonne felt strangely exhilarated about torturing a little girl. She tried to fight it, but it just overwhelmed her. "May I?"

"Of course, but I want to watch."

They took the little girl named Angelique through a hole in the cave's wall. A passage wound its way down into the darkness. It got colder the farther the group descended. And it was damp. Rats could be heard scurrying around the path, seeming to be oblivious to the spirits. They finally got to the bottom.

Chamberlain found some matches and lit a candle that cast a dim light in the room. He normally shied away from light, but he liked to clearly see every step of the Transformation process. The process that would take away her innocence and replace it with pure evil.

The room was simple and small. There were four rock walls and a rock ceiling high above them. There were no other exits from this space. A stone altar stood in the middle. It was four feet high and only four feet long, specially made for children.

Yvonne picked up the little girl to place her on the altar. But she hesitated. She could remember holding another spirit child in her arms. Her name was Julie, and she was also three, but that was in happier times with Gary and the rest of her spirit children in Canada.

"What's going on?" Chamberlain wanted to know.

To his surprise, Yvonne then changed back into a white spirit and made the little girl also change over. She tucked the child into her spirit and flew up the path.

Chamberlain watched in stunned silence before he pulled himself together. He turned into a black spirit and followed. When Yvonne reached the top, she was confronted by a room full of black spirits. Chamberlain stopped behind her. She turned to face him.

"You are good, Yvonne. You really tricked me, but now you are going to pay the price for eternity," Chamberlain growled.

One of the other dark spirits implied, "Our leader does not get tricked, Chamberlain. We have decided to..."

Chamberlain interrupted, "How dare you, you little insect. I will crush you!"

He raised his arms and lightning arced between his hands like an angel can do. He then pointed his hand at the offending spirit. A bolt hit him in the chest, and he disappeared to be scattered across the Universe.

"Anyone else want to challenge me?" Chamberlain quizzed.

The cave remained silent.

Chamberlain continued, "As you can see, I have the powers of an angel, and no one will ever defeat me. NO ONE!"

He then turned to Yvonne.

"What have you learned, Yvonne?" He angrily asked.

"What have you learned, Yvonne?" the angel gently questioned. They were back in the bright and friendly confines of Heaven.

Yvonne replied, "I've learned that evil spirits from the dark side prey on the spirits of children who have just died. They torture these child souls until they have been turned into evil spirits themselves. They hate the light and hide in the darkness where even angels cannot go."

"We prefer to think of the spirits on the dark side as those who have lost their way and have chosen not to cross over," the angel corrected. "Through God's wisdom, we can't control these misled souls, but we can control those who have crossed over."

"What else have you learned?"

Yvonne carried on, "I've learned how terrible and destructive nightmares can be. Physical beings have no idea how bad they are. My job is to be part of my human life form. To help it and not to harm it. I know I have the power to give my human dreams and nightmares, but I will not do that. Only the Dream Factory can safely manufacture dreams to be given to my physical form through me."

The angel laughed and clapped her hands. "You have always come through for God, Yvonne. This time is no different. Some spirits, after this exercise, have strayed. But you never have, Yvonne in all your physical lives."

She added, "Have a long and flourishing life on Earth, Yvonne." Then the angel disappeared.

CHAPTER FIVE

Rouj's Books

Rouj was the top angel in Heaven and was next in line to become an angel. She had been to Obliiv as a physical being several thousand times and had since retired from that calling. Rouj now studied Earth from Heaven. She believed it was the next planet in all of God's Universe to experience a revelation on a cosmic scale. Other planets, such as Obliiv, had been helped by such events. Now it may be Earth's turn.

Rouj summonsed the angel, Joyce, who had been one of the longest-serving spirits to take on the human form on Earth. Joyce was white with a long flowing gown, large white wings, and long blonde hair.

"I have been watching Earth and I think the people are ready for the spiritual awakening like what had happened in Obliiv," Rouj stated. She was in the form of a spirit – just a whiff of smoke.

She continued, "Before you became an angel, you were a human. What must I do to get the process started for the awakening, Joyce?"

Joyce replied, "The process is simple, and I will help you. First, the five most senior spirits in God's Place must agree to investigate the human race for this honour. Second, the five spirits must come forward with proof that the people on Earth are ready for the awakening and will benefit from it. Third, I will take your proof to God for his approval."

A scroll appeared in Joyce's right hand. She handed the scroll to Rouj and said, "You are the most senior soul in God's Place. Here are the names of the four behind you. I will come to you when I feel you need my help." Joyce disappeared.

Rouj looked at the names on the scroll. All four were in God's Place or Heaven which was a break for Rouj. She summonsed all four to her location and they appeared together as the usual whiffs of smoke. Language was no problem because spirits communicated only with thoughts.

The most senior spirit in Heaven behind Rouj was a primitive life form from the Muhad world and he did not have a name. Next in line was a very early human, also nameless. Number four was a being named Zop from a planet called Doub in a distant galaxy. The last being was called Tribi from the Cous world in a very distant galaxy.

Rouj explained, "I asked you to meet with me so that we can bring the spiritual awakening to a planet called Earth. I need your unanimous support so that I can begin the process."

Tribi was the first to respond, "I have never heard of Earth. I do know of worlds in galaxies close to mine. So, that probably means our worlds are very far apart. But I do know you, Rouj. You are a very experienced and knowledgeable soul. On that basis, I will support you." Then he disappeared.

Zop revealed, "I also know nothing of Earth, but I will support you based on your spotless reputation in God's Place. I will leave it to you to gather the proof." And he was gone.

The last two spirits had no names for a reason. They had no language. But both of these souls entered Rouj's soul, and she could feel their endorsement. They left, leaving Rouj to come up with enough evidence to convince God. She decided to travel to Earth as an invisible spirit to see what she could come up with. Through her studies, she was already familiar with this planet.

* * *

As these thoughts entered her mind, a porthole appeared in front of her. She entered it and crossed over onto the world called Earth. She found herself in the middle of a corn field.

Rouj flew up high into the air to get her bearings and all she could see were endless fields of corn. She flew towards the rising sun. Passing over several villages and towns, she finally found a large city. Flags with white stars in one corner, plus red and white stripes seemed to be flying everywhere.

Looking for a place of worship, she found a mosque. Rouj remembered that this building was of the Islam religion that worshipped only one God. It was a large white building with two miniature minarets standing at the main entrance. A school for Muslim children was built adjacent to the mosque.

Walking though the outside wall, she found a very large open space with no furniture at all. Just a decorated red rug laid on the floor. She went through another wall looking for humans and found two in a small office with no windows. She was invisible to them. There were two men, dark in complexion, who had short black hair and black beards. Both were wearing long casual pants and white long-sleeve shirts. One was sitting in a chair behind a light-brown wooden desk. The other was standing in front of the desk on brown carpeting. The white walls were completely bare.

The man behind the desk asked, "Are you sure we can trust these two. I don't want the FBI getting too close to us."

The other man replied, "They are Muslims who were born in America. Both were secretly trained in Pakistan and know explosives. They just want money to carry out jihad against the American infidels."

"What target do you have in mind?"

"They want to become martyrs for Mohammed. They will carry high explosives onto two separate subway cars in New York City during rush hour. It'll be at the same station, so one may be caught but not both. With Allah's blessing, they both will get through."

"Alright, give them what they need and do not mention me or this mosque. And if this is an FBI trap, you will say nothing."

"Understood." And he left the office.

Rouj thought, "Muslims plotting inside a mosque to commit mass murder."

She left the building and soon found a large Baptist church. Rouj knew this building was of the Christian faith that worshipped only one God.

The old-brick building was over one hundred years old. Two huge solid-oak doors lead inside. After walking through a coat room, two more large doors opened up into the church itself. There were twenty rows of wooden pews on each side, each one was able to seat about ten people. A red carpet in the centre led up the Baptistery. The choir sat on each side, with the pulpit at the very front on the right side. Large stained-glass windows adorned both sides, depicting Jesus, his disciples, and his mother Mary.

You could almost hear the choir sing hymns to the congregation that had packed the church in its heydays many decades ago. At a time when black families had worked and had played in safety and had given thanks to God in the Baptist Church. Those times were long gone when the neighbour gradually deteriorated into what it is now.

Rouj walked through the wall and immediately found two men talking in an otherwise empty structure. They were sitting in the pews. One was seated forward while the other was in the row in front looking back.

Both men were wearing dark suits and white shirts with ties. The tall man looking back was the minister of the church. He was black with short black hair and a slim build.

The other man was white with short brown hair. He was less than six feet in height and had a sizable beer belly.

The black man wanted to know, "Can't you give us a break? You don't have to foreclose. The congregation will come up with the money."

The white man said, "Are you kidding? This church can hold four hundred people. You have a total of thirty-five members. Today's service will be the last one here."

"What's going to happen to the church?"

"It'll be torn down with all the old houses around it to make way for a very large liquor store."

"These buildings go way back. They're part of history. They should be kept as heritage sites."

The white man chuckled and revealed, "An old black neighbourhood in this town is not considered a heritage site."

The white man got up and left.

Tears fell down the black man's face. After serving the lord for over one hundred years, the church was going to be torn down. And it was going to be torn down on his watch. And that moment, the minister deemed himself a failure as a clergyman.

Rouj pondered, "A Christian church closing because of declining enrolment in a growing population."

She left this city, flew to the south and found an enormous church. It was round with several huge windows around the building. Skylights on the roof bathed the congregation in sunshine. The main area inside housed hundreds of pews that were padded with blue comfortable material. The pulpit was on an actual stage where the congregation were treated to songs and dances praising the lord.

There must have been over a thousand people inside and they were just now filing out. Rouj flew over their heads to an office in the back. It was a huge luxurious room. Red shag carpeting covered the floor wall-to-wall.

A large mahogany desk stood in the middle with a chubby white man sitting behind it on a soft black-leather chair. He had short thinning brown hair and wore an expensive tailor-made suit. He was the minister of the People's Community Church.

Another white man was sitting in a comfortable wooden chair, where the seat and arms were padded in a red material, in front of the desk. He had a thin build and short brown hair and had the same taste in pricy clothes. He was the assistant minister.

The walls were white with several diplomas hanging on the wall behind the desk. An original oil painting hung on another wall with a soft light shining on it. At the far wall was a comfortable sofa. A statue of Jesus stood on a four-foot solid-oak stand beside the sofa.

The chubby man pointed at the twenty collection plates sitting on his desk and remarked, "Look at all the cash there. It'll be thousands once we open the envelopes and count the money."

The other man agreed, "Yep, we really hit the jackpot. Do you want to do the same thing with it?"

"Yeah, we'll put half in our slush fund. It must be getting pretty big."

"Hundreds of thousands. And the money is as clean as a whistle."

The chubby man looked at his watch and disclosed, "The treasurer will be here in two hours. Let's get busy and count the money for him. He always appreciates the extra work we do for him."

Both men laughed.

The chubby man threw his coat over the statue of Jesus.

He revealed, "I just feel better if he's not watching me."

They laughed again.

Rouj observed to herself, "A Christian minister stealing from his own church."

She continued, "I've had enough of this. Things may be different on another continent."

She flew east across a great ocean to a country that practised mainly Judaism. It was surrounded by other countries that practised mainly Islam. She stopped at a very large and a very old city where the three religions that worshipped one God laid claim.

A mob of angry young Muslims were throwing stones at Israeli soldiers. The soldiers fired tear gas at them and were pushing the group back along a narrow street lined on both sides by ancient buildings. A Palestinian was on top of one of these buildings with a rifle. He peered through his scope at a soldier below. He squeezed the trigger and the soldier fell to the ground dead.

The other soldiers thought that the shot came from the mob. In unison, they lowered their automatic rifles on the crowd and fired. Several civilians fell to the ground - some dead and some wounded. The others scattered as the soldiers fired at them. Several more fell to the dusty ground before the others finally disappeared.

Rouj silently said to herself, "The human race even kills at a holy city for three major religions. And these three religions are essentially the same – they all worship only one God. The God that created what they call Heaven."

She was then drawn to another nearby country that was at war within its own borders. She was looking for men that made bombs. She found one group in a small village. There were five men with dark complexions and black beards in a dirty house. The house appeared to be made out of mud brick. The floor was dusty. There were four small windows that were covered by thick black curtains. A naked light bulb hung overhead shedding a weak light. An old wooden table was in the centre covered with chemicals, rifles, ammunition.

One handed a backpack and car keys to another man. "You will be a martyr in the eyes of Allah."

The man with the backpack nodded and left.

He entered a rusted red car and drove it into a large city. He knew where he was going, and he saw it ahead. He gunned the engine and drove into a crowded outdoor market. The car got stuck with crates under it. That's when he detonated the bomb. A fiery explosion tossed fruit, vegetables, and body parts in all directions.

"Is this possible? A Muslim killing Muslims to free Muslims from a foreign invader," Rouj asked herself.

There was one place she wanted to see. She heard about it in her studies but wanted to see if it was true. She flew to Northern Ireland and came down in an old city. She invisibly walked around, listening to people's conversations. But one caught her attention. She walked through the wall of a small pub. Two men were sitting in a booth at a window and she beside one.

The pub could hold only about fifty people, but it still made money. Its patrons were heavy drinkers. The wooden bar was short with several bottles of hard liquor displayed on a cabinet at the back wall. Behind the bar were three beer taps and stools lined the front. There were ten wooden and very uncomfortable booths, four of which had a view of the street through windows.

They were young white men with short brown hair and wearing working clothes of jeans and light jackets. They softly spoke to each other.

One man remarked, "Sean, the war's over. They made peace with England."

The other man responded, "Well, I didn't. We should be part of the Republic of Ireland. Instead, a few Protestants are keeping us apart. I say kill them all."

"Are you forgetting what Father O'Reilly said at yesterday's mass about the Catholics and Protestants getting along just fine now?"

The angry man drained his glass of beer and asserted, "This Catholic ain't one of them. I might bag myself a couple of Protestants before they kill me." He got up and left the pub.

"I guess the material I heard was correct. Two branches of the Christian religion killing each other based solely on religion. If any race needs God's help, humans should be at the top of the list.," Rouj revealed to herself.

Rouj found the porthole and crossed over into Heaven.

* * *

The angel, Joyce was waiting for her. "What have you come

up with, Rouj," She asked.

Rouj replied, "I have more than enough to prove that all religions on Earth are in decline after several Earth-centuries of
growth. Even though the human population has greatly increased, those actually attending a place of worship has continued to dwindle.

"Wars between religions has been happening for centuries,
but it has recently picked up substantially. Right now, it appears that Islam is at war with Christianity and Judaism. But at
the same time, Muslims are killing Muslims and Christians are
killing Christians. But the attacks and fighting are the worst in
human history. Millions are being slaughtered. And the strange
thing here is that the ordinary people in these religions are
against this violence.

"And some leaders of these religions are actually stealing
from their congregations and other leaders are preaching violence to their followers. Humans have lost their way and are
failing in their spirituality. They need our help."

Joyce smiled and remarked, "You have done well, Rouj.
Have you decided who will write the books?"

Rouj looked puzzled and questioned, "The books?"

The angel replied, "Yes. The books. Don't you remember the
three books that were written on Obliiv that changed the planet?"

Rouj answered, "Just barely. That was hundreds of generations ago."

Joyce carried on, "If God approves of your plan, you must
have someone to write three books with words that come from
inside God's Place. The first will describe the spirit world on
Earth and make it less frightening. It will also disclose that God
does not demand prayer or worship, and that every spirit will
be admitted into what humans call Heaven. That there is no
hell or Satan.

"The second book will describe what the inside of Heaven
really looks like and how spirits and angels function here. It

will also reinforce some aspects from the first book.

"The last book will give humans a look into their future."

Rouj asked, "That sounds straight forward. How do I pick the humans to write these books?"

The angel responded, "These humans must be kindred spirits living on Earth. Do you know anything about kindred spirits?"

"A bit, but not much."

"Kindred spirits are very rare and are protected by God. They are loving partners who spend eternity together. There are very few. Some are here right now – others are scattered across God's Universe. There are a handful on Earth as we speak. Can I give you a suggestion?"

"Please."

"There is a couple living in what humans call Canada. Yvonne and Gary. Through a mistake, they were parted before their conception. It has taken years for their spirit guides to finally get them back together. To write these books, one must be a living human who will write the books and get them published. The other's human body must have recently died, with the spirit crossing over into God's Place. The spirit who crossed over will feed the words from Heaven to the mate left behind.

"This couple would be the logical choice. As things stand now, Gary will live on Earth for at least ten years – long enough to write the books. Yvonne, however, is going to die from liver cancer in two years. If you pick these two kindred spirits, I can arrange for Yvonne to die from cancer in just a couple of months."

"I'm anxious to get this started. I can remember now. I personally saw the great benefits the spiritual awakening brought to Obliiv. I believe it can do the same for Earth. I pick Yvonne and Gary to write these books."

The angel revealed, "I have just asked the other four members of your group. They all agree with your choice. I must now ask God."

Joyce disappeared and materialized in front of God who sat on his throne in a huge round room filled with splendor. There were columns around the circumference of the hall, covered with gold from one world. A large statue, donated by a primitive race, stood to one side. Scratchings carved into a flat rock hung on the wall. Paintings and other artwork presented to God as gifts from several different races around his Universe decorated the walls. The floor was white marble, and the walls were a dazzling white. The ceiling was a white dome where the images of the spirits God had personally sent to help other worlds were engraved. The throne was made from mahogany on top of a high platform shaped from a precious stone from a far-off planet.

His angel, Joyce disclosed, "Your top spirit in your Place requests your permission to start the spiritual awakening on Earth."

God observed, "I can see the evidence that Rouj has collected. She is a very resourceful spirit and I am very proud of her. Do you agree with her, Joyce?"

"Yes, I do, God."

"And she picked Yvonne and Gary to write these books."

"Yes, she did, my Lord."

"Very well. Rouj may go ahead with her plan."

But God cautioned, "I want you to be sure that the love of these two kindred spirits does not die. You know how I feel about their kind and how I will protect the few that have survived."

His angel promised, "I will watch them very closely. Your kindred spirits will be kept safe."

She disappeared from God's presence and reappeared in front of Rouj.

Joyce divulged, "God has approved of your plan. But keep this in mind. This is risky for Yvonne and Gary. The eternal love they share with each other could be severed in the awakening. This would make God very angry. So, I will be watching you very closely. If I see any warning signs, I will personally cancel the spiritual awakening. Be careful, Rouj. Be very careful."

"Thank you. And I will be careful."

* * *

As promised by the angel, Yvonne was diagnosed with liver cancer in February 2010. But she was not receiving treatment because she had to wait to get a biopsy in the middle of March.

One night while Yvonne was sleeping, Joyce appeared to her as a dream.

She revealed, "You will die from this cancer, Yvonne. But when that happens, you will be greeted by your mother and taken into Heaven. However, you must not fight this disease. You must set your soul free as soon as possible so that you and Gary can write three books that will change your world. They will be words from Heaven. Your words to your kindred spirit, Gary."

Yvonne did not remember that dream, but it was stored in her subconscious. Following the angel's directions, Yvonne did not fight the cancer although she did not realize what she was doing at the time. In February, she started to deteriorate very fast. She was admitted to hospital in London, Ontario where a team of doctors took tests to begin treatment. To their surprise, however, Yvonne died on March 2, 2010.

On March 2, Yvonne was alone in a partially dark hospital room on the sixth floor in tower D, Room 402B. It was a semi-private room, but the other patient was sleeping with a curtain drawn between the two beds. Gary had given the hospital staff orders not to resuscitate when she died, so she was not hooked up to a monitor. She knew that her physical body was going to die that night, but she held onto life until Gary left at 8:00 P.M.

She felt what she had thought was fear, but it was really apprehension about going into the unknown. Then her heart stopped. Yvonne was now standing over her dead body looking down. She looked up and saw figures on the other side of the bed. There appeared to be a translucent curtain in front of them. The curtain gradually disappeared revealing Yvonne's mother, Jean, and Yvonne's seven spirit guides.

Jean was an English lady who had chosen to appear before her daughter as she had looked while in her fifties. She was tall with an attractive figure and short brown hair. Her face carried the air of nobility.

She walked around the bed and stopped in front of her daughter, who was a grey-ghostly image of her physical body. Yvonne looked at her mother with uncertainty in her eyes. Jean smiled and took Yvonne in her arms. Yvonne tightly hugged her back as tears flowed down her cheeks.

She pulled away from her daughter and revealed, "Welcome home, sweetheart. I'm going to take you into Heaven, and you will soon remember that you have been there before. Your spirit guides will stay with you until you get comfortable. You must now change over into a spirit."

Yvonne saw that her mother had changed over into a whiff of smoke. Yvonne looked down at herself to reveal that she had also changed. Jean put her arm around Yvonne and lead her to a porthole. Both entered the porthole and crossed over. Yvonne was now in Heaven.

Yvonne was summonsed to appear before Rouj's group. They were all in the forms of spirits; just whiffs of smoke.

"I trust that you have got reacquainted with God's Place?" Rouj asked.

Yvonne replied, "Yes, I have. I'm so happy to be here. I just wish that Gary could have come with me."

"You will be together, but first you two must write three books."

"Three books?" Yvonne was confused.

"God has decided to allow us to write these books as the spiritual awakening on Earth. It will allow humans to choose the right path if they wish. This group and you will help Gary to write these books. They will be published by Colleen."

"I have to tell Gary about this. He's open to spirits and will do as you have asked."

"I know he will. And you two will be given an awareness only possessed by the angels. You will see God, you will see where he resides, you will see miracles beyond the belief of spirits. This will be passed onto the humans through these books."

The first book had only taken five months to write and was about Gary's and Yvonne's experiences in the spirit world on Earth. Aside from the fact that it was a real tear-jerker for Gary to write, otherwise it was an easy task.

But the second book was much different. It was about Heaven and those who resided there. Gary had no knowledge of these things at all. And Yvonne's knowledge was limited. But the book was being written at quick pace. Gary heard nothing with his ears or in his mind as he wrote down the words on his computer. The script just seemed to flow through his body to his fingers by some unseen force.

He was starting to feel chronically tired. He got little sleep at night. Bouts of depression became more common even with the anti-depressant pills that he had been taking for years. And he began to worry about minor things. Yvonne was starting to see these changes taking over Gary – physically and mentally. And she was worried. If only Joyce had seen this building up.

* * *

Then disaster struck. The date was September 28, 2010.

The entire family was in the basement of their London, Ontario home. Gary, his spirit wife Yvonne, and their eleven spirit children. They got together here every night to watch T.V. A television stood on a dark-coloured wooden desk in front of the only window. A sofa stood against the far wall facing the T.V.

The door to the patio was open revealing a forested ravine behind the town houses.

Gary sat on the sofa with the younger children – Julie, Jason, Leigh, and Debbie. They watched the T.V. and played with their toys. Two young boys – Oliver and Anthony – sat on the floor and played with construction toys. A one-year-old-toddler, Gabriel happily walked and crawled around the room. Yvonne sat on a chair holding five-month-old Christopher. Three teenagers – Shirley, Stephen, JoJo – sat on the floor in front of Gary. They were all in the ghostly forms of their last human bodies, but Gary rarely saw them except in his mind.

These children had been directed by spirit guides to Gary and Yvonne for protection and guidance. Nine children were murdered by a parent, one was accidentally shot, the baby died of neglect. They all would be the couple's children in their next life together.

Yvonne was worried as she watched Gary. Before the second book, he would get into conversations with the teenagers, especially Shirley about UFO's, life on other planets, what spirits thought of disasters on Earth. Now his glassy eyes silently stared at the T.V. She could feel his depression, she could feel his weariness. She had to do something to snap him out of that.

Yvonne smiled and cheerfully asked, "Why don't you order out? KFC sounds good."

Gary listlessly replied, "I'll put on weight."

"You've been good. Just once won't hurt."

Gary came to life. He jumped at the chance, but he went over the top. He ordered the family mega meal. Yvonne hit the roof.

She shouted, "I thought you would have ordered something you could eat in one night! You can feed an army with that! I hate you!"

And she left with the baby to a place where she felt safe and could be alone. It was dark as she sat on the trunk of a fallen tree. She knew what had happened. It was more than the chicken. It was something that had been brewing since they started the second book. Their eternal love was gone, just like that. Several lifetimes together on Earth were now just history and there would never be another one.

Yvonne cried at the loss.

That night, Gary got up at 2:30 A.M. to urinate. He returned to his bed and just sat on the edge. He was having trouble sleeping again.

A female voice revealed, "I'm one of God's angels. My name is Joyce. We were afraid this would happen with the spiritual awakening on Earth. You and Yvonne are no longer kindred spirits. And I have cancelled the awakening. The second book will never be finished."

"Wait," Gary pleaded, but she was gone.

"Lord God," Gary appealed. "Please don't let the tragedy that happened to me and Yvonne be in vain. Please allow us to finish this book."

A male voice gently replied, "I am very pleased with you and Yvonne. You both have made huge sacrifices that will benefit others. You may finish the second book, but the third will not be started."

"Thank you, Lord God," Gary uttered.

Then Joyce's voice returned. "I'm very happy that God has granted your request. We will help you to finish this book. And the spiritual awakening will continue on Earth."

When Gary laid down, God spoke to Gary once more. "I will allow you and Yvonne and all your children to be together one final time. It will be long and happy lives. And once your body dies, you will not have to go through the process. You can begin your next life right away."

"Thank you, God."

Yvonne returned the next morning and found the family in the darkness of the upstairs living room. In here was a fifty-inch T.V., a relatively new sofa and love seat. A China cabinet stood to one side filled with Yvonne's special items from her previous life. The brown rug, however, was old and worn.

It was 5:00 A.M. and Gary was ready to take the dogs for their usual early-morning walk.

"I love you," Gary remarked when he saw that Yvonne had returned.

Yvonne corrected, "You don't love me. Deep down inside, you know you don't love me."

Gary knew she was right.

The children were sitting in front of the big T.V. waiting for Gary to turn on TVO/Kids at 6:00 A.M.

Three-year-old Julie asked, "Will we be together as a family in the next life, Mom?"

Yvonne replied, "I don't know, Julie. I don't know."

Gary then divulged, "God told me last night that Mom, myself and all you guys will be a family in our next life."

Julie cheered and said, "Thanks, Dad."

* * *

God had summonsed Joyce, Rouj and her group to his room. Joyce appeared as an angel. The others were spirits – whiffs of smoke.

God declared, "Because of your carelessness, I have lost two spirits that would have been in love for eternity. There are so few kindred spirits that the loss of even two is a tragedy. I must punish all of you for your serious inattention.

"Zop, Tribi and the nameless two from the Muhad and Earth worlds. The four of you will spend one Earth month on the moon that over looks Earth. During this period, you will know time. You will spend the entire term looking at Earth where you helped to destroy two kindred spirits. And you will pray to me on a daily basis asking for forgiveness. When your time expires, you will return here."

The four spirits vanished to begin their sentence.

God continued, "I am deeply disappointed in you, Rouj.

You were the leader in this mess, and you will be punished more severely. I was tempted to cancel your promotion to become an angel. But, despite your lapse in judgement, I need your advice and experience with me. So, you will become an angel after your punishment is over. You will join your group on the moon and everything I told them will apply to you, except that you will remain there for one-Earth solar cycle."

Rouj disappeared.

God lamented, "You, Joyce have disappointed me the most. You have delivered me faithful service in all tasks that I have directed you to complete. Not once have you let me down – until now. And you have cost me something very dear to my heart. Two kindred spirits. I considered making you a spirit for eternity, but that would be a loss for me. Instead, I will temporarily strip you of your powers as an angel."

The wings on her back disappeared and she turned into a spirit.

"Because your mistake was on Earth, you will go to Earth and haunt a convent there as a spirit. As with the others, you will know time. You will spend your time there asking everyone you see for forgiveness. When someone finally forgives you, you will materialize as a nun using your last physical appearance on Earth. You will not sing. You will not speak. But you will complete any chores the other nuns give you. You will attend every service they offer. They will give you just enough food and drink to survive. And you will pray to me everyday asking for forgiveness. When Rouj completes her sentence, you will return here as an angel."

Joyce vanished.

* * *

The family was in the basement T.V. room that evening. Gary was on his first beer when he showed his family a new talent he had acquired.

He simply said, "Elvis Presley." and Elvis Presley's spirit appeared; a thin Elvis Presley.

Elvis asked, "What's up, man?"

Gary replied, "I've always wanted to meet you. You are the king of rock and roll."

"Well, Thank you. Thank you very much."

Gary and Elvis laughed.

Gary then enquired, "Why haven't you started a new life."

Elvis responded, "I just haven't decided what I want to do. I was thinking maybe a singer. What do you think?"

Gary answered, "You will, no doubt, make a great singer. Thank you, Elvis."

Elvis Presley disappeared.

Gary wanted to know, "Did you guys see him?"

Yvonne and Shirley indicated that they had, indeed, seen him.

"Can you get Martin Luther King Jr or Malcolm X here, Dad," Shirley requested.

Gary mentioned their names, but they did not appear.

"Their spirits have to be in Heaven. These two have probably started new physical lives," Gary explained.

Then he had an idea. "Michael Jackson."

Michael Jackson appeared.

"Hi everyone. I'm Michael. Who are you?"

Gary replied, "I'm Gary." He pointed at Shirley. "My daughter, Shirley wanted to meet a famous black person. And they don't get any bigger than you."

Michael smiled and approached Shirley. He took her hand and kissed it.

Michael remarked, "The pleasure of meeting you, my dear, is all mine." Then he vanished.

Gary asked Shirley, "Did you notice something about him?"

She responded, "Yeah. He was black."

After a period of silence, Yvonne mentioned, "I care about you, Gary. Maybe when our next life on Earth has ended, we can choose to be with each other. There is a lot of freedom in Heaven."

Then she questioned, "Will you sleep in my bed tonight?"

Gary answered, "No. You said it's over."

"I love you. Do you love me?"

"Yes, I do." He could never refuse her. "I'll sleep with you tonight."

Julie queried, "Are you making up?"

Gary replied, "Yes, we are."

Julie carried on, "Will you kiss her?"

Gary walked over to Yvonne's chair. His lips gently caressed hers which made his soul boil with passion.

Yvonne declared, "I love you, Gary."

Gary uttered, "I love you, too. Will our love ever die?"

She professed, "No, Gary. It will never die."

God heard this and he was pleased.

CHAPTER SIX

The Expected Return Of Colleen

There was a buzz throughout Heaven. Trillions of spirits gathered around and over a single porthole. There were spirits from inhabitable worlds stretching from one end of the Universe to the other and some from worlds that have ceased to exist. Things got so tight that spirits temporarily merged into each other to get a better look. Those who couldn't get that close lined the route of honour.

Three angels appeared in front of the porthole forcing the crowd of spirits to back up. The angels were in the form of Earth beings since the spirit that was about to cross over was from Earth. They all had the typical appearance of angels: long, white, flowing gowns and large white wings on their backs. The two males had short black hair, while the golden hair of the lone female was long and softly beautiful.

The crowd, through their collective thoughts, cheered when Colleen stepped through the porthole. She had the standard spirit appearance – a whiff of smoke. She stood in front of the porthole frozen in place by uncertainty. She knew her physical body had died, but, as with all returning spirits, she was momentarily confused.

Colleen thought, "Why are they all so happy to see me?"

Her thoughts could not be heard by any of the spirits over the merrymaking of the heavenly souls.

The female angel walked over to Colleen and gently touched her. Colleen stepped back, still unsure. But with the touch, she was transformed into her old physical form. She was a white woman, a bit overweight. But she was thinning and rapidly loosing weight, probably due to cancer. Her height was about five foot six inches. The shoulder-length hair was coloured blonde. She was wearing the flowing white robe of the angels.

This female angel was one of the oldest Earth angels in the service of God. She had been a physical being on Earth several hundred times, starting before the dawn of civilization.

She spoke out loud to Colleen in a in silky voice, "Welcome home Colleen. You are among friends. Your arrival had been anticipated and all of Heaven's souls turned out to see one of the top spirits in God's Universe."

The angel smiled and swept her arm in a wide arc. "Look at them rejoicing. Hear their joy. It's all for you, Colleen. It's all for you."

The angel stepped away to give centre stage to Colleen, who slowly turned in a full circle to face as many souls as she could. It was all coming back now – she remembered who she really was. Their acclamation filled her with jubilation. She smiled and raised both arms. The multitude went wild.

The female angel approached her and softly uttered, "Follow me, Colleen. Many other souls are waiting to see you. Then you have a council to attend where God, himself has an interest."

With the female angel leading the way, Colleen walked down Heaven's centre path, paved with gold. The path was out of bounds to all spirits without God's permission. It had been used by Abraham, Jwottf, Cxx, Jesus, Mohammed, long-serving spirits like Colleen; to name just a few.

With the two male angels behind her, Colleen waved to the acclaim and applause of the countless spirits along the parade route. Fairies flew around Colleen leaving colourful ribbons behind them. Sparks lit up the path ahead of the female angel creating a rainbow effect. Colleen was showered with tiny diamonds that sparkled with brilliant colours as they fell around her. Overhead, orbs of all sizes dashed in all directions and angles.

The spectacle, however, came to a halt at the never-ending pillar. It was blocking the path.

Then a powerful male voice loudly echoed throughout Heaven, "Welcome back Colleen. It is very rare for me to speak to spirits, but you are one of my most trusted souls in my Place. You have done well. I am very pleased."

The crowd of spirits silently cheered. It was not often that they heard God.

The never-ending pillar disappeared, and Colleen walked alone to the next porthole. She stopped at it and turned toward the crowd. She lifted both arms and they rejoiced, giving her a final ovation as she disappeared into the porthole.

Colleen was one of the top spirits in Heaven. As a matter of fact, she was the only one of the top-ten souls still having a physical life on another world. In the spirit hierarchy, Colleen's soul was number six. Very close to becoming an angel.

Her life on Earth, however, was not nearly as spectacular. Despite the fact that she entered university when most children her age were still in elementary school, she lived a very modest life in the shadows. In university, she earned five doctorate degrees including one in divinity. She was a talented writer and published several books, none in her own name.

Colleen was one of the best clairvoyants in the world and, according to Yvonne's spirit, she was the best on Earth. But the masses never heard of her. She was never invited to attend radio and T.V. shows. That's because she preferred to live a humble life out of the spotlight. She quietly did free clairvoyant work for police departments all over North America, but her passion was to help society's insignificant folks while charging them a very small fee. Sometimes no fee. And this was how she lived on a fraction of the income she should have had. Sometimes she didn't have enough money to pay for the basics. This was the role Colleen had chosen.

Colleen appeared in the room where the Test for Gary had been carried out. Waiting for her were five other spirits in their old physical forms and an angel standing in a group on the lower floor. The stool on the high stage was empty.

One soul was the top spirit in Heaven. Her name was Rouj. She will be the next spirit to become an angel. She was short with the ash-grey skin of the Obliiv world. She was bald with very large eyes. Her mouth had no lips and two holes for a nose. Her body was short, as were her two legs and two arms. The grey and white clothes she wore seemed lifeless.

The number-two spirit had been a primitive life form on Muhad, known on Earth as Mars. He was a fish with six short legs growing out of the belly. Except for the legs, he looked exactly like a fish. Silver scales, gills, fish eyes, fins. But he was a big six-foot fish. He did not have a name, but on Muhad he did have a functioning brain; the only requirement for spirits. He could receive and give thoughts but had never spoken out loud.

Next was a human, a very early man. He had a huge hairy and naked body. The mouth area was very large and filled with teeth. The upper skull that housed the brain was small. Because he had lived so early in human development, he also didn't have a name. He too could do the thought process, but when he tried to physically speak, all you heard was a grunt.

Number four was a past resident of the Doub world in a distant galaxy. It had been an advanced planet torn apart by wars between people who looked different. The planet was wiped out when a distant supernova exploded. The scientists saw it coming, but they could do nothing. They were not capable of space travel because of the wars. His name was Zop. He expertly hopped around on one leg. His two arms were about half the size of humans, although he towered to over eight feet tall. His head was in his chest with a small hole where he fed. His internal organs were way out of whack with those of humans. His skin was a glowing green colour. His physical body died in the supernova.

The last spirit in the room was a being from the Cous world. His name was Tribi. He was only about two feet tall with pink skin. He had no arms or legs but had a huge head twice as large as a human. There were two small eyes that became permanently shut through evolution. There was no nose and a small slit for a mouth. This race was one of the first to be civilized in God's Universe and they are still thriving. They have not physically spoken for several thousand generations. They use the brain to communicate and to give them their wants. If they want food, all they have to do is think about it and food will appear. If they want to be entertained, all they have to do is think about it and entertainment will appear. And they are very peaceful, content with their physical world. Tribi's world was in a very distant galaxy, out of the reach of Obliiv. But they still had enemies. When they had been rarely attacked, however, these beings had destroyed the aggressors with just a thought.

The single angel present was the blonde female who had led the parade in Colleen's honour. Her name was Joyce. She would remain speechless and just observe with a smile.

It must be explained again that the names given to these worlds are not their real names, but names given to them from those in Heaven for simplicity. And because of language difficulties, the names of the beings are as close as the authors can get to what they actually are.

Because of language difficulties, only thoughts were exchanged among the group.

Rouj revealed, "We all are very happy to have a spirit of your stature back home, Colleen. As with all spirits, your memory is a little fuzzy when you crossed over into God's Place. And the parade we had in your honour probably made it worse. But listen very closely. You are going to have to make a very big decision.

"We were actually expecting you, Colleen. When you were in hospital, we took the unusual step of stopping your heart. The doctor is now working on your body. Whether he is successful or not will depend on your answer."

Colleen groggily asked, "If he doesn't bring me back in a few seconds, I'll be brain dead."

Rouj smiled and replied, "You are still linked to Earth. There is no time here, so there's no rush for us. You will be back in time if that's what you want."

Rouj carried on, "These books that Yvonne and Gary are writing are very important to us. The first one will let beings on Earth know about the spirits on their world. The second is the most important. It will show what is inside God's Place. Or Heaven to the human race. The third will give Earth beings a glimpse of the future."

"Why are you doing this for Earth and not other worlds?" Colleen questioned with stronger thoughts.

Rouj responded, "Oh, we have done this for many worlds, but God must approve any such action first. That's why the angel is here to observe us and to report back to God. My own world of Obliiv was graced with such literature that changed the planet. My people learned to live with the spirits and to be their friends. And death was no longer feared, because we all learned about God's Place which is our true home. I'm not saying that Earth will change like that because they are totally different people."

Rouj disclosed, "Here is the choice you must make, Colleen. We want you to return to Earth and continue to guide Yvonne and Gary as you have done in the past. But this time, you will be in charge of the books. But in God's Place, spirits have almost absolute freedom. So, if you decline our offer, you will remain with us."

Colleen was quick to answer. "I have guided these two for years and it would make sense for me to continue to do so. I really had no idea how important these books really are. Even with a spirit helping a human, it never dawned on me. Yes, I'll go back."

Rouj added, "The words for the second book are coming through Yvonne's eyes to Gary. She is describing her experiences in God's Place, plus the experiences of other spirits and angels in God's Place."

Joyce, Rouj and her group didn't realize it at this time, but these books would turn into a disaster that would result in their punishment.

* * *

Colleen nodded and left the room through the porthole. Before leaving Heaven, however, she wanted to contact Yvonne and Gary. She sensed that they were walking the dogs.

While on Earth, Yvonne did not look like a spirit. She had taken on the ghostly form of her old physical body. She was under six feet tall with a full figure. Her hair was long and pre-mature-grey for her forty-seven years. Her face, which had never seen makeup, was clear and fresh.

Gary was sixty-three years old and was six feet tall. He was still overweight, but he had lost thirty pounds by exercising and following a diet set up by Yvonne after her death. His moustache and short hair were grey.

Colleen called out, "Gary, Gary..."

Gary heard someone call his name in his head over and over.

"Who is this?" Gary questioned.

"I am the spirit who has been chosen to guide you two," Colleen replied.

"Are you my spirit guide?"

"No. I am more advanced than them. Just as your children are novices to Yvonne, Yvonne and spirit guides are novices to me."

"Are you Colleen?"

"My name means nothing now."

"Are you in Heaven?"

"Yes."

Colleen commanded, "I will guide Yvonne and yourself for the rest of your life. When it comes to the books, you will not make a move unless I tell you. If I tell you to be at a place at one-fifteen, you will be there at one-fifteen and not one-sixteen. These books are not yours, but they belong to those in Heaven. Both of you will listen to me and obey me."

Gary was still puzzled about who he was talking to. He didn't recognize the voice.

"What do we call you?" Gary asked.

"She's gone," Yvonne revealed.

* * *

Later that afternoon, Gary fed the dogs at their 4:00 P.M. routine time. As usual, he put Princess's dish in the living room of his house.

His house interior was not the neatest on the block. The living room was painted in an off-white and contained a relatively new red sofa, with a matching love seat. There were also a recently purchased dark-wood coffee table, two end tables, and matching lamps. A fifty-inch T.V. stood in front of them. The brown carpet, however, had seen better days. It was very worn and shredded in places. Although the room had been recently painted, his dog Oakie, a brown German Shepherd mix, had scratched the paint off the wall where she had slept.

Princess, a black Labrador Retriever, would typically dive right into the food and have it quickly gobbled up. But today, she seemed to lose interest in the food. Instead, she just watched the kitchen from the living room. And once she did start to eat, it was unusually slow.

Gary was standing in the kitchen washing some utensils.

The kitchen was equally in disrepair. Three brown cupboard doors had fallen off and had not been replaced. The brown linoleum floor had a large hole, exposing the wood underneath. The walls varied in colour from white to off-white to a bit of yellow. There were two large windows giving a view of the wooded ravine behind the house.

Gary heard a voice call out, "Hi, Gary."

It was definitely Colleen's voice.

Gary reasoned to himself, "These are just my thoughts. Colleen is going to call me tonight or tomorrow."

The voice remarked, "It's me, Gary. Sorry about the way I talked to you two earlier."

Colleen's spirit was now with Gary and Yvonne in their kitchen. Unseen to Gary, Colleen continued, "These books are important to us. More important than I had thought earlier. When I had crossed over, the top spirits had been very glad to see me. They had put me in charge of your two because of my stature in Heaven and our previous relationship."

Colleen said, "I'm sorry that I scared Princess. I'll leave you alone with your family." And she was gone.

"What did she look like, Yvonne?" Gary enquired.

Yvonne answered, "That was obviously Colleen. She looked only about ten years younger and had blonde hair. She looked like she did before she got the cancer, except for the hair."

"Colleen's body has died, Gary," Yvonne concluded.

* * *

Colleen's spirit flew from London to Woodstock General Hospital. The hospital is an old red-brick full-service hospital located in the north end of the city. It's small with only 113 beds and dates back over a century.

She walked through the walls into the semi-private room where her body laid dying on a bed. As promised by Rouj, this was the moment when Colleen's remains died. The room was brightly lit. Two nurses and a doctor were at her bedside. A heart monitor was at the head of the bed to one side.

"We're losing her," the doctor told the two nurses as he watched the irregular heart beats on the monitor.

Then the heart monitor flat lined. Colleen was dead.

The doctor began Cardiopulmonary Resuscitation, as another nurse rushed in with a defibrillator which was the last-ditch attempt to restart her heart.

The doctor continued the CPR on Colleen as the nurse readied the defibrillator.

Unseen to them, Colleen's spirit guide left the corpse. Then her own spirit entered her own body only about ten seconds after she had died. Her heart started and the heart monitor picked up normal activity. The doctor smiled. He thought that he had just brought Colleen back from the dead.

CHAPTER SEVEN

The Angels

Becoming one of God's angels is no easy task. Rouj from the Obliiv world was one such example. She had worked her way up from a novice that had just been created by God to the top spirit in Heaven.

Rouj was no longer interested in returning to her home world as a physical being. She had done that thousands of times. As with all spirits that had travelled to other worlds to become solid people, she had retained the physical characteristics of her home planet whenever she must take on a solid form. Otherwise, she was just a whiff of smoke.

* * *

After her sentence on the Earth moon had ended, Rouj stepped through the porthole to the silent cheers of the crowd of trillions of spirits. She had looked just like them – a whiff of smoke. She had been surprised to see this event in her honour. She'd had been part of the crowd for other spirits, but never the guest of honour. Three angels, who had always kept their physical forms, were waiting for her. A female and two males who had been part of the Obliiv world as spirits.

They had short white gowns because of their stature and large white wings on their back. The wings looked too heavy and too big for these short people to carry, but the wings were light and were proudly displayed. These angels were dwarf-like beings with the grey skin of the Obliiv world. They were bald with very large eyes. Their mouths had no lips and two holes where the nose should have been.

The female angel, known as Ysebbi, had been to Obliiv several thousand times. She started out on that planet before the great civilization was founded. She fought against the wars that followed and was there for the revered spiritual awakening. Ysebbi read the first literature published describing the spirits that lived on Obliiv and then the description of God's Place that came after. When her last life ended, she became a spirit guide. And then an angel.

The female angel approached Rouj, who was still confused, but was able to overcome this handicap quicker than a human. The angel gently touched Rouj who immediately took on the physical appearance of an Obliivian. She wore the flowing white robe of the angels and looked exactly like them, except for the wings.

The angel smiled. That was something Rouj never saw on Obliiv.

The angel spoke out loud in a soothing voice, "Welcome home, Rouj. Do you plan to visit Obliiv as a solid being again?"

Rouj answered, "No. I have been to that world thousands of times. There are no more lessons for me to learn from another life. I am a complete spirit."

"Will you become a spirit guide?"

"No. I have just decided to serve God right here in his Place."

"Very well," the angel said. "God has given spirits great freedom in his Place."

The female angel turned to the spirits crowded around them and raised her left arm. The multitude went silent. Then she pointed her right arm at Rouj and said, "Rouj's soul has returned home to stay."

The mass of spirits exploded in silent jubilation.

Ysebbj started to lead Rouj down the path paved with gold to the din of joyous celebrating spirits around them. Rouj could hear nothing, but she heard it and felt it in her mind. She raised her arms and smiled for the Heavenly souls. Colourful ferries circled around Rouj's head and orbs flew overhead. The faint aroma of the heaju flower surrounded her head, as the orange and blue blooms showered Rouj and the delighted crowd. In front of the guest of honour, the gold on the path melted. She entered the liquid without pain. When she continued, the gold hardened leaving her bare footprints on the path for eternity.

They stopped at the never-ending pillar which blocked their path.

A hush went over the spirits as a booming voice thunderously rocked Heaven, "Welcome home, Rouj. All is forgiven. You have been a faithful and obedient servant to me, even before the enlightenment on your former world. I have given your soul a special spot in my chambers that has been reserved only for the prophets that I have sent forth to help the people on other worlds. And you will be at my side as an angel once you have completed the Examination."

The throng of spirits roared their approval of God's words.

The never-ending pillar disappeared, leaving a porthole in front of Rouj. She turned and gave the souls around her one last look. She took the time to survey individual spirits before her and was pleased by what she saw. After smiling and waving at the assembly, Rouj entered the porthole to begin the Examination.

* * *

Rouj, still in her physical form, entered a room that had no bounds. But it was still a room. It was totally plain with nothing insight except for the endless floor. There were no walls and no ceiling. The visible floor was the same colour - a brilliant white. Dazzling white lights were everywhere, but then nowhere. Rouj could see beams of light as far as she could make out, but they had no beginning and no end. They were just there.

Then the angel, Ysebbi suddenly appeared in front of her.

Although Rouj knew she had to expect the unexpected in God's Place, she was still startled.

The angel asked, talking out loud in the Obliivian language, "Why did you jump when I became visible?"

Rouj replied in the same manner, "I didn't think someone would appear that way."

"Ah. So, I surprised you?"

"That's right."

Ysebbi looked deep into Rouj's eyes and asserted, "As a direct servant of God, don't you think angels are presented with miracles all the time? Don't you think angels see things materialize out of nothing? Don't you think angels are given impossible tasks by God? Don't you think angels have special powers that would even puzzle a spirit of your stature?"

The angel questioned, "Are you ready to become an angel? Can you handle it?"

Rouj responded, "God wants me to become an..."

Ysebbi angrily declared, "God is not here! God will not help you! This is the only world in his Universe where God has decided to never venture."

Rouj enquired, "Another world? This isn't God's Place?"

"Are you that stupid where you can't tell God's Place from another world?" The angel teased.

The angel added, "I don't think you're worth the trouble, but God instructed me to give you the Examination. So, here we go."

* * *

Ysebbi raised both arms and disappeared. The whiteness instantly vanished and was replaced with darkness. She could barely see the outline of naked trees. She heard animal growls and chirping insects. Something from above silently brushed her head.

Then beings burst through the bushes and seized Rouj. They

tied up her arms and put a cloth over her eyes. They lead her to a village where she was able to see light though the cloth. She was then roughly thrown into some structure and left alone.

Her mind was running very fast.

"How do I get out of this?" she silently asked herself. "I'm not a physical being like them. I'm a special spirit with thousands of generations of experience. How could physical life forms seize a spirit?"

Then she had an idea. Just as she changed into just a spirit – a white whiff of smoke, five males entered with burning torches. They were large humans, dark in colour, with short black hair. Their faces were hairless, and they wore only enough cloth to cover the penis and bum.

They looked at Rouj's form and laughed. All five of them turned into spirit forms, but these forms were black. Blacker than a dark hole. They quickly enveloped her and were still laughing.

She could hear the thoughts of one of them. "You are now part of the dark side. We are always looking for stray spirits like you, but we prefer children. They are more easily molded into our ways. This is one place that angels dare not tread. And God will not harm us in order to preserve the balance in the universe. So, you are forsaken by your own kind, Rouj. You will forever be part of the dark side."

Rouj thought to herself, "They know my name. How did they know my name? This is not real."

Rouj found herself back in the bright room before Ysebbi.

"Wow. You certainly figured that one out," the angel remarked. "But just one warning and this is the only warning that you will get during the examination. Some situations are fictitious like this one. Others are not."

The angel continued, "What did you learn here?"

Rouj answered, "I learned about something that I didn't know existed; the dark side. It's necessary to keep God's Universe in balance, but it is out of bounds for angels and God's spirits. And we must keep a protective eye out for spirit children whom the dark-side spirits covet."

Ysebbi conceded, "Well, that's right, I guess."

Then the angel brightly asked, "Is the dark side on all the worlds?"

"I don't know."

"I thought you didn't. The dark side is on only a few planets, like Earth."

"So, the dark side is not on Obliiv."

"If it had been, Rouj, I think you would have heard about it."

Ysebbi continued, "Would you like to take a breather to compose yourself before the next one? No pun intended."

Rouj uttered, "That would be nice."

The angel laughed and declared, "Well, you can forget that."

* * *

She raised both arms to reveal a living room inside a nice house on the planet Earth. The room was tastefully decorated in an early twenty-first-century fashion. A fifty-inch flat-screen T.V. stood alone against one wall on top of a large silver-coloured stand. Against another wall, facing the T.V. was a dark brown leather sofa. In front of the sofa was a brown coffee table with a glass top. At each end of the sofa was a brown end table with matching lamps on each. An original painting of a forest winter scene hung on the wall behind the sofa. Against another wall was a matching love seat. On the wall behind it hung an original painting of a clown's face. A large window revealed an overcast sky. The room was painted in an off-white colour with light-brown wall-to-wall shag carpeting.

The angel had disappeared leaving Rouj alone, invisible to the Earth beings inside the house.

A human man and woman were seated on the sofa. The white man was in his late forties with short brown hair. He was about six feet tall with a large belly. The black woman, the man's wife, was about his age with long black hair. She was slightly shorter than him with an attractive figure.

The man named Bill asked, "Do you feel another presence in the house?"

The woman named Hillary replied, "No. How about you, Nathan?"

Where was Nathan? They were alone.

Then Rouj heard a child's voice in her head, "Yes. There are two other spirits with us."

That's when she saw the spirit of a young boy, around ten years old. He was white with shoulder-length hair. He stood about four feet with a slim build. He looked very nervous.

Then she saw a spirit that sent shivers up her spine. It was a male adult. He was white with short black hair and a full-length black-leather coat. His shoes were also black. He didn't seem to notice her. He was staring at the boy with a smile on his face.

The boy whined, "There's a very bad man here. I'm afraid."

Bill jumped to his feet and somehow pulled Nathan toward him. Then she saw that Nathan was in a bubble of some sort.

Bill sat back down and closed his eyes. A bright light appeared around his waist, and he said over and over, "Spirit from the dark side, enter my light and do not return."

The man in black lost his smile. He struggled against the light's pull, but he was no match. He disappeared into the light. Sunshine flowed through the window.

Nathan said, "He's gone, Dad."

Bill then questioned, "Who are you, spirit."

Rouj replied, to her surprise, in her own voice, "I'm Rouj. I have been sent here from God's...from Heaven by an angel to observe as part of my Examination to be an angel myself."

Bill queried, "Is that true, Rishmond?"

A male voice replied only through thoughts, "She is correct."

Bill said, "Well, an angel in training. Have you learned anything from us?"

Nathan interrupted, "She looks funny, Dad."

Bill growled, "We don't talk about people or spirits like that."

Rouj wanted to know, "Are you the boy spirit's father?"

Hillary revealed, "We are his parents now, but not always. He was stabbed to death by his own father. His spirit guides brought him to us for protection and he will be part of our next life on Earth. We have been guided for years in the spirit world by our clairvoyant and so we know the ropes. Bill and I are kindred spirits."

Rouj had heard about kindred spirits, but they were very rare.

"What is that bubble that surrounds the boy?" Rouj queried.

"It's a protective barrier against such things as spirits from the dark side. When there is danger, we can mentally pull Nathan to us," Hillary disclosed.

"Who is Rishmond?"

Hillary answered, "He takes any child who is not supposed to be with us to Heaven."

At that moment, three spirits from the dark side entered the room. They looked exactly like the first one. Child spirits were very valuable to them. Bill and Hillary were overwhelmed. As they were trying to remove two of the spirits, the third approached Nathan, unhindered. Nathan stood frozen in fear.

"Come out of your bubble or I will destroy your parents," the dark spirit demanded.

Nathan, in an effort to save his parents, obeyed. He was crying. Rouj had seen enough. She flew in between the spirit and the boy, to the dark spirit's surprise. As she pushed the boy out of the way, she faced the dark spirit and commanded, "Be gone spirit. Go back to the dark side and never return to this place. As an angel from God, I command you!"

The dark spirit sneered, "You are not an angel. You are just a spirit."

Rouj turned into her physical form and pointed her right hand at the dark spirit. Before he could move, lightning shot out, hit him, and he was dispersed across space.

The other two dark spirit also disappeared, and order was restored.

Rouj told Nathan's family, "They won't bother you again." And she was gone.

***

Again, she found herself in the never-ending room in front of Ysebbi.

Ysebbi snarled, "Why don't you answer the question that Bill asked you? Did you learn anything?"

"Anything at all?" she repeated.

Rouj replied with respect, "Yes I did. I learned about the efforts of humans and angels to protect child spirits from the dark side, but not all attempts are successful. I also learned that I have been given the powers of an angel."

Ysebbi mockingly clapped her hands and said, "Well done, my dear. But those powers that God has given you are just temporary."

"If I had failed, would Rishmond have intervened?"

"Of course, he would've. I wouldn't trust you to protect that little kid. But now that you know about your powers, you won't be given any more backup. We'll see if you can handle those new powers of yours."

***

To Rouj's surprise, the angel vanished leaving her alone in the never-ending room.

Then a male voice loudly thundered, "Rouj, I have a task for you to complete."

She had heard this voice before. It belonged to God.

She answered, "Anything, Lord God."

"One of my angels has become envious of me. She believes that her powers have grown greatly. I want you to defeat this angel in battle and cast her into hell."

Rouj was confused and asked, "Lord God, is there a hell?"

The voice angrily shouted, "How dare you question me! You are nothing but a puny little spirit that I could crush. If I say there is a hell, then there is a hell! DO YOU UNDER-STAND ME!"

Rouj fearfully replied, ",, Lord God. I'm sorry." She forgot any doubts that she had

"That's better, Rouj. The Examination will be complete once you cast the angel into hell. Then you will sit at my side."

"Thank you, Lord God."

"The angel's name is Ysebbi. She will reappear shortly."

At that moment, Ysebbi materialized. Rouj thought she would take her by surprise. She held up her right hand and shot an invisible force at the angel. Ysebbi was knocked to the ground, but she was able to fire back at Rouj, who danced out of the way. Rouj then shot the force again at the angel who withered on the floor in pain. Rouj was proud of herself as she walked up to the prone angel and shot her again. Ysebbi's back rose up and fell as she screamed in pain. Rouj was ready to finish the job when those doubts returned.

In a moment, she offered Ysebbi her hand. The angel took it and was pulled to her feet.

The angel declared, "You have just disobeyed God."

Rouj replied, "That voice wasn't God."

"How do you figure that?"

"You had said at the start of the Examination that this was the only world where God had decided to never venture," Rouj responded. "And there is no hell. And there never has been a hell. And there will never be a hell."

Rouj continued, "God is gentle and loving, and preaches mercy and forgiveness. If an angel did something wrong, God would confront them himself. Plus, the voice had never said that he was God."

"But the part that really got me thinking was how easily I defeated you," Rouj deduced. "You are an experienced angel who would have easily defeated a novice like me."

Ysebbi remarked, "Impressive reasoning. Maybe I was wrong about you before, but let's see how you make out with this."

* * *

The angel raised her left arm and Rouj found herself on one of Obliiv's only three porthole bases. It was easy to tell what it was because of the twenty gigantic porthole buildings used to transport space craft to distant worlds in a blink of an eye. Each of these black structures was about five miles long and two thousand feet tall. There were no windows in the buildings at all. Three doors that an Obliivian being could enter could be seen along each side. Two large doors were visible at each end. They measured about two thousand feet wide and one thousand feet tall.

Five extremely tall towers were scattered around the base. They had the colour of plain- silver with no doors or windows visible. Each one was about one thousand feet in diameter and towered about three thousand feet above the base. These structures were where the fuel for space and air vehicles was manufactured.

Space craft were constantly being moved around the base. To and from the porthole buildings. To and from the several hundred hangers. Small launch pads were at the centre of the base for space craft to go on missions close to Obliiv. Since all vehicles went straight up, the area was very compact.

Armed guards patrolled the perimeter and inside the base.

They were dressed in a black-cloth type material over their entire body, including their head. The uniform was light and allowed the body to breath through it, but it was capable of protecting the soldier from most battlefield injuries. Their helmet was also very light and very protective at the same time. Once the helmet was placed on the soldier's head, he could exchange words with others just by thought. Also in his brain, the soldier could see anything he wanted from his own immediate area to an entire battlefield.

Rouj was standing beside one of the towers in the darkness. Sirens were sounding and she could hear thoughts from some of the workers, "A spirit is inside the base." The soldiers were trained not to reveal their thoughts to the spirits.

A huge black machine was slowly approaching her. A big dark hole in the front showed sparks flying in the darkness.

"I'll just wait until an angel comes to rescue me, Rouj reasoned. "They're always monitoring spirits on other worlds."

Then she remembered what Ysebbi had said, '...you won't be given anymore backup.'

She was ready to get out of there when the machine sucked her inside. She was surrounded by sparks. It was like being stuck in a primitive porthole, unable to go to the other side.

"They can trap spirits, but not angels," Rouj thought.

She spread her arms above her head. Lightening arced between her hands and then into the machine. It exploded in a fireball. When the smoke cleared, Rouj was standing surrounded by the machine's wreckage. Some pieces of metal were on fire. Soldiers ran at her, and they levelled their weapons. Rouj pointed her arms at them with the palms up. When they tried to shoot her, their weapons failed to fire. But one soldier crept up behind her and fired point blank. She was hit, but it only served to irritate Rouj. She pointed her finger at the soldier, and he flew backwards through the air.

"I'll teach them not to fool around with angels," she angrily threatened.

She approached the first porthole building and raised both arms toward it. It was about to be destroyed, when Rouj lowered her arms. She flew out of the base and found a porthole nearby. She crossed over into the never-ending room.

Ysebbi was waiting for her and asked, "Why didn't you destroy the base? You have the power to do that."

Rouj responded, "I know I do, but I'm a servant of God. I must show the mercy and forgiveness that God shows. I will only use my power to carry out God's will and nothing more."

The angel smiled and hugged Rouj. "You have come a long way, Rouj. I knew you could do it. The bitterness I had shown you at the start was just an act. I am very pleased with you."

"Then it's over?" Rouj hopefully asked.

"No. You have one more Examination. Some of the past ones were real, some were not. This one is definitely real, and it will test you to the limit. If you fail, your spirit will disappear forever. Do you wish to continue?"

Rouj smiled and replied, "Of course I do."

"Just one more thing," the angel added. "You have the power to control whether you are invisible or not. I conveniently forgot to tell you."

The angel smiled and simply nodded her head once.

* * *

Rouj found herself floating in space just inside a solar system. She was watching a small star with three planets orbiting around it. The two outer ones were gas giants, while the inner rock planet was much smaller and blue in colour. It seemed to be similar to Earth, but it was not Earth. And the star was not the Sun. This solar system was in a far-off galaxy just inside God's Universe. She could also see other stars and galaxies beyond his Universe.

"Does it ever stop?" Rouj questioned. "I must ask Ysebbi when I return."

"If I return," she quickly correctly.

She descended, invisible to any beings, toward the blue planet, coming over the side facing the star. There was an immense ocean that covered most of the planet. Just a single land mass took up about ten percent of the surface. She could see a few lakes on the land with several rivers, but otherwise it was covered in a green forest. Not a jungle, but a forest. Both poles were ice-free.

She landed near a clear inland lake with a nearby stream gurgling toward it. The temperature was in the mid-twenties Celsius, with low humidity. She walked into the forest where the star's light speckled on the dark-dirt floor. The tree trunks were huge, and the trees were very high. There were no branches at the ground level. But smaller trees were growing where they could; probably the offspring of the tall trees. These little ones had a few small leaves at the very top. These leaves were in different shapes from tree to tree. They ranged from heart-shapes to round to triangles. The floor, however, was rich in flowers of every conceivable colour and shape. There were also berries growing on nearby bushes.

She watched as a hairy creature roamed close to her. It walked on two stubby legs but had very long arms. And she could see why. He walked up to a bush and had to stretch the arms to reach the berries at the top. The head was also hairy, with a very large nose and a small mouth filled with molar teeth. It did not have eyes. The creature stopped eating and sniffed the air.

It smelled danger but was no match for the four-legged creatures pursuing it. With sharp claws on its hands and feet, it started to climb a tree, but it was not fast enough. The four-legged creatures pulled it down – and stabbed it with a knife several times.

There were three of them. They had very little hair and yellow skin. They wore clothing made from animal skin that covered most of the body. At the end of each leg was a hand with six fingers and two thumbs. Each hand was protected by leather gloves. The head was bald with a few hairs growing here and there. Each creature had an extremely small nose and a mouth filled with razor-sharp teeth.

Each creature had four small eyes. One on the forehead, one on the back and two on one side. The side of the two eyes varied with each creature. In this case, one had the eyes on the left side, while the other two on the right side.

One removed the gloves from its forelegs and cut down a six-foot sapling with a saw-like tool. It then tied the dead animal's arms together with some cord. These beings slipped the tree between the dead creature's arms and tied one of its stubby legs to the other end of the tree. The being lifted one end of the tree over the back of one friend and the other end over the back of the second one. After replacing the gloves over his hands on its forelegs, all three slowly walked away on all fours.

Rouj followed them to a small village. There were several huts built from reeds found on the shore of a shallow lake. A fire was burning in the centre of the village. A wooden spit was over it, probably to cook the dead creature. Little beings were running around on all four legs, laughing as they played. The women, who had large breasts, were gathered around the fire. The men dropped the beast in front of them and the women began to butcher it.

Rouj stopped calling these people 'it'. They were an obviously intelligent race, although very primitive. The woman rushed to cut out a large piece which was put on the spit over the fire. One woman turned the meat. The other women took the rest of the carcass into a hut where they probably prepared it for long-term storage. It was quite a while before they came out. The meat was cooked by then.

These beings formed a line with the adults only. One by one, each one presented the woman with a large leaf. She carved off a piece of the meat and placed in it in the leaf. They settled down on the ground and ate with the hands on their forelegs.

All had removed the gloves. The adults shared their meals with the children.

As their star began to set, these people scrambled to get the last work done before heading into their individual huts. The only person left outside was a male who carefully put out the fire. Then he disappeared into a hut as darkness fell over the village.

"They seem to be afraid of the darkness," Rouj guessed.

She settled in the forest outside the village to watch. She had a short wait. Two dark shadows entered the village and she recognized them as spirits from the dark side. The spirits materialized into beings resembling the villagers, except they walked on their hind legs only. They wore black leather clothes and black leather gloves on all four hands. Walking between two rows of huts, the pair stopped at one. They entered and exited shortly with the spirit of a child. The spirits laughed as they walked away.

Rouj dashed after the pair. One task of angels was to stop child spirits from being taken to the dark side. But she must do it before they got to their haunt. She flew after them and jumped in front blocking their path. They were still in the village. She materialized into the form of a spirit to the amusement of the dark spirits.

One taunted, "What do we have here? A spirit that has obviously lost its way."

Rouj declared, "You will not take the child spirit."

The second dark spirit remarked, "It will take more than a spirit to take this child from us."

"How about an angel?" Rouj suggested.

To their surprise, Rouj raised her arms with her palms pointed at the pair. A bolt of lightning struck both in their heads. They disappeared, dropping the child. Rouj heard the sound of a rushing wind speeding her way. She quickly picked up the child spirit, held it high above her head, and sent it to God's Place inside a brilliant beam of light.

Just after the child was gone, the wind Rouj had heard reached her. She was picked up by the wind and transported to a large room that was a dazzling white in colour. There were no walls or ceiling, but the floor was black made from a precious metal from a distant world. Four-feet-high white objects shaped like pyramids were scattered around. These were precious stones from another world. She was unceremoniously dropped to the floor. In the distance, Rouj could see a red object rapidly approaching. It stopped within inches of hitting her. The object was a platform made from a rare wood found on only one planet in the entire universe.

A spirit, just a whiff of red smoke, was on top of it. But this was no ordinary spirit.

She heard his thoughts in her head, "What are you? You look like a spirit, but you have the powers of an angel. What are you?"

Rouj replied, "I am a spirit taking the Examination to become an angel for God."

"Yes, my neighbour, God. But you are no longer in his Universe. You are in mine."

"I was in God's Universe until you brought me here."

"That world is mine and you destroyed two of my spirits, although they were dark."

"God..."

"Enough of your God. I am the Maker of this universe, and it is all mine. I am going to crush you for entering one of my worlds."

The Maker materialized into what looked like a single amoeba, but this one was over ten feet tall. What was inside the Maker moved against the outer membrane like a liquid. It was green with brown spots moving around inside. Angry sparks started to fly from it as it approached Rouj. Claws appeared from its body. She held up her arms and lightning flew from her palms to the Maker.

The Maker laughed, "Do you really think a puny little thing

like you could harm me? I have no equal."

"How about my God," she asked.

"I'm not sure. We have always respected each other's universe," the Maker replied.

"If that's the case, do you honestly think my God would allow me to go to a world in your universe?"

"ENOUGH!"

In a blink of an eye, the Maker sent Rouj back to the village surrounded by the strange beings. She was still visible. Next thing she knew, Ysebbi brought her back to God's Place. Ysebbi stood in front of her.

The angel commented, "That was a close call. I never expected the leader of another universe to intervene. We try to avoid any such confrontations. God will not be pleased, but that was my fault."

Ysebbi continued, "You have succeeded in the Examination and will become one of God's angels."

She smiled and hugged Rouj.

"Just one question. How far do the other universes go? Is it for eternity?" Rouj asked.

The angel replied, "God himself is still pondering that question."

The angel nodded and a porthole appeared. She led Rouj through it to the other side. They entered a great white hall that was decorated with items from other worlds. A painting from a master artist on Earth, a statue from clairvoyant on Obliiv, a piece of pottery from the ancient Ofd people on the Rukdsa world, a potted plant from a simple woman on the Geth world. There were large golden pillars placed around the circumference of the round hall. Jewels were embedded into the wall and the faces of all those God had sent to other worlds to create peace were on the ceiling. The floor was white marble. In the centre of all this was a single throne sitting on a ten-foot-high round platform, white in colour. Stairs all around the platform ran down to the floor. The throne was made from mahogany with a white cushion on the seat. Angels were standing at the base of the platform.

Rouj just stared at what she saw on the throne. It was a spirit – a white whiff of smoke.

God spoke to Ysebbi first. "You have done nothing wrong. It was the Maker who mistakenly thought that world was his. Now he knows better. You have been one of my finest servants and I am very pleased with you."

Then he turned to Rouj and laughed. He revealed, "I get the same reaction from every spirit that is becoming an angel. Shock. Because spirits have never seen me, they get a preconceived notion of what I look like. It's usually a physical being."

He carried on, "But I have created all spirits in my own image. Some spirits then become physical beings and I do not create these. I have chosen to retain my original form. So, you now see me as I have been since the very beginning."

God added, "Rouj, you have now been given knowledge and power. You can now answer the question that you asked in the last part of your Examination."

Rouj bowed her head and softly said, "Thank you, Lord God."

God continued, "I want all my angels to treat me with respect, not awe. I have never asked for worship or prayers, only obedience. I will call you Rouj and you will call me Light. All things that happen between us will stay with us unless I direct otherwise.

"So, pick up your head and look proud. You are now one of my angels."

Rouj was instantly covered in a white gown and white wings painlessly grew out of her back. The angels around her smiled and hugged her one by one. She was now God's angel.

CHAPTER EIGHT

the dark side

It came into existence alone in the dark and had no name. It could not speak, but it could think. It was a life form that consisted of pure intelligent energy.

"Where am I?" the new being thought after it had awakened.

"I don't like this darkness. I must find light."

The creature searched for a very long time, but time meant nothing to it. The entity finally found a bright universe that was just forming. It was teeming with galaxies. Each galaxy contained countless stars and even more planets, but the being was the only life form in it. In this light, it appeared simply as a six-foot-high white whiff of smoke.

The creature declared, "This is my Universe, and it will be named after me."

"But I don't have a name," it thought.

"What can I call myself? In my Universe, I am the almighty. No. I am the creator. No. I am god. Yes, that's it. It's short and to the point. My name is God," it happily thought.

Then it noticed that its Universe was surrounded by other universes. These universes beyond his also supported an untold number of galaxies, each with its own stars and planets. Some were claimed by entities of his equal. With all the powers God had, these universes continued farther than he could see or sense. Was it endless? Even God could not tell. As a pure intellect, however, it was curious and went to investigate these alien places.

It crossed over into another universe and was confronted by a strange life form. Unlike God, it had a body and a voice. It was like green jelly held together in a membrane. Dark spots floated around inside. It was very tall.

"Who are you?" God asked through thoughts.

The other being replied out loud, "I am the Male and the ruler of this universe that you have just invaded."

"I'm sorry," God said. "I was just exploring. I want nothing more with you than peace."

"I can feel your presence, but I can't see you. Why?"

"This is the way I found myself when I awakened."

The male fired a blast of small particles, but God stopped them.

"I see that you have great power. Are you going to attack me, now?"

"No. I forgive you and I will show you mercy."

God added, "I have learned much today. I will never trespass in a universe belonging to another being, except to defend my own."

God continued, "Before I leave your universe, tell me, what is a male?"

"A male is the supreme leader of all he surveys. In my universe, I am the Male. "

God kept his word and left.

"I will become a male because I am the supreme leader over all of my Universe," God thought to himself. "But I would like a body for others to see, like the Male."

He concentrated and his body appeared. He was very tall and was pure white. A brain stuck out of where the stomach should have been. A mouth sat on the back of his square head. Two eyes were on the top of each foot, that were shaped like claws. God did not like his new physical body and changed back into a whiff of smoke.

He promised himself, "I will keep stay in this form for eternity."

God then thought to himself, "I'm lonely and I need companionship, but the other leaders will have nothing to do with me."

He looked down at himself and thought, "I am powerful – the Male told me so. Can I create life?"

"Yes, I can!" he declared.

"But first, I must make a home for us."

God created a sanctuary without end in a dimension different from his Universe. The inside was white and brightly lit from unknown sources. He built a pillar that climbed upward forever, and its circumference was infinite. It would only appear to show the others that his Place and his powers were without bounds. Time and space would not exist there. He made portholes that would allow the others to enter and to leave his Place.

He also made himself a round great hall that only he could enter. But he left it empty, except for pillars around its circumference, waiting instead for gifts from those that he was about to create.

He left his great hall. Large arms protruded from him, and lightning arced between his hands. He gathered the bolts into a ball and threw it to the ground. It split into hundreds of pieces of pure energy.

"What form shall I give these beings," God pondered.

"They will be created in my own image!"

He stared at the energy dancing around on the floor, with an image of himself in his mind. They all turned into white whiffs of smoke like God.

"Can you hear me?" God thought.

They answered together, "Yes, we can."

God revealed, "All of you have intelligence. From now on, you will act as individuals."

He heard a confusing mix of voices. And that was good.

God disclosed, "I am your creator, and you will serve only me. I will call all of you spirits. Like me, you will live for eternity. And you will also carry out my will and practice forgiveness and mercy as I do. I will give you all great freedom in my Place. You can stay here if you wish, or you can travel to any world in my Universe through my portholes. All you have to do is think of a world and a porthole will appear through which you can cross over to that world instantly."

At the start, the spirits and the worlds did not have names. There was no need for them until one of his spirits discovered something. This spirit was very fond of going to a far-off world. As with all the other spirits, she just had to picture the planet in her mind and the porthole would appear. Then she would just simply step through it and immediately cross over to her chosen world. She found it soothing. When God created his beings, some turned into males and others into females. But this made no difference as all of them were equal and they had no desire for each other.

Anyway, this world she visited was full green forests and babbling brooks that ran into rivers. And the rivers ran into lakes and seas. Flowers of all different colours and sizes grew everywhere. Then one day, she sensed new life forms in the water. They were very small. She left, but this new life form puzzled her.

On her next trip to the same planet, she went straight to a lake. This time, she saw larger creatures swimming in the water. She saw that they fed on aquatic plant life and each other. She left intrigued by her discovery.

When she returned to the world, she saw that some these aquatic beings had crawled onto the land. Because time meant nothing to her, she stayed to observe these living things evolve on land. They grew legs, they changed shapes several times, teeth of all different sizes grew according to what they ate. Some fed on plants. Others ate smaller creatures. This violence troubled the spirit.

But what really fascinated her was the fact that some of these beings had intelligence. For example, she saw a group of five hunters checking out a herd of plant eaters in a meadow. These hunters were on four legs, covered with hair, were low to the ground, and had large sharp teeth.

The plant eaters were very large and walked on two muscular legs. Despite their size, they could easily outrun any predator. Their teeth were like molars that were useful in eating grass. The skin was covered in scales.

Three of hunters quietly went around the meadow and hid in a nearby forest just off the well-worn path. Then the other two rushed at the herd from the opposite end. The herd ran for the safety of the forest along the path. That's when the three hunters who were hiding in the forest attacked and killed one of the plant eaters. The five hunters then quietly ate their prey.

If intelligent creatures were evolving on one world, they must be evolving on others. She must tell God what was happening in his Universe.

The female spirit stepped through the porthole into God's Place. Because spirits were forbidden from entering his chambers, she called out through her thoughts, "God, I have an important matter to discuss with you about life on your worlds."

God answered through his thoughts, "What's going on?" She could not see him.

"Your worlds are teeming with life," she replied.

"I expected that."

"But some of the life is growing more and more intelligent."

"You saw this on the world you have chosen?"

"Yes, my Lord."

"How long did it take for the intelligence to show itself?"

"I have no sense of time, but I have observed this one world before animal life even appeared."

"It would only make sense that if it is happening on one world, it would be happening on many others," she added.

God ordered, "Go back to this world. When one species has grown to dominate the others, let me know."

The spirit nodded and stepped through the porthole to the world she had chosen.

The female spirit stayed on this world observing the animal

life. She was captivated watching them evolve. Then one life form started to pull away from the others. At first, this animal was a predator and hunted plant-eaters. They were covered in purple fur, had six legs, and a hairy flat face full of razor-sharp teeth. And it could run like the wind.

As the millennia passed on this world, this animal greatly changed. It stood up on its four hind legs. Hands with a thumb and two fingers developed on its fore legs. It lost its fur revealing purple skin. The sharp teeth remained except for four that were lost to molars. They formed settlements and a language. This being was definitely more intelligent than any of the other animals.

The female spirit crossed over into God's Place through the porthole.

She could not see God, but he called out to her in a booming voice, "Welcome back. I've been waiting for your report."

No thoughts for God at this time, but thoughts were the only way spirits knew how to communicate.

"My Lord, I have found a superior being on the world I have chosen. It has a growing intelligence that the other animals cannot come even close to match."

"Other spirits on different worlds report the same thing. A superior being has risen above the others. I must control these intelligent creatures before they cause me trouble. I have chosen five of my top spirits to come to my chambers to discover how this could be accomplished. You are one of them."

She disappeared and reappeared in God's great hall. God had done some decorating. The columns around the circumference of the hall were now coated with gold that a spirit brought back from one world. A large statue, made by a primitive race, was to one side. Scratchings carved into a rock hung on the wall. God, however, sat on a mahogany throne. The throne was placed on a high stone platform. The floor was now white marble that another spirit had given God from a different world. The five spirits stood in front of him.

God said, "You know why I called you here. Any ideas?"

A male spirit suggested, "Have spirits go to each world and force them to comply to your authority."

God replied, "Remember that I want a peaceful Universe. Forcing them to do something will only create tension."

The female spirit conveyed, "You were right that spirits must be a part of our plan, but in a gentler way. I think that spirits should occupy the bodies of the intelligent beings from conception to death. After the physical body dies, the spirit would return to your Place to start a new life. That way, the spirits would guide all of these life forms according to your wisdom. Namely peace, forgiveness and mercy."

God responded, "I like that idea, but I would have to create many more spirits. How would I be able to instil my ideals on so many? And to keep them in line?"

There was just silence.

God divulged, "I need my top spirits to do my bidding, both here and on other worlds. You will be special from the other spirits with authority over them. I will give you more power than anything in my Universe, except for me. I will call you angels and you will be the only beings allowed to come to my chambers. But I must change your appearance so that all spirits and all life forms will know that you are my special agents."

"Each one of you will show me a picture in your minds of the superior beings on your chosen worlds."

The five spirits were instantly changed over into five different physical beings that matched their thoughts. The female spirit, for example, had purple skin, four legs, and two arms with hands. Long grey hair grew from her head.

Despite their differing appearances, all fives shared two similarities. Large white wings had grown out of their backs, and they were all dressed in long flowing white gowns. God liked the colour white because it reminded him of the light that he had sought for so long.

God was pleased with his new angels and told them, "All of

my spirits have the freedom to decide whether or not to go to other worlds and to occupy physical bodies at conception. Because I made all the spirits different from each other, it will be up to you make sure each one is a good candidate to occupy physical bodies. This will be one of only two times where a spirit will be judged."

An angel, who looked like a human but was not, asked, "If a soul chooses to go to another world just as a spirit, will that soul need to be examined by us?"

"No. Except for occupying physical bodies, spirits are free to come and go as they please."

A second male angel, who was short with a bald head, urged, "My Lord, because there are going to be many spirits, it would be wise to give them names to tell them apart. And also, names for each planet."

God turned to his purple female angel and ordered, "You will be in charge of matters in other worlds. You will give each and every planet a name and enter that name in a catalogue so that each spirit can view it mentally.

"Also, when the physical body of a spirit dies, that spirit will carry the name of that being into my Place. And if a spirit needs to show a physical form, that form will come from its previous life on another world."

The same male angel with the bald head had another suggestion, "My Lord, with an increasing number of souls to fill life forms all over your Universe, you will also need more angels to watch over them and to protect them on other worlds."

God was impressed with this angel. "What do you recommend?"

"Have a system like a pyramid where each soul is ranked according to knowledge and experience. The beginners would form the base. Souls would move up as knowledge and experience were gained until there was only one at the top. Then this one soul would be put through a series of tests by one of your trusted angels. If that soul passes, with your blessing of course, she or he would become an angel."

God declared, "That sounds like a lot of work."

He looked at the bald-headed angel and added, "You will carry out the examinations for future angels. And for the record, this is the second and last time where a spirit will be judged. I will not judge spirits, but I will judge angels."

* * *

As the millennia passed on his worlds, however, God saw two things. One pleasing to him and one that troubled him.

On Obliiv, for example, God was troubled with many buildings that were being constructed to worship him. One such place of worship was a grey building in an early democratic country on Obliiv. There were doors and windows. The people inside were dressed in colourful clothes. They were short beings with bald heads and their skin was ash-grey in colour. These numerous people gathered inside on comfortable chairs in a hall decorated with symbols of their religion. The leader stood up front.

He pointed at a huge circle behind him. It was brown, made from a precious metal. A smaller circle was inside.

He shouted, "That represents the prophet that God had sent to lead us on the true path of righteousness. Those other religions in the pagan countries do not worship God as we do. And all of them will be tortured in damnation for eternity."

His voice softened as he carried on, "But we, fellow worshippers, will be taken to God's Place where we will spend eternity, eating and drinking. There will be no pain. There will be no wars."

He closed his eyes as did all of his followers. "God, please watch over and protect us from the evil people that surround us. We follow only you God because we fear for your judgement of us all."

When they opened their eyes, everyone jumped to their feet

and shouted. Then they happily danced out of the building with smiles on their faces, confident that they would not face eternal damnation.

God was not happy with religions that had spread on Obliiv and called on his angel who had been to this planet. The angel had the form of an Obliivian – short stature and a bald head.

God revealed, "There are different religions spreading on your planet whose sole purpose is to worship me and to pray to me. I have never demanded any of this from the physical beings. They are also spreading lies about me sending people who sin to eternal damnation. And it is not my will to have these things."

The angel replied, "I have presented myself many times on Obliiv as your servant, my Lord. They have given me great respect and honour, and have several times come close to worshipping me."

"I believe the problem here is with the leadership," he continued. "Your spirits that have occupied physical beings and those spirits dedicated to guiding them, have instilled into the physicals that you are the creator who preaches forgiveness and mercy.

"A few individuals, however, saw this as a chance for power and money. They formed religions with willing followers to worship you. And to keep their followers in line, their leaders have painted you as a terrible God who would throw all sinners into eternal damnation. Sins include not attending a place of worship and not giving much money to the religions. A few leaders have greatly profited from this."

God revealed, "I could stop these foolish religions in the blink of an eye, but I will not interfere with any world in my Universe. Angels, however, are able to carry out my will anywhere I please."

The angel sadly remarked, "My Lord, there are too many religions on too many worlds, and they are spreading fast. We did not realize the effect that your spirits would have on physical life forms. The only way for your angels to stop these religions is by using violence. And we will not do so because your will is to show mercy."

"Your decision, of course, is quite right," God conveyed. "The only alternative is to have my spirits give these life forms a different message that religions are not my will."

"That will take much time in your worlds, my Lord."

"It will take as much time for religions to fall as it did for them to rise. It's a good thing that time does not exist here, or I would become very impatient."

* * *

But God was happy with a new class of spirit that was just forming. It all started with Henry and Jill.

Henry's soul was in his wife's room on a planet called Earth. It was a small room that was painted a soft blue. Her bed was like a queen-size with a canopy over it. She was sleeping in the bed with a hand-made quilt covering her. On a scuffed wooden brown dresser was a wash pan with a jug inside. A fireplace was to one side, but there was no fire. It was a warm sunny day. But the curtains were drawn on the only window creating a semi-darkness. Voices could be heard in the kitchen just outside her room.

She was a human and was dying. He had taken on his former human appearance to comfort his wife when she passed. He was white, six feet tall, black hair and a black beard. His wife's name was Jill. She was white, about five feet, eight inches tall, with long grey hair. He had died thirty years ago, but the two of them had stayed in contact.

About two months after his death, Henry had first visited Jill as a spirit. She had been sitting on a comfortable red chair reading a book. He had approached her. She had black hair back then. He had touched her, but she had recoiled from the touch. Henry, however, had still loved Jill so much that he would not stop. He could not stop. Even Heaven had not seemed like Heaven without her.

"It's me, Henry. I love you and I will always love you," he gently thought.

Jill received his thoughts and had understood. She smelled the same cologne that he had always worn. But it took many more such encounters before Jill finally believed what was happening and began to communicate with her husband's spirit through thought.

"I miss you so much, my love. Not a day passes that I don't think of you. Are you here because my time is coming soon to join you?" she finally asked.

Henry replied, "No, it is not. You must live your life until your time comes. Then, and only then, will your spirit leave your body. Then you will be in my arms once more. But that is many decades in the future. Until then, I will talk to you every so often, if that pleases you?

"Oh, it does. To hear your sweet voice would be heavenly. And to express our love for each other. Our love will last forever. I can feel it, my darling."

"With the knowledge I have gained since the release of my spirit, I will guide you. You are very young, and I want you to remarry so that you will not be lonely."

"I will not do such a thing."

"You must. Do it for me."

Jill had remarried and had raised a family of three girls and one boy. She had loved her entire family and had kept her undying love for Henry a secret. When she had been alone, Henry's spirit had come to her. They had kissed and had touched each other. They had expressed their eternal love, a love that just wouldn't die.

Now, Henry was watching Jill die. Her laboured breathing ended when her heart finally stopped. Her soul left her body as a beautiful young woman with long black hair. She stood on the floor and looked down at her body. She had been expecting this and was looking forward it. She looked around in the darkness and her eyes locked onto a grey curtain. She could see a form behind it. The curtain gradually disappeared and revealed her love, Henry. They rushed into each other's arms, and their lips met in a soft warm kiss. Then they pulled away from each other, but still held hands.

"Finally, we are together again. I have missed you so much," she said

"I have also missed you. I will love you always," he replied.

They both changed into their natural forms – just whiffs of white smoke. Then they crossed over into Heaven.

As they were planning for another life together, Henry disclosed, "I have a deep feeling that our spirits have a special love that will last for eternity. We will always be together, whether it's here or on Earth."

Jill agreed, "Yes, I can feel the same eternal love as you do. By the grace of God, we are bound together forever in love."

After these first two, other couples were formed with love that would last for eternity. Depending on the world, they were called by different names. But God called them kindred spirits. They were not created by God and were only drawn together by intense love.

After giving his purple angel some instructions, he asked her, "Have you detected a new class of spirits that I call kindred spirits?"

She joyfully replied, "I have, my Lord. A couple who are bound to each other in eternal love. Such an arrangement is very comforting."

"Yes, it is. These couples represent the two things that I have always sought since my awakening – eternal love and eternal light."

"But they are few in numbers. Do you wish special protection for them?"

"All spirits are safe in my Place and angels protect spirits on other worlds. I don't see the need."

The angel respectfully bowed and left. God, however, would

come to later regret his decision.

* * *

God summonsed his five angels to his chambers to discuss a matter of great importance to his Universe.

God explained, "My Universe is incomplete. It has developed according to my wishes, but something is missing. As I was pondering the missing ingredient, I saw what it was in the universe next to mine. The dark side. All intelligent life forms in my Place and in my worlds are based on the light and the love that I have desired. They have chosen my principles of mercy and forgiveness. Have you noticed this?"

The Obliivian angel, as usual, was the first to speak up. "I have, my Lord. I have observed life forms on many different planets. Though they differ in appearance and customs, all of them experience only love and happiness. With the possible exception that some fear you. They do not fight. They do not hunt. They do not fish. They only consume vegetation that they have grown or found growing in the wild."

"Did you not think this was odd?" God asked.

The angel replied, "I thought nothing of it, my Lord. I believed that's what you wished."

God revealed, "To experience true life, there must be more than love and light. There must also be hate and darkness. Spirits are not capable of such emotions, but physical beings are. Life must be balanced."

His purple angel uttered, "My Lord, I do not wish to question your wisdom..."

God interrupted, "Spirits will not dare to question me, but as my angels I expect more from you. When I ask for your counsel, I want to hear the truth as you see it. If your opinion conflicts mine, so be it. You may continue on how you see this matter."

She carried on, "We have people on many worlds living

their lives in peace and contentment. Can we not just let them continue with their happiness?"

God replied, "A very good question. I want people of all races, on all planets to live life to the fullest. How can they know what love truly is until they experience hate? How can they know what light truly is until they experience the dark? How can my spirits gain enough knowledge to one day become my angels? The simple answer is that they can't."

God stopped to look at each one of his angels. He was pleased to see understanding in their eyes.

God added, "We need the physical life forms to live balanced lives in both the light and in the dark. This is essential so that not only will physical beings grow, but those that occupy my Place will also grow."

God remarked, "I would like to balance my Universe by introducing a limited dark side. I would like suggestions on how to accomplish this."

All five thought this over very carefully before one, a large hairy human, replied only by thought because his race had not yet developed language, "I have noticed that the dark side is already on the world where I had lived several lives. But I have not seen it in the other worlds where I have visited. You are right, my Lord. All worlds need a limited amount of the dark side. I recommend that the five angels here be sent by you to the other worlds to create a dark side on each one that will counter the light and the love."

The ancient ash-grey Obliivian disagreed. "That would lead to the darkness overtaking the light and that could lead to terrible tragedies all over your Universe. I suggest that one angel among us go to ten well-placed planets and introduce the dark side. That way, the darkness could be kept under control and slowly spread to other planets."

God responded, "I like the last idea, but we need the right angel to do it properly. It would have to be the one that has entered the dark side already. The human angel that had killed an animal life form for food in a previous life is my choice."

The human angel, unaware of Godly protocols, interrupted, "My people were starving from a crop failure. I was their leader, so I chose to kill animal life to feed them. It was hard to do and hard to eat, but it was necessary."

God divulged, "No one is judging you for your actions. You are not the only human to kill for food. You do not have to defend yourself, but you are the best one among the five to carry out my directions."

"I will follow your instructions. My Lord, just one request."

"You would like to be able to speak out loud."

"Yes, my Lord. That will allow me to communicate directly with the beings on other worlds."

God pointed his finger at the human angel and declared, "It is done."

Then all five disappeared.

Unknown to everyone present, including himself, the human angel would complete God's task well. Too well.

* * *

The human angel decided to start his task on Earth to carry out God's instructions. This planet had a very limited dark side that he must increase. As he thought of his former-home planet, a porthole appeared. It was six feet by six feet and the inside was black. He stepped into it and found himself on Earth, but much had changed. He was in a temperate wooded area. He was standing on a well-worn path which was about ten feet wide. Oak trees were growing on both sides of the path as far as he could see. But he was sure that he would find different trees nearby, such as maples and pines.

He could hear and feel several horses approach him. There were five horses with a man on each. They were soldiers dressed in uniforms, except for one. They all carried swords and had manicured beards. As they drew near to the angel, the men pulled up on their steeds and stopped just short of hitting him. The angel stood his ground, studying these unfamiliar humans.

The man without a uniform spoke with an old-English accent and was wearing the clothes of a noble person. He appeared to be the leader of the soldiers. This man looked alarmed as he stared at the hairy angel in front of him.

He asked, "What sort of beast are you?"

The angel replied, "I am an angel sent here by God."

"You have the white wings and clothes of an angel, but your body seems to have come from hell itself. You are not an angel of my God. Out of my way, devil!"

With that, all five horses galloped over the heavenly being. He was not hurt, only confused. Angels should not be treated this way. He decided to find follow these men and take more drastic action, but he would not use his powers to hurt or destroy. Vengeance was forbidden by God who taught forgiveness. He flew above the trees and followed the trail to a large city surrounded by walls of stone. Around the city were cultivated fields.

He landed in the city's central common area to the horror of the townsfolk. The buildings inside the walls were also constructed with stone. There were several small houses with smoke rising from their chimneys. The roofs were thatched with dry straw. A crowded outdoor market stood down the dusty cobble-stone street. Stables, filled with horses, stood in the far corner. In the centre was a three-story palace made of stone with a wooden roof. Stone stairs ran up to the second floor which was the throne room. It was guarded by soldiers armed with swords and spears. Soldiers also stood on wooden ramparts near the top of the wall.

Two men were in a wooden balcony on the third floor of the palace. The one man who had previously met the angel revealed, "That is the beast I told you about, sire. He claims that he is an angel of God."

The other man was the ruler who wore a small black beard

and long well-groomed black hair. His tailored clothes consisted of a long scarlet robe, black pants, a fluffy white shirt, and a narrow silver crown on his head.

He declared, "An angel of God. Really? Well, we will go down there and converse with him."

He kissed a large silver cross that hung from a chain around his neck and took the inside stairs to ground level.

He approached the strange being and defiantly questioned, "Do you mean us harm, angel?"

The angel gently answered, "Of course not. God sent me here to complete a task on his behalf. Once I have done his will, I will be gone."

"You have the wings of an angel, but not the body."

"Angels in Heaven come in all shapes and sizes, according to God's will."

That seemed to satisfy the nobleman. He declared, "I am the lord over all that you see and beyond. You were wise to come to me to carry out God's will."

He nodded his head once and continued, "How may we be of assistance, angel?"

The angel responded, "Can we go inside so that I can explain my mission from God."

The lord turned to his underling and ordered, "Prepare a feast with the deer they killed today. I want my consort, my guards, and the clergy to attend."

The underling bowed, "Very well, my Lord." And he backed away.

The lordship and the angel climbed the outside stone stairs to the second floor and retired through a pair of large solid-oak doors to a large chamber made of stone. It was round with a high wooden ceiling. A large padded wooden chair stood at one end on top of a three-foot stone platform with stone stairs. There was a shield behind the chair with what appeared to be coat-of-arms. There was nothing else on the wall and there were no windows. The lord settled into his seat. There was no where else to sit.

The angel stood in front of his lordship and questioned, "You mentioned killing a deer. Do you hunt?"

The lord laughed, "Of course we do. How could we survive without food?"

"Grow crops."

"We do grow crops to make wine and beer. Maybe some corn, but meat is our main source of food. And I must say that the animals we kill in my forest are especially sweet."

"Why do you have guards?"

"You are very naive for an angel. I have guards and soldiers to do battle with my enemies and kill as many of them as possible."

The human angel thought to himself, "These people are more deeply into the dark side than I had thought. There must be other planets that are similar to Earth. I just have to find a few more worlds like this one, convince them to go even more deeply into the darkness. Then the practices of these shadowy worlds will spread across God's Universe."

He became excited at that prospect, but angels do not get excited. He was changing. With this visit to Earth, the thrill of the hunt and the joy of the kill returned from a far-distant time – when his spirit actually enjoyed taking life.

That night, the nobleman held a feast in the angel's honour. Although angels do not eat or drink, this Heavenly being did not want to insult his new friends by not enjoying the festivities. As a physical life form, he was able to eat the cooked deer meat with his bare hands and drank cup after cup of red wine. The area around his mouth was covered with grease from the meat. He laughed with the others as they watched the entertainment of dancers and musicians. There was even a joker. The party continued well into the morning until the lord was tired and decided to retire to bed.

The following afternoon, the angel met with his lordship alone in the stone throne chamber.

The lord observed, "I have never seen any man drink as much wine as you and still remain standing."

The angel replied, "I must admit that I did, indeed, relish your flavourful wine and your meat was too sweet to resist."

"I'm happy that you enjoyed yourself. Now, tell me why you came here."

"As I said, I was sent here by God. He has another angel in your realm, but he does not look anything like an angel. God expelled this angel from Heaven for performing dark deeds. But God still loves him and wishes to get him a following to worship him. He is now called the devil."

"The devil! By God, I will never worship the devil!"

"Hear me out. If you and your subjects worship the devil, you will defeat all your enemies in battle. You will be able to slaughter as many as you wish. You will take their land, their jewels and gold, their women. Think about it. You will be richer beyond your dreams and with the power to govern nations."

"Will I not burn in hell for eternity?"

"You will live with the devil for eternity, but not in hell. When the time comes for the devil to conquer the world, he will make you the sovereign over entire countries.

"I must think this over."

The angel warned, "Don't think this over for too long. In a fortnight, I will take this offer to your enemy."

Then the angel disappeared and reappeared in the forest nearby. He went through the complete catalogue of other worlds that all spirits and angels now possess within themselves. He picked out four other planets that may have entertained similar dark habits. He found his porthole and quickly crossed over into Heaven. Then he thought of a planet named Hrotyij. Another porthole appeared and he crossed over to that world.

Hrotyij was a planet about half the size of Earth. It had an orbit well out from a star that was much bigger than the Sun. It took the planet several Earth-years to complete one orbit. Two other rock planets were closer and baked in the star's heat. As with most habitable planets, Hrotyij also was protected from cosmic objects by two gas giants on outer orbits.

This world was rocky and barren around the planet, except for a strip of land only about one thousand miles wide. This was the only place where life flourished. In this area, the temperature remained in a constant range of 70 to 85 degrees Fahrenheit. It received an adequate amount of rain to grow the crops planted by the inhabitants.

The people throughout this world were very dark in colour due to the high level of sunshine. Both females and males were built the same; about eight feet tall, over three hundred pounds, and with equal strength. Black hair grew all over their bodies, except for the head. They had three legs about two feet in length. The third leg was only a foot long, between the two good legs. Their arms were similarly short with hands that resembled lobster claws. The people had learned to grasp tools over millennia with these hands.

These beings, however, had no sexual organs. To reproduce, the female would cough up a small soft round egg. The male would carefully take it in his mouth, dig a hole in the ground, and place the egg inside. He would then bury it and sit beside the hole. He would not leave, even to eat. He dug it up when he just knew it was the right time. After washing off the dirt, the fifty-pound toddler was able to breath, walk and eat solid food.

They grew mainly crops for their seeds. Some were kept for future plantings, but most were consumed. They also ate fruit from wild trees. But they harboured a secret. Their religion demanded that one adult person be sacrificed per month to please God. Because there were different tribes around the world, the number of deaths added up quickly. But they did this deed at night in total darkness because they ate the raw flesh of those sacrificed.

The human angel searched the planet and found the largest

village made up of several hundred huts constructed from vegetation. At midday, he appeared in the centre of the village out of no where to the astonished villagers. They fell back but did not run away – even though these people did not have any weapons. An old male carefully approached the angel.

Because thoughts can overcome any language barrier, the angel said from brain to brain. "I am an angel sent here by God to punish you."

The old male did not quite get it and tried to speak out loud. The angel revealed, "Do not speak. Just send me your thoughts."

The old being asked, "Have we been disrespectful to God?"

"Yes, you have and God wants to destroy all of you!"

The male fell to his knees and pleaded out load for mercy. The other villagers joined him.

The angel waved his hand in a circle and swords appeared around him on the ground. He picked one up and walked over to a villager. He plunged the sword into her stomach. She fell to the ground bleeding and would die within seconds. He felt a strange sensation of joy.

The angel turned to all the people surrounding him and declared, "God will forgive all of you, but first you must show your loyalty by slaughtering your neighbours. Eating their bodies. Taking their females as slaves. Hunt animals for food."

The old male nodded to his people. The villagers, both male and female, picked up the steel swords. The angel showed them how to use them. How to kill with them.

A few nights later, the villagers crept up to a smaller village. A male was standing outside and smiled as he saw them approach. Friendship had grown between the two people. But he lost his smile when he saw the swords. He curiously stared at the strange objects until one was rammed through his chest.

The invaders shrieked with delight as they entered the huts. Screams of terror rose from their defenceless victims. They chased down the prey and stabbed each one multiple times.

Males and females were all the same to this race, so they killed them all. But they did spare the children who would serve as slaves.

It was daylight by the time the rampage was over. The victors wandered through the devastated village with smiles on their bloody faces. Bodies lay everywhere. They found where the harvested seeds were kept and loaded them into sacks to be taken home. As a final touch of contempt, the village was set on fire. The dead people were left for the wild animals to scavenge.

The angel smiled as he saw the looks on faces of the victors. They thoroughly enjoyed murdering innocent people. The dark side was well onto its way as a balance to the light. God is going to be so pleased, the angel thought. He did not realize what he had just done.

The human angel entered the porthole and crossed over into God's Place. Then he thought of Earth and another porthole appeared. He crossed over onto Earth and found the city where a nobleman was considering his offer to live on the dark side. And to serve something that did not exist – the devil. He flew to the double oak doors of the palace and walked into the throne room. The lord was sitting on his chair which was perched on stone.

"Have you made a decision?" the angel asked.

The lord responded, "I have. I will accept your offer. I have dispatched all my clergy and have turned the church into a place to worship the devil."

"That's very good. In three days, you will march to your enemy's city before first light. The wall will come down. Your soldiers will be able to enter unopposed as most of the enemy's soldiers will be sleeping. You will be able to ransack the city and carry away all its treasures. This will only be the beginning."

As the lord's troops approached the city of his enemy in the predawn darkness three days later, the human angel held up his right hand. Lightning shot from his palm and struck the stone wall. The wall crumbled to the ground starting at the place where it was hit and continuing all the way around until the entire city was exposed. Before the lord's troops entered the city, the angel was able to kill dozens of enemy soldiers with lightning bolts.

Then he sat back and listened to the fear coming from the city. The shouts and the screams. The troops of his new friend were able to easily rout the enemy soldiers. Then they turned on the people. They entered houses and killed the men before raping the women and girls. They stormed the stone palace and killed the ruler. Then they gang raped his wife. The soldiers plundered the palace of all of its treasures and carted them off down cobblestone streets filled with blood and bodies. They took the livestock and the surviving women and girls. The angel smiled when the city was finally set ablaze late the next night. He watched as the palace came crumbling down in the intense heat.

The angel returned to Heaven through the porthole. There were three other planets he wanted to visit, but instead he appeared in front of God who was sitting on his throne in his chambers. He was surrounded by several other angels.

"What have you done!" God thundered out loud.

"I carried out you wishes to encourage the dark side on other worlds," the human angel replied.

"You have lied to those beings. You told them that the devil and hell do exist. You have enjoyed dead meat. You have killed and destroyed. My angels do not do such things. You have gone against everything that I have taught," God angrily pointed out.

The angel lowered his head in shame. He now realized what he had done and that he had betrayed God. But it was too late now.

God carried on, "Thanks to you, I can see the dark side going beyond what I had wanted on two worlds. They will mistakenly worship something that does not exist. Their dark souls will remain on their worlds collecting more souls to join them. The dark side will spread slowly to other worlds and in time it may overwhelm the light. I can only hope that other life forms will not embrace the dark side as they have on Earth and Hrotyij.

"You have greatly disappointed me, angel. If there was a hell, I would cast you into it. But I must follow what I have taught my spirits and my angels. Forgiveness and mercy. You are forgiven for your evil deeds, but I must punish you while showing mercy at the same time. You will be stripped of your wings and powers for eternity."

The wings of the human angel disappeared, and he turned into a spirit – a whiff of white smoke.

"To complete your punishment, you will go to any world where the dark side is flourishing to protect child spirits from being taken by the evil spirits to the dark side. You will know time on these worlds. And you will find a place of worship and pray to me for forgiveness everyday. When I have decided that you have been punished enough, you will return to my Place – never to leave it again forever."

Then the former human angel disappeared.

* * *

As God had said, the dark side flourished on two worlds and will spread to others, but God was, strangely enough, pleased. His Universe was now getting into balance. Earth, however, became the darkest of them all.

On Earth, the nobleman who had agreed with the human angel's offer to worship the devil and embrace the dark side, was growing in power. He had conquered several cities and became the largest landowner in the country. Lord Chamberlain's forces even exceeded that of the king.

On a day that will become pivotal in Chamberlain's future, he could be found in his private chambers with a woman captured in his last attack on an enemy's city. His room was small with stone walls. A large bed was the only piece of furniture. The ceiling was made of wood.

The woman had long blonde hair and blue eyes. She was in her late teens and was barely five feet tall. Her weight did not exceed one hundred pounds.

Chamberlain ripped all of her clothes off and punched her in the face. She fell hard to the ground with her long blonde hair flying in all directions. Blood poured from her mouth and nose. At a mere five feet and a slim build, she was no match for Chamberlain. Before the battle, she had been the wife of the now-dead ruler.

Chamberlain stood over her, smiling. He was enjoying her suffering. The woman screamed as he pulled her to her feet by the hair. Some came off in his hands. He brushed it off before he picked up the woman and threw her in his bed. He pulled down his pants exposing his large stiff penis. As he joined her in bed, she tried to escape. He slapped her face several times and then pulled her onto her back. He climbed on top of her and rammed his manhood into the female's dry vagina. She cried out in agony.

Then came a knock at his door.

"This had better be good," he shouted. He climbed off the woman, as sperm exploded over her naked body.

He got up, pulled up his pants, and unlocked the door. Chamberlain was over six feet tall with a small black beard and unkempt black hair. He wore a dirty white long-sleeve shirt and long black pants. His black-leather boots were scuffed. Since his battlefield victories, he came to care little for his appearance.

He opened the door to his top aide. This man was neatly dressed in a white shirt, black pants, and a grey coat. His black-leather boots were polished to perfection.

"I'll have your head for this," Lord Chamberlain warned.

The man had seen the temper of his lord and master before

and he was not afraid.

"A messenger from the king has just arrived, my Lord," the man announced.

Chamberlain smiled. He had been expecting something from the king who was badly out matched by Chamberlain's forces.

"I will greet him right away." The lord looked at the woman bleeding on his bed. "Give her to the guards and burn my bed sheets," he ordered.

He buckled up the belt carrying his sword and went down three-flights of stone stairs and found a man of obvious-noble heritage standing beside his white horse. The man was extremely well dressed displaying an ornate sword and wore a fancy hat covering a white wig. He was less than six feet tall, but was extremely fit. This man also had few peers when it came to the sword. Chamberlain looked jealously at the man. But the horse caught his attention.

"What a fine animal," Chamberlain thought to himself. "I must have it."

The king's courier took off his hat and bowed expertly before the lord. He took a large book from a bag on the horses back. It contained loose fine paper and words hand-written in ink. The king's wax seal was burned into the paper at the bottom.

The courier read from the paper sheets, "I, the king, demand that you attend my castle where I will consider your surrender..."

The lord interrupted, "He wants me to surrender? My soldiers outnumber the king's by two to one. Here's my answer and you will write it down."

The courier took out an ink well and a feather pen from the bag. He looked around and saw a fountain. He marched over a sat on the ledge. He opened the ink well and set it down. He dipped his pen into it and looked at the lord.

Chamberlain dictated, "I will never surrender. We will

march on your castle in five days. Once we have defeated your puny soldiers, I will watch with glee as I see you beheaded in front of your own subjects."

Chamberlain took out his sword and commanded, "Get up."

The courier rose to his feet only to be cut down by Chamberlain.

He turned to his aide, "Take his horse as my own. He won't be needing it anymore. Pin the paper he just wrote for me to his clothes over his chest. Then drop the body in front of the gates to the king's castle. Prepare my troops for battle."

Chamberlain and his large army were approaching the king's castle seven days later. Thinking that victory over the king was certain, Chamberlain had a casual attitude toward the battle itself. He was on the white horse in front of thousands of his soldiers. His aide was beside him on a brown horse. Everyone else was on foot, with swords, spears, and shields as their only weapons. They wore round helmets and armour over their chests. Chamberlain, however, was the only one to wear a long colourful feather out of helmet. They stopped at the edge of the forest as the castle came into view. For two miles, there was nothing between the tree line and the castle walls. The king's soldiers were no where in sight.

The white wall surrounding the castle was tall and very strong. A pair of thick wooden gates, reinforced by metal, sealed the entrance. The doors were secured by three thick metal rods as long as both gates. The enemy could never force their way in, so the king's advisers had suggested that they not fight them head-to-head. The king, however, would not hear of it.

The king had said, "I would rather die in battle than to hide behind walls."

Chamberlain's aide pleaded, "My Lord, it would be best if you did not lead us into battle. Your death or injury could result in our defeat."

Chamberlain smiled, "You are such good soul caring for my welfare, but I will not loose one drop of my blood. Did I not lead in all the other battles?"

"You did, my Lord, but that was against feeble opposition. The king's army has fought against soldiers from other countries and won. He has expert horsemen, archers that have been training all their lives, and well-armed soldiers."

"My blood will not be spilled. The devil will not allow that to happen. Everything I have, every victory that I have won is because the devil has ordained me to be his Earthy king. I worship the devil. I have ordered my subjects to worship the devil. He will protect me even if I face certain death."

Chamberlain and his aide climbed down from their horses. A soldier led the animals away. Chamberlain raised his sword and marched forward. After coming out of the tree line into the open field, the troops spread out to the left and right as they had been ordered by Chamberlain.

Chamberlain smiled and thought to himself, "What a beautiful summer day for a battle."

The king, dressed in full battle gear of a silver helmet and silver chest armour, watched from a guard tower through a narrow slit in the brick structure. He turned to his general and offered, "Chamberlain is standing out like a peacock with that feather in his helmet."

The general, dressed in a grey helmet and silver chest armour, agreed, "He is, your majesty. If we manage to cut him down, his entire army will flee. I will give the horsemen the first chance to kill him. If they fail, the archers will concentrate their arrows on the evil lord. But my soldiers will not fail. They have fought against larger armies and better armies and have always emerged victorious."

The castle gates opened, and fifty horses came trotting out with the riders' lances high in the air. As the horses picked up their speed in a charge at the enemy, the lances were lowered. Chamberlain stopped and smiled at the sight. The horsemen went straight into the other army. Three lines of soldiers jumped in front of Chamberlain and were cut down, but their leader was spared. The lances took out several other men and others were trampled under the horses' hooves. But new soldiers poured in and pulled some riders from their mounts. Other horsemen lost their lances.

Some riders, however, saw Chamberlain's feather and rode straight for him. The first rider was brought down by the aide. But then the aide was slashed by another horseman. More soldiers gathered around Chamberlain. The horsemen tried to slash their way inside, but the soldiers would not yield. The horsemen left the battlefield leaving behind over two hundred bloody bodies.

Chamberlain returned to the front, stepped over the body of his aide, and continued to march forward. As they drew closer, one hundred arrows fired from the battlement, streaked high overhead, and then descended into the troops. They saw them coming. The soldiers went down on one knee and covered themselves with their shields. Only a few arrows found their targets because the odd soldier was too slow. After a few more volleys, the archers discontinued the barrage because Chamberlain still lived.

The castle gates opened once more and shouting foot soldiers charged out. These soldiers had grey helmets and grey chest armour. Their shields displayed the king's crest. Chamberlain and his army started to run toward them. The enemy, however, was able to identify him and went straight for their target. As the smaller army attacked Chamberlain's centre, both of Chamberlain's flanks surged forward past the enemy. Then the flanks encircled the rear of the king's soldiers. Chamberlain's army pushed the enemy soldiers tightly together and then attacked them from both sides and the rear. Fighting a larger army on the front, rear, and two sides; the king's army was doomed. And therefore, so was the king.

After seeing the battle turn against him, the king retired to the large hall that served as his throne room. The walls were made out of stone. Swords and shields decorated them with the odd suit of armour. The room was brightly lit by candles and scented oil lamps.

The general burst in. "Your majesty, I have a horse and several guards waiting for you. You will be spirited away while the battle still..."

The king, sitting on his large throne padded in red, held up his right hand, "I will not desert my subjects nor will I desert my army when we are facing defeat. Bring the guards in here with me and we will defend my throne until the last man has died."

On the battlefield, Chamberlain could sense victory. He was fighting enemy soldiers at close quarters. He laughed as he struck down man after man. Before a kill, he would sometimes ask, "Where's the king?"

He swung his bloody sword at the enemy like a lunatic. Some soldiers fled at the sight of the madman, but the battle around Chamberlain finally ended when a soldier stabbed Chamberlain in the back with his sword. As he fell to the ground, Chamberlain thought, "This can't be happening. I worship the devil."

As the soldiers watched, Chamberlain hit the ground and his assassin pounced on him stabbing him in the back with a knife time after time. Even after his death. Chamberlain's soldiers were horrified. They expected him to live forever serving the devil. But the devil let him die. Being a superstitious lot, the soldiers now felt threatened themselves. They didn't care that victory was theirs. They fled the battlefield and others followed as rumours of Chamberlain's death spread.

In short order, the last of Chamberlain's soldiers disappeared into the forest, leaving behind a bloody battlefield littered with the dead, the wounded, and the startled soldiers of the king. They were too tired and too weak to pursue.

When the king was advised of the unexpected victory, he

marched out onto the battlefield and was led to Chamberlain's body. The feather was still in his helmet.

"Take off his helmet," the king ordered.

The king then kicked the body onto its back. He looked carefully at the face, eyes still open, before he raised his sword and sliced off the head in one blow. He put the point of his sword into the open neck and lifted the head high above his shoulders, facing his castle. His subjects lining the battlement roared with approval.

But Chamberlain's spirit, standing nearby, was not pleased. He was just a whiff of black smoke, and no one noticed him. His spirit guides stood nearby.

The door keeper, the leader of his spirit guides, approached Chamberlain and said, "We will guide your soul to Heaven."

Chamberlain vowed, "I will not go to Heaven, and I know now that there is no hell or devil. But I will spend eternity starting a hell of my own. And I will be the devil. Begone spirits. I do not want your counsel any longer."

His spirit guides then disappeared.

* * *

The sunlight was starting to bother Chamberlain's spirit. He was feeling hot, oddly enough, and he had trouble seeing under the sun's glare. He had to find a place that was cool and dark. He flew off to the night skies in the east.

Chamberlain searched the world for a place he could call hell. For evil souls that would worship him. For evil souls that would follow him into hell. He did find corrupt spirits – there was no shortage of them. But some went to Heaven, others refused to worship him, while others just laughed at him when he said he was the devil. Days turned into months, months turned into decades, decades turned into millennium. Still, he searched.

Late one evening, he found himself over a large city; one

that he had never seen before. The night was warm, but he felt more comfortable with the sun gone. But he must find a dark place to stay while the sun was up. Finding the right location that he could call hell was more difficult than he had ever imagined.

Then he spotted a black spirit below him. The spirit was tormenting a little human girl who got separated from her parents. She was about five-years of age, maybe three feet tall, and long blonde hair that stretched down her back.

Chamberlain watched as the other spirit, just a whiff of black smoke, jumped around the girl. He touched her back and when she turned, he would jump over her. At her back again, he would speak to her. She turned again and he would materialize as a ghostly man with his face ripped off and blood dripping to the ground. His eyes were out of the sockets bouncing around with a piece of flesh holding them to the eye sockets

The girl screamed and started to run away toward a crowded street. The spirit jumped in front of her again as a skeleton with red pieces of flesh sticking to the bones. She turned and ran farther into the darkness of the bad part of town.

Chamberlain thought to himself, "What a vile and disgusting way to treat an innocent little girl."

He laughed, "He's my kind of spirit."

He flew down to him. The other spirit was watching a human man talk to the little girl. The human was about six feet tall, had a grey beard and hair, and wore shabby and torn clothes. He smelled like a wine barrel and a sewer at the same time.

The man told the girl, "This place is full of evil ghosts. I'll take you to my place and once the sun rises, I'll take you to your parents."

The girl felt relieved, and her blue eyes looked up at the man. She smiled. The man put his arm around the girl's shoulders and lead her away. Her torment was just beginning.

The spirit was startled when Chamberlain landed beside him.

"Who the hell are you?" he asked.

"I'm the spirit who's going to change your future, but you must worship me as the devil," Chamberlain replied.

"There is no devil and I worship no one."

He was about to go after the little girl when Chamberlain questioned, "Where are you going?"

"That man just took my little girl and I want her back."

"I've got a better idea. Let him keep her. We'll watch him and then there'll be the surprise of your life."

Chamberlain thought that over and added, "Poor choice of words."

The other spirit was intrigued. "I'll follow you. For now."

"You may call me, my Lord."

"You may call me, John."

They followed the man and the girl to an abandoned ten-story brick building. It had once been a grand hotel, but the city had gradually shifted its centre away from the hotel. It had become unprofitable and had exchanged hands several times. Finally, the city had gained possession due to nonpayment of taxes, but the administration had been unable to find a buyer. The hotel now sat as a ghostly image of its former glory. The once-proud yellow bricks have turned into a grimy-black. Some bricks have loosened and fallen off.

The hotel now catered to new guests who aren't so fussy about poor service. It provided shelter to the homeless who lived in the worst part of town. The man and the girl entered through an unlocked side door into darkness, but the man knew his way. They walked down a long corridor lined with doors. He stopped and looked back. He had a strange feeling that they were being followed.

They continued to the last door on the right. He opened the door and they walked in. He went to a table and lit a candle revealing dancing shadows of the table and a small bed. Another man was sleeping on it. The girl's false friend angrily picked up the man and threw him out into the hall.

"I told you to stay out of my room!" he shouted before slamming the door shut.

He then sat on the dirty bedsheets that crawled with all sorts of bugs. He patted the bed beside him and softly uttered, "Sit beside me. I won't hurt you."

The girl reluctantly obeyed his request.

He gently revealed, "Your clothes are so dirty. We can't let your parents see you looking this way. I'm going to wash them."

As saliva dribbled from the corner of his mouth, he tenderly removed her white top. Then he took off her long black skirt. She was becoming more frightened as he finally removed her black stockings, black leather shoes, and her underwear. He then roughly kissed her on the mouth. After pushing her back onto the bed, he laid on top of her and rammed his hard penis into her tight vagina. She screamed in an agony that she had never felt before. Blood poured onto the sheets as he pumped in and out. In and out.

After releasing his sperm, he got up and turned the limp body of the girl onto her stomach. She was becoming drowsy and could not feel the pain anymore, even when he drove his penis into her small rectum causing more bleeding. As the blood drained from her body, her blood pressure dwindled. Finally, her heart stopped.

That's what Chamberlain had been waiting for. As the man still assaulted her dead body, the girl's spirit rose up and descended to the floor. It was a white whiff of smoke and was immediately surrounded by her seven spirit guides. Chamberlain charged at the other spirits and broke through their line. He gobbled up the girl's spirit inside of his and flew off. His partner, John followed.

They set down on the roof of a house as the eastern sky turned to a light blue – the sun was getting ready to rise.

The girl was crying, and she was frightened. And she had good reason to be frightened. She was about to enter the dark side where she will be held prisoner for eternity and tortured.

"What are you going to do with her?" John asked

"You'll see. But I need a cool dark place to call home for now."

"I'll take you to where I live."

They both laughed at the last remark as they flew to John's home. As the sun began to peak over the horizon, they quickly flew to the south at an unimaginable speed. They reached a desolate area with high cliffs and a bubbling plateau where molten rock released stream. They flew up a hill where an entrance to a cave was concealed.

They floated down the steep incline to a large cavern with a very high ceiling and rock walls. The floor was dust-covered rock. It was dark and cool. Chamberlain looked around – spirits could see very well in the darkness. Scanning the walls, he noticed a small opening.

"Where does that hole lead to?" Chamberlain asked.

"I don't know," John replied.

"Well, let's do a little exploring."

With the girl reduced to sobs, they entered the opening. They went downward again until they reached a very small chamber. It was about the size of a modern garage surrounded by rock.

Chamberlain observed, "This will make a very nice room where I can begin to train the little girl."

"Train her? Train her for what?" John asked.

"I have to bend her will so that she will become a willing member of my realm. She will eventually become a dirty vile little girl who will follow me and obey my commands. Child spirits can be molded to suit my needs, but their only problem is that they will remain at the age of their death. This little girl will be five for eternity. That's why I would rather have an adult."

Chamberlain looked around and divulged, "I need an altar."

Then he began to concentrate, picturing a small rock altar in his mind. Without knowing it, he raised both arms where they came within inches of touching the ceiling. The hands turned so that the palms were facing each other. Lightning arced between the hands and a blinding flash resulted. When the brightness faded away, a stone altar was in the middle of the room. It was about four feet high and was the right length for a child. A stone table had also appeared with candles and matches on its top. He had also been thinking about candles so that he could clearly see the agony on the girl's face.

Chamberlain smiled at his new-found abilities. John, however, was cowering against the wall.

"What's wrong?" Chamberlain queried.

John responded, "The only beings I've seen that have such power are angels. I know this because of the run ins I've had with them."

"You don't have to worry about angels anymore. If they show up on the dark side, they will have me to deal with."

Chamberlain then lit one of the candles and a flickering light cast shadows against the walls.

"I thought you didn't like the light." John pointed out.

"I don't, but I want to see every minuscule fragment of the suffering she will endure."

Chamberlain pulled the little girl's soul out and gently put it on the altar. She began to fearfully cry once more. Chamberlain was getting excited just by hearing her cries. As he looked at her, his mind conjured up the girl's ghostly body. Now he could see the torment on her face. How her mouth twisted. How her eyes squeezed shut. Those tears rolling down her flawless white cheeks.

He began the process to destroy the girl's innocence and convert her to the dark side forever. John watched and learned from his dark master.

Leaning over her, he turned himself into a grey version of his former self. He showed the girl an evil grin and said, "I am the devil. You are going to burn in hell for ever and ever. Do you understand? FOREVER!"

The girl screamed as Chamberlain climbed on top of her. He thrust his rock-hard penis into her vagina, but it felt like a white-hot poker. It burned her. She screamed in terror and pain until she lost her voice, but her mouth remained open in a silent scream. Finally, he took out his penis and stepped down to the dusty floor. She became quiet.

Next, Chamberlain held up the girl's arm before her eyes. They widened as he cut off her hand at the wrist with a knife in one-clean motion. Blood squirted out all over her face. She quietly stared at her severed hand.

Her torturer then changed his appearance in the same form, but with human colour. He softly spoke to her, "What have they done to you? I will make you better."

He replaced her hand on the wrist. She was able to wiggle her fingers. Then he changed back into the evil Chamberlain.

He revealed, "He can't help you. I will torture you forever. And your mother, too."

He stepped aside to reveal a woman with a battered and bloody face. She was just over five feet tall with long blonde hair.

The girl looked at her and asked, "Mommy?"

The evil Chamberlain crept up behind the woman with a large sword and gleefully cut off her head. Blood sprayed from her neck all over the girl.

She screamed, "Mommy!"

Then Chamberlain approached the girl. He held up the bloody sword high above her. As he was about to bring it down, he was pulled out of the way. He was replaced by the good Chamberlain.

He confided, "He's wrong. I can help you, but you must do as I say."

The girl settled down to listen to him when he was pulled

out of the way.

She shook her head and shrieked, "NOOOO!"

The evil Chamberlain was back. He showed her a white-hot knife and placed it on her stomach. She screeched as her skin broke out in red painful bubbles. Then he took the same knife and cut off her ears and nose, laughing as he did so.

Then the evil Chamberlain was pulled out of the way and replaced by the good one.

His gentle face came close to the girl's. "He's coming back. I can help you, but you must tell the evil devil this message – I worship Chamberlain. I will obey him. I like doing evil to others because Chamberlain will protect me."

She sat up on the altar as the evil Chamberlain returned. For a girl of five, she was able to repeat what she had been told, word for word.

She calmly looked at the devil and repeated, "I worship Chamberlain. I will obey him. I like doing evil to others because Chamberlain will protect me."

With those words, the devil disappeared in a ball of fire. The little girl did not blink an eye. She closely watched as the good Chamberlain approached her and then smiled. He replaced her nose and both ears as good as new. Then he roughly kissed her, and she kissed him back as she tried to wrap her arms around him. He pulled away and she smiled at him. An evil smile.

Chamberlain was happy with his first conversion of a soul from pure good to pure evil. He didn't realize it at the time, however, but these events in the cave had set him on a collision course with Heaven itself.

* * *

In God's chambers in Heaven, God had called his four senior angels.

He disclosed, "Some bad news on Earth. An evil soul named Chamberlain has taken over the dark side on that planet as its lord and master. But somehow, he has the powers of an angel. I could increase your powers to defeat him, but that would not be showing mercy, would it? I could easily eliminate him myself, but I will not interfere in the affairs of my worlds.

"So, here's the simple solution. You will never enter the dark side on Earth. And I mean for eternity. I do not want to see a deadly confrontation that could cast souls into oblivion."

The angel with the Obliivian appearance asked, "My Lord, will other souls from the dark side appear with powers equal to your angels?"

God replied, "Not on Earth – Chamberlain will not allow that to happen. But on other worlds, I really don't know. The dark side is new to me, and my senses have not yet adjusted to it."

The angel with the purple skin pointed out, "But my Lord, you first became aware in the darkness."

"That's true," God admitted. "But there was no evil in that darkness. There was just me and nothing more."

The angels nodded their understanding and disappeared

* * *

As the centuries passed on Earth, now that he had found his hell, Chamberlain was able to gather more souls on the dark side. Many were spirits who had lived evil lives and did not want to enter Heaven after the death of their physical bodies. They wanted to continue their evil ways and were drawn to Chamberlain and his hell. But his favourite were the child spirits because of the torture he inflicted on the innocent. He still hunted children into modern times.

The dark side was where wicked spirits hid in the shadows. These spirits now knew that there was no hell and no devil, but still they worshipped the darkness in the shadowy world they called home. They were safe from God's angels because that was one place where they dare not tread. And best of all, they had God's blessing.

Lord Chamberlain continued as the leader of the dark

spirits on Earth, but leadership was tenuous at best. These dark creatures were looking for the evilest among them, and Lord Chamberlain fit that bill – for now. Not to mention that they feared his powers. They appeared as all spirits look like. Whiffs of smoke, except these ones were black. And they were easily missed in the dark by humans.

When Chamberlain changed his appearance, he always looked the same – a full black beard and unkempt long black hair. He wore a dirty white long-sleeve shirt and long black pants. His black-leather shoes were scuffed. He savoured the blackness and was true evil, more than anything that the human race could devise.

It was now past midnight and Lord Chamberlain was tormenting a five-year-old boy in his sleep. Adults called it a nightmare, but it was closer to hell.

The boy's mind pictured the black thoughts from the evil spirit. There was a car crash. His mother was laying in a ditch with her eyes hanging out. His father was still in the car, but his brain was laying on the hood. Blood was everywhere. Then he saw his own body broken in two. The bottom half was laying on the roadway, with the top half five feet away. His skull had been crushed in.

Cars and trucks kept running over his body, turning it into a bloody pulp. No one would stop to help. He screamed, but there was no sound. Then he saw the devil approach him. He wore black clothes with a black cape. There were horns on his head and a tail behind him. A black beard grew on his face, and he was smiling a wicked smile, revealing decayed teeth.

Satan declared, "You are mine. I'm going to take you into hell to burn forever. You sinned, Billy and God have cast your soul away."

Billy asked, "What did I do that was bad?" He was crying and shaking with fear.

Satan replied, "You didn't finish your supper last night."

Satan laughed and grabbed the boy with his claw-like

hands. That's when the boy woke up screaming.

Chamberlain went back to his dark kingdom. A kingdom that he called hell. It was nothing to mention, except it was dark. Black candles lit up a portion of a chamber carved out in the bowels of Earth. Dark souls waited for him.

One of the black spirits, John greeted the ruler. "That was a good dream for the boy, my Lord."

Chamberlain answered, "Yes, it was. A few more nights and he will die. And I'll be right there to take his soul here for eternity."

Then Chamberlain asked, "How many child souls have you collected tonight?

Another spirit replied, "None, my Lord."

"What! No children!"

The other spirits were afraid of Chamberlain's wrath. "My Lord, the angels from Heaven have been protecting the prime candidates. We could get many in the poorer countries where God has chosen not to protect the children."

"Why do you think God does not protect the children dying from disease and hunger?"

"Because..."

"Because he knows we don't want them. Spirits which come from bodies that have died under such great stress are of no use to us. These spirits just act like zombies. They have no will that we can bend to freely worship with us. Only children with safe lives have wills that we can mould to our ways."

The dark ruler then questioned, "Who is this spirit that does not know our ways? Is he new? If so, he has not earned the right to talk to me."

A different spirit replied, "She is not new and has an envious evil record as both a human and as a spirit. This is her first time talking to you and she was nervous."

Chamberlain slyly remarked, "A female, eh. You come with me, and we can change into our physical bodies. I'll give you some lessons in the dark side. The rest of you go out and do not come back with out the spirit of a child."

The shadowy creatures returned just as the sun was rising. They hated the sun as well as all light. They came back empty handed again. Chamberlain was annoyed, but he had a new member of the group to introduce.

Chamberlain announced to the group, "I am pleased to present a spirit whose physical body recently died in the United States. He was a man who spread child porn all over the internet. He took great passion when he had sex with children online. He was put in jail several times, but always returned to his life's obsession – his lust for children. His name is Max."

He went on, "He will show you how to get the child spirits that we can really use. And to show my confidence in this spirit, he will not have to go through the training and evaluation before being able to speak to me."

He finally declared, "This depraved spirit will target a family living in Japan. The parents have six spirit children ranging in age from two to eight. Both parents are also spirits, living at a Buddhist temple."

The next night, the new paedophile spirit flew to a temple on a mountain northeast of a city in Japan. It was built in that direction to keep evil spirits away from the city. It may have not worked for the city, but it did work for the temple complex. The spirit family stayed quietly in a red tiered building and the monks ignored them.

The sinister spirit had a plan. He flew down to just outside the compound. He dared to go no farther. As he stood there, he could feel the presence of God. He turned into a physical being resembling a Japanese monk.

Using thoughts, he called out to the spirit family, "You must come to me at once. An evil spirit is roaming the grounds looking for you, but I can take you to a safe place. Please come at once before it's too late."

The spirit family flew to the disguised spirit. The parents stopped inside the perimeter. They were suspicious and tried to stop their children. They stopped the four of them, but the two youngest flew to what they thought was a monk. When they were in reach, however, the monk turned back into the foul spirit. His form enveloped the two child spirits. With them crying for help, he took off for the dark side. The parents could do nothing but watch. The family had learned a lesson that night – a hard lesson."

The immoral spirit returned to Chamberlain with two frightened child spirits. He was laughing. When the other dark spirits saw the children, they too, began to laugh.

Chamberlain asked the demonic hero, "Do you wish to lead the inquisition of the children?"

The paedophile spirit answered, "No, I have another family in mind. A few spirits here have told me about a family of three spirit children, a spirit mother, and a human father. What makes this family special is that God has taken a personal interest in them. It's almost like fighting God. I have to think over my plan."

Chamberlain warned, "We must be careful when dealing with God. It would be devastating to me if I lost a dark soul of your calibre."

Six dark spirits lead the frightened children away even deeper into the black depths of the Earth to begin a terror that would transform these youngsters into spirits as corrupt as their captors.

Max, the porn spirit left for Canada the next night. The family he was seeking lived in a city nestled in the lower Great Lakes. They seemed to be easy prey, but the other dumb-ass spirits couldn't get through whatever was blocking them.

He penetrated a townhouse in the south end of the city early in the morning as a spirit. The structure was a three-story brown-brick house with light-brown siding.

He expected the occupants would be sleeping and it would be easy for him to snatch all three kids. But he was surprised to find everybody awake in the living room. Wide awake. The living room contained a fifty-inch T.V., red sofa and love seat, wooden coffee table and end tables with matching lamps.

He witnessed a confrontation between a seventeen-year-old spirit boy, named Steve and the five-member family. The teenager had long scraggly hair, a thin build, and a six-foot frame. His unshaven face was covered with scars and blemishes. He smirked at the parents. He was powerful and evil. His spirit would make a great addition to the dark side.

"My kind of lad," the porn spirit thought with a smile.

The spirit mother shouted, "Send him away, Gary. Send him far away."

The spirit mother's name was Yvonne. She was a few inches under six feet tall, with long premature-grey hair. Her figure was described as full. Also present were the souls of a teenage boy, and a young boy and girl.

Gary, the human father, was six feet tall and weighed close to three hundred pounds. He had short grey hair and a grey moustache, wearing black track pants and a grey top. He sat down on the sofa with his hands out and palms up. He closed his eyes and could see the red light. He ordered, "Come into my light, Steve. Go far away and don't come back."

Steve could feel the pull from Gary's light, but he resisted. His rage turned into fear. He got on his knees in front of Gary and pleaded, "Don't send me away. I'll cross over and change. Pleeeze."

Gary did not believe him. He repeated his words, "Come into my light, Steve. Go far away and don't come back."

Steve was drawn into Gary's light and disappeared. Max left the house before they could sense him. He didn't expect the power of the human father and was afraid of him.

The evil spirit returned to the dark side empty handed. Chamberlain was surprised and asked, "What happened?"

The paedophile spirit relied, "I didn't expect anything like that. You know about this family in Canada?"

"I do. My band of evil spirits claim that they cannot grab

those children."

"I saw the human father dispatch a depraved teenage-spirit boy. Good thing that kid was there, or I would've been the one to disappear. I'm going to appear to them tonight to see how they react. Just a quick in and out."

That night, he found the family in the basement watching T.V. The three spirit children were sitting on a sofa beside their human father. One spirit was a three-year-old girl with short blond hair. The next was a boy a year older with short brown hair. The third was a chubby fourteen-year-old teenager with long brown hair. The spirit mom was not in the house. That was good for the corrupt spirit.

The T.V. room was small. A couch against a wall and a T.V. on an opposite wall. There was only one window with a view of the wooded ravine that behind the townhouses. The inside door, which lead to the patio, was open.

He took the form of a tall white man wearing a long black leather coat and black shoes. His hair was short and black. He was still a spirit that only another spirit could see. And saw him, they did.

The girl cried out in horror, "Do you see that man?"

The older boy shouted, "I see him!"

The spirit children gathered around their father and urged him to get up, but there was no response.

The evil spirit smiled and thought, "He's drunk." He moved a step to seize the children but stopped.

"If he woke up, I'd be a gonner."

To be safe he left the house but remained outside to see if the kids were ever left unattended. Around 5:00 A.M., he saw Gary and Yvonne take their dogs for a walk. The children were with them. Max, the evil spirit materialized so that they all could see him but using the same appearance that frightened the kids. They were walking along a sidewalk beside a large hospital. He crossed the street about fifty feet in front of them and stopped on the sidewalk. He turned his head to look back at them and smiled. Then he disappeared before their eyes.

Max watched for a reaction. Neither parent batted an eye. Gary did look into an empty parking lot, but that's it. The parents did not fear spirits, evil or otherwise. And the children did not show the fear they did last night. They felt safe with both parents' alert. The evil soul decided to just watch them. They might get careless.

The black spirit did not return to the dark world. He became obsessed with this family and waited outside the house, day and night, looking for a chance to grab the children. The parents did not give him any opening at all, and he was getting agitated.

One day, the spirit family got into their blue Ford Escape and drove thirty miles to a nearby city. Max followed them to where they pulled up outside an old brick house. They all went inside a small white-frame addition built on the side. It was small with a sofa and three chairs. Yvonne and Gary sat at the dining room table with a clairvoyant doing a reading for them. Her name was Colleen.

Colleen had shoulder-length red hair tied in a bun on her head. She was well over five feet tall and a bit overweight. She wore a black pants and a red top.

The evil soul waited outside, but soon he had enough. He entered the house as a spirit. The dining room light dimmed as he entered. Colleen saw the light dim and immediately knew why.

She announced, "There's an evil spirit in the house."

She closed her eyes and mentally targeted Max. Things happened so fast that the dark soul did not have a chance to flee. Then he was no more. Colleen dispatched the spirit, and he was scattered into oblivion.

Colleen told the group, "He's gone."

Then Colleen and Yvonne put all the children in unseen protective bubbles that would let the parents know when an evil spirit was nearby. But that would never happen again. Chamberlain was dealt a severe blow by God's forces, and he would never send his spirits there again.

* * *

Back at the dark side, Chamberlain revealed, "The newest member of our world is gone. Missing in action trying to penetrate that growing spirit family in Canada. That one is now off limits to us."

But he carried on, "I was thinking. Why should we put ourselves at risk with these spirit families? The easiest way to get spirit children is to be there at the moment they die. That way we can snatch them before their spirit guides can lead them to a family."

"Here's the plan," he explained. "You will spread around Earth, but just the good countries. Check out human families, see if they're in some sort of distress where the children maybe in danger from their own parents. Children die at the hands of relatives more than strangers. Then watch that family. Be there when the child is killed and immediately take possession of the soul. The spirit guides are not strong enough to stop you."

"Good hunting," Chamberlain remarked. Then he laughed a terrible vile laugh.

Thousands of evil spirits descended around the world that night on a hunt for the souls of children to be converted into devilish spirits.

Two such spirits checked over a very large city in the United States north-east. They entered houses and apartments looking for children who could be murdered by a relative. Finally, they hit pay dirt in a large apartment building in a run-down area of town. The apartment itself was dirty and dingy. There was an old sofa and chair in the living room. The floor was covered by an ageing carpet covered with stains. There was one bedroom with a double bed long past it's prime and a baby's crib. A six-month-old boy was inside the crib and was wailing because he was hungry.

There were baby bottles inside the refrigerator that would have quieted the child, but the lone occupant was not thinking clearly. He was of average build and height with long brown hair, sunken cheeks and a face covered in stubble. His mind was clouded because he had just smoked a joint. Now the baby's crying was getting on his nerves. He paced around the living room, getting more and more enraged.

Finally, he had enough. He had to stop that kid from crying. He entered the bedroom and picked up the child when the door to the outside hall opened.

A female called out, "Hi. I'm home."

She was around five feet tall and weighed about 120 pounds. She had an attractive figure and face, with long blonde hair. She married her husband because she was looking for excitement and he was bad. She has regretted that decision now for the last two years.

He put the child back to bed and went to the living room to meet his wife. "Can you shut that kid up?"

She replied, "All you had to do was heat up a bottle and give it to him. He's just hungry, that's all."

She went into the bedroom and brought out the baby, still sobbing. She went into the kitchen to get a bottle when her husband asked, "How was work?"

"Fine. But you need to get a job. We can't live like this."

He said nothing, but her comment made him stew in his own poisonous juices.

One of the spirits said in thought, "If she didn't show up, he would have killed the baby. So close."

The other one replied, "We'll keep an eye on this place. When she goes to work again, he'll probably kill the child. Maybe we can slip some cocaine to this guy. He'll find it and think that it just slipped his mind. He'll get really high. That should ensure success for us."

They left for the dark side, confident of success.

Another gruesome two some were scouring houses in a village in northern England. These fiendish souls found a house of interest. It was a small old house with three upper bedrooms. A kitchen and a front room were on the main floor, both neat as a pin. There were three people, however, in the dirty damp basement.

The basement had four small windows that were covered with black curtains. A root-cellar entrance was in the middle of one wall, opposite the wooden stairs. In the middle of the basement, however, was a six-foot long wooden altar that stood about four feet high.

A six-year-old girl was sitting on an old wooden chair, crying. She was tied to the chair with blue clothesline. Her hands were tied behind the chair.

"Auntie Rose, please let me go. I won't tell anyone," the girl pleaded. She was short with a plump build. Her brown hair was tied in a ponytail. Her name was Catherine.

Rose replied, "You'd like that, wouldn't you?" She was also short and plump with long grey hair tied on her head in a bun.

"We have plans for you, my dear," the girl's uncle John revealed. He was thin with a bald head. A full black beard was covering his face.

A knock came at their front door. John put a dirty rag over the girl's mouth to gag her.

John revealed, "That's probably your brother. I promised him that I would join a search party looking for Cathy."

"Just don't make any promises for tomorrow," Rose remarked. "The others will be here at sundown for the sacrifice."

The hideous spirits were excited.

One happily remarked, "This is going to be easy. When her auntie plunges the knife into the girl's heart tomorrow, we'll be right here to take her soul." They left for the dark side, laughing.

The dark spirits returned to the English house the next night and were surprised to see three police constables and a sergeant talking to Cathy's uncle outside the front door of the house.

The spirits were worried and with good reason.

The sergeant pointed out, "Your brother-in-law, sir, claims you have a group that worships Satan and makes sacrifices. And judging by the look of the people here, that appears to be correct."

People were silently entering the house dressed in black robes with black hoods.

The man replied, "We do worship Satan. Is there a law against that, sergeant?"

"No sir, there is not. Your brother-in-law, however, further claims that you may have sacrificed his missing daughter."

"That's rubbish, sergeant. We sacrifice small animals, not people."

May that as it be, we would like to search your house and inspect your yard, just to be on the safe side."

"Do you have a search warrant?"

"No, sir, but I can get one in short order."

"Very well sergeant, help yourself."

"Thank you, sir. We'll be out of your hair in short order."

One constable, with a powerful torch, searched the yard looking for recently disturbed ground. Another constable searched the main floor while the other was on the second floor. The sergeant searched the basement, being hounded by the group of Satan worshippers.

One woman threatened, "We'll have your job for this, sergeant."

A man declared, "I'm a lawyer. I'll see you in court over this, sergeant."

The sergeant ignored the comments. He tapped the wooden altar, pot marked with the point of a knife, and asked, "Is this where you sacrifice animals?"

Cathy's aunt Rose replied, "Yes, it is, sergeant."

He looked around the basement. There wasn't much to search, except for the root cellar. He walked over to it and looked for a light switch.

Rose disclosed, "There's no light in there, sergeant, but here's a torch."

"Thank you, ma'am."

He thought to himself, "These people are actually helping me to search. There's no corpse in here, I'm sure."

The root cellar was filled with large cardboard boxes. He half-heartily pulled a few out and looked inside them. They were empty.

The sergeant went upstairs and waited for his men to finish their jobs. The two inside the house reported that they had found no evidence of a kidnapping.

The constable came in from the outside and said, "No graves out there, sergeant."

The sergeant turned to Cathy's uncle and remarked, "Sorry about the disturbance. Just doing our job. Have a good night, sir."

"Thank you, sergeant. Keep up the good work."

When the police left, he smiled, went into the basement, and asked, "Where is she? I was ready to pack myself off to jail."

His wife laughed and pulled out all the boxes from the root cellar. Behind them was an old ice box. She opened the door to reveal Cathy, gagged and tied up.

She pulled Cathy out and disclosed, "Remember when you wanted me to throw out all those boxes.

Good thing I didn't listen to you, dear."

Two men placed a terrified Cathy on the altar on her back. She shook with fear as her eyes darted back and forth. They all lit black candles, and someone turned out the electrical lights. A woman with a red hood walked up to the altar and raised a four-inch knife above her head and slammed it into Cathy's chest. The point went right through the body into the wood. The girl's head and legs jumped up with the force of the blow. The worshippers started to collect blood draining from the back of the dead body in silver cups. They drank the blood as if they were dying of thirst. Blood dribbled from the corner of

Aunt Rose's mouth.

The relieved evil spirits leaped out and grabbed Cathy's spirit as it rose from her body. Her spirit guides tried to block them, but they were not powerful enough. Young Cathy had faced two horrors that night but being taken to the dark side would be a never-ending nightmare. The demon souls giggled with delight as they took her away. The worshippers never noticed a thing.

Meanwhile, five hours to the west, the baby's father went to the closet and took out his coat. It was still late afternoon in the eastern U.S.

"I'm going out to check on a couple of job leads," he called out to his wife.

She responded, "Don't be too late. I have to leave for work in two hours."

As he was putting on his windbreaker, he felt something in his pocket. He pulled out a medium plastic

bag containing a white powder. He opened it, wet the tip of his right pinky, and dipped it into the powder. He put the finger in his mouth and smiled.

He thought to himself, "That's coke, alright. I don't know how it got into my pocket, but who cares. I'm going to party tonight."

The man left the apartment and returned as his wife was ready to leave.

"Any luck on the job situation?" she enquired.

"Not today," he said.

"When the baby cries, change him. And if he still cries, heat up a bottle and feed him."

"Okay, okay."

He waited ten minutes to make sure she wouldn't return, then the man began to snort the white dust. After a couple of hours, the baby's father sat in the dirty easy chair, pretty much wasted. He was hot and his hands were trembling.

Then the baby started to cry. He was felling mellow, and

that lousy kid ruined the whole experience.

"I'm going to shake the fuck out of you!" he angrily shouted.

The man got up and walked unsteadily toward the bedroom.

The foul spirits had just arrived, and they were getting excited. The kill was near.

Halfway to the bedroom, however, the man felt a shooting pain in his chest. He fell to his knees in torture and then rolled onto his back. He hugged himself in agony. His suffering ended when his heart stopped.

The evil spirits watched as the man's soul rose from his dead body.

One said, "Oops. Too much cocaine."

Then the spirit continued, "Well, he is an immoral prick. Just our kind of guy."

The other one agreed, "And he's better than nothing."

They darted out and went through the ring of spirit guides surrounding the man's soul. They engulfed the man's spirit and flew off to the dark side. A fitting place for this evil man.

CHAPTER NINE

The Wars

In God's Universe, Heaven was the only place where time and space did not exist because it was in a different dimension created by God. But they did exist in the rest of his Universe. And as time had marched on, life forms had increased in numbers – some to be blessed with his spirits and counselled by his spirit guides. Soon, a few of these life forms had become civilized and intelligent. And beyond that, they had rose to higher levels with weapons and space travel. The trouble had started when these beings, not created by God, had overrode the wishes of the spirits that had been created by God.

* * *

Three ancient worlds were the first to travel in space. The first to do so was a planet called Cous. Its development was light years ahead of any other world, even those in neighbouring universes outside of God's realm. Being on the edge of God's Universe, Cous was a lightening rod for a ruler of a nearby universe who was as powerful as God himself. This ruler called himself the Maker.

Cous was a planet a bit bigger than Earth. It's star, however, was twice the size of the sun, so Cous was orbiting farther out from its star. It would take seven hundred Earth days to complete the orbit. There was one rock planet closer to the star and three gas giants beyond Cous.

Because this planet was not on an axis, temperatures were more uniform. The equator was the hottest and cooled off to the north and south, but it never dropped below 45 degrees

Fahrenheit.

Mrs. Ibtmi, the first Leader of a united Cous, had gathered with his cabinet in his office. It was a small room with a steel desk and eight steel chairs, including the one behind the desk. There were no pictures on the wall, no decorations. If an object did not serve a practical purpose, it did not exist on this world.

Mrsibtmi asked the Leader of the Defence, "Have we been able to slow down the attacks against us? I've noticed fewer strikes on our world."

The Leader of the Defence replied, "That's because we have developed better weapons, better space craft, and better tactics. The races that the Maker have been sending against us do not present much of a challenge. As a matter of fact, in a few more months, they will not be able to come within firing range of Cous before we destroy them."

The Leader of Religion revealed, "We should ask God for help. The Maker is attacking his Universe."

Mrsibtmi remarked, "We can handle this ourselves. They are of little threat to us."

The Leader then told the group, "The development of deadlier weapons and more advanced space vehicles are our number one priority. We need to stay well ahead of our enemies."

As hundreds of generations had passed on Cous, along with its Leaders, a day of reckoning approached this planet. The Leader at this time was called Oubyix.

The leader summonsed his Council to the Chamber. This race was short with very large heads that got larger as the generations passed. They had two large eyes, a small nose, and a slit for a mouth. These ones were all males and were dressed the same way to signify their position. A grey top and pants with a red collar around their necks.

The Chamber, as with all buildings on Cous, was mainly bare. Anything that was not needed did not exist. There was a large steel table and nine uncomfortable steel chairs. On Cous, there was no art, no physical sports. Engineering, however, was at a very high level, developing machines and instruments that gave the race the necessities of life, including defence.

"A raiding party from the Mo world has attacked the destroyed a small town in the southern region of our planet. I thought we had this problem solved generations ago." Oubyix revealed.

In a world where free speech was encouraged, one of councillors shot back, "That's nothing new. It's happened before, although not for generations. The Maker just found a way to penetrate our defences. We can fix the problem."

Oubyix claimed, "The problem here is that the Maker was not involved. The beings from Mo have developed flying war craft that can reach us with advanced weapons. And they have technology that can render our defences useless. Suggestions."

The same councillor replied, "I've been saying this for a long time. We should attack Mo and show them what's it like. We are still far ahead of them."

"And why didn't we pick up on Mo's development of their war craft?" he added.

Oubyix responded, "Who knows? We don't have people on their planet watching their every move."

He carried on. "And as far as attacking another planet, have you forgotten our Constitution? It was forged through the blood of our own people and one article reads, 'The people of Cous shall never do unnecessary harm to each other or to those beyond our world.'"

Another councillor offered, "Why don't we ask God for help? Mo has been given help from the Maker for several hundred generations."

Oubyix pointed to an individual sitting in a dark corner. "Will God help us, Master Clairvoyant?"

The clairvoyant stood up and walked to the table. "If we needed God's help against these raiders from outside his Universe, he would have been here only in defence. But God believes in the Light and in peace. He will not offensively strike against another power, no matter what the price might be.

"But consider this. The fact that God is not here to help in our defence, means that we are quite capable to defend ourselves. We must not attack Mo and we must not ask God for help. Our people are very ingenious."

The clairvoyant took his seat again in the dark corner.

"There you have it," Oubyix observed. "Any other suggestions?"

A third councillor took the unusual practice of rising to his feet. "I have been monitoring the Generation Device being built well below our surface. The engineers and scientists have been working on it for generations and it's..."

The first councillor interrupted, "That machine was being built only to serve the Cous people. What does this have to do with defence?"

The third councillor disclosed, "That's true, but it could also be used in defence. It's almost ready for use by our entire population. They're just testing it now. I can explain how it would work all day but seeing it with your own eyes will give you your answer. Accompany me to this device."

Oubyix declared, "We will go with you, but this had better work."

The Leader and his councillors walked outside the chamber to a large waiting vehicle. It was like a huge silver box in the form of a rectangle. There were several windows on both sides. A door slid open as the council members approached. Once the doors closed, the vehicle rose to a designated level and flew at a very high rate of speed. It slowed down as it approached its target and gently lowered to ground level.

The door slid open to reveal a small building on an otherwise barren landscape. The metallic building was about ten feet high and shaped like a disc, with no windows. There were no guards. The leader put his hand on top of a small stand outside the door, but nothing happened.

The third councillor to speak at the meeting came forward

and revealed, "I'm the only one here cleared to enter."

He put his hand on the stand and said, "I am Bfsiz. I have nine visitors."

A voice replied, "You are, indeed, Bfsiz – the master of this project. I have scanned your visitors. They all are council members, including the Leader. I have also scanned your bodily functions and you are not under any duress. Your visitors may enter, but they must wear a detector."

The door slid open, and they walked into a very plain white room which was brightly lit. A table was just inside where the detectors were kept.

Bfsiz told the group, "Put these on your wrist. They cannot be removed until we return here."

The leader asked, "What do they do?"

Bfsiz answered, "It monitors for any erratic behaviour. If it detects anything dangerous to the project, it will destroy the subject in a small explosion that will not damage anything out-side the length of an arm."

The only other thing inside was a square silver structure. They walked over to it and the door opened. And they walked inside. The door closed.

"Control station," Bfsiz ordered. The entire structure moved down at a high speed and quickly stopped at the control room. They got out and the structure returned to its original station.

The control station wasn't much to look at. For a facility that controlled massive technologies built over several genera-tions well below the surface of Cous, the control station was merely a white room about the size of a large living room. Bright overhead lights revealed a small steel table in the middle of the room. There were no buttons or levers. It operated on the verbal commands of a few carefully chosen people.

Only one being was present when the councillors arrived. She was the chief engineer of the project, one of many over its long construction period. Because of her high position, this in-dividual was dressed in the same grey pants and top as the councillors. Except her collar was orange.

Bfsiz asked the engineer, "Are things ready to show my colleagues?"

The engineer replied, "Everything is ready for your demonstration."

Bfsiz turned to the Leader, "Think about something you want. Don't say it, just think it."

A cup materialized on the table. The Leader reached for it but was hesitant. He looked at Bfsiz who smiled. Oubyix picked it up and drank it.

He was excited. "That's the best green wine that I have ever tasted."

"Every citizen on Cous will soon be able to get anything they want with just a thought. There will be no limit on the number of people able to do this," Bfsiz revealed.

He continued, "Now I'm going to think about killing our Leader."

All the councillors, especially the Leader, were surprised and alarmed. Before they could move, Bfsiz completed his thought. A white mist encircled his head and then disappeared. Oubyix was happy to see that he was still alive.

"There is long safety protocol," Bfsiz explained, "that prevents any harm to any living being. And I mean ANY living being."

A small monitor was lowered from the ceiling. The screens on both sides came to life as the councillors crowded around. It showed a large space craft high above Cous.

He carried on, "This was ready to be salvaged, but I decided to use it for this demonstration."

Bfsiz concentrated and the vehicle blew up in a large flash that quickly dissipated. There was nothing left – the entire vehicle had been vaporized.

He pointed out, "If there had been a life form on that craft, the Generation Device would not have destroyed it."

Another councillor wanted to know, "This is a very nice

demonstration you have put together, but if we can't destroy invading space vehicles carrying beings, what good is it?"

Bfsiz smiled and pulled out a weapon from his pocket – a rare sight on this planet. It was two inches long and an inch wide. He pointed it at the engineer and fired. The engineer went down but returned to her feet without help. She had been expecting this.

Bfsiz then thought for a moment and then fired at the councillor who had asked the question. The councillor was startled, but nothing happened.

"I had this weapon at its lowest level, but it is, indeed, capable of killing. The weapon, however, was disabled by just a thought from me. We can use the Device to disable weapons on any enemy craft with just a thought. And we can destroy any unmanned craft."

The councillor who just had the weapon pointed at him complained, "Well, that's just great. Our people will be able to run around destroying property. If a person got a rotten piece of fruit, he could wait until the store was empty and then destroy it with just a thought."

Bfsiz answered, "The engineers have thought of everything and have covered all contingencies. The power to use the Generation Device to destroy will be in the hands of a few senior military personnel. They will need the Leader, however, to be there in person. To destroy an object or objects, the Leader and a chosen military officer must think the same thing at the same time."

The engineer now disclosed, "Myself and councillor Bfsiz have now lost our control over the Generation Device. I have given the power to destroy to five senior officers and Leader Oubyix. The Device is now in control of itself and will perform any needed maintenance. It will not allow ANYONE to interfere with its operation. It will know if the Leader or any of the military personnel have been replaced and will revoke the power to destroy from them and issue the power to their replacements."

Another councillor questioned, "So, we have this machine that no one can now touch. What happens if it malfunctions and starts to kill and destroy? How can we stop it?"

The engineer answered, "There is a destruct switch hidden in a secure vault on the other side of our world. If the Device needs to be destroyed, the Leader with one councillor and two officers will need to display their codes that will reveal the switch. Once the switch is pulled, the Generation Device will be destroyed along with a quarter of our planet. That's why it was built in such a remote area."

The councillor lamented, "I just wish that we had been kept up to date on this matter. I just don't like surprises coming at me like this. Why do we even have a council if important matters like this are kept secret until it's too late to change them."

The Leader touched the councillor's shoulder and remarked, "Come on, Bov. This is the way things have been on Cous for generations. Each councillor tends to his own ministry in secret, except for the Leader. I know for a fact that you have several important items that are secret. You know how our system operates."

Bov lowered his head and conceded, "I know."

It didn't take long for the new defence system to be put to the test. Several space craft from the Mo world rapidly approached Cous.

They were detected early by the defence force on Cous. Calls went out to the leader and the senior military staff. Oubyix rushed to the control room of the Generation Device and met the military there.

"Who's the senior officer here?" Oubyix wanted to know.

A man in a uniform came forward. He was wearing black pants and top with a red belt. The belt signified the rank and red was the highest.

"What do we have?"

The officer replied, "There are twenty heavily-armed enemy vehicles heading our way. They won't be in striking distance for some time."

A junior officer wearing a brown belt interrupted, "We have detected 125 unmanned missiles headed our way. They have just passed the enemy's space craft and will be here shortly."

"Alright commissioner," the Leader ordered, "we must think the same thoughts to destroy the missiles. Think over and over, 'destroy the missiles.'"

The control room went silent.

The missiles, black in colour, like large tubes, about twenty feet long and five feet in diameter. One missile could destroy a small city and there were 125. As they rapidly approached the planet, the missiles spread out so they could inflect as much damage as possible over a wide area.

As they neared the planet, one blew up. Then another. Then three more. All 125 missiles were destroyed before they could enter the atmosphere around Cous.

The occupants of the Mo space craft saw the destruction of their missiles. These beings were shaped like an upside-down pear with no limbs showing. When they needed to eat or work the controls, a black offshoot darted out of various regions of the body. There was a large opening at the mid-section to eat and for speech. These beings had no eyes, but they could accurately picture any situation in their brains using powerful senses. They wore no clothes but had different-coloured hats shaped like beanies on the top of their bodies.

The black Mo space craft were shaped like very-large black cylinders and the beings operated the craft in the dark. The entire interior of each craft was dark.

The commander of the fleet observed the destruction of the missiles in his mind. He wore a green hat.

"I had no idea they could do that," the commander disclosed.

His second in command wearing a yellow hat said, "Those missiles were supposed to weaken the beings on Cous. Shall we retreat?"

The commander replied, "No. We'll bombard them with our own weapons. Are we within range?"

"Yes."

"Alert the six craft in front of the formation to fire on the planet. NOW!" the commander ordered.

But nothing happened. Then all twenty of the space vehicles slowed to a stop when their propulsion shut down.

"Have you tried to restart the drive mechanism?" the commander asked.

"Yes, but without success. The crew is baffled."

Back on Cous in the control room of the Generation Device, the people inside burst out cheering.

The junior officer had announced, "All the craft from Mo are now drifting in space."

The senior officer ordered, "Send up our prison craft to take the creatures from Mo in custody."

But the junior officer quickly declared, "All twenty of the craft have been destroyed."

An enraged Maker had destroyed the useless Moian creatures. He thought to himself in his invisible sky palace, "With all the help I had given them, they still could not take Cous. Well, I'm finished with trying to get creatures to do a job meant only for my greatness."

The Maker's personal room was filled with the finest gems, klov and hginx, and a huge throne of solid gricaav! Pictures and statues donated by various races in his universe adorned his great hall. Countless spirits – just like black shadows – scurried around doing his bidding. He sat on his throne as a ten-foot tall being that looked like a single giant amoeba. A clear membrane over his body covered a green gel that moved inside.

He loudly declared, "I will now destroy that puny little world like it was made of feathers."

He raised a pair of claws that had appeared from his body. Sparks flashed from them to the terror of his shadow subjects; powerful beings in themselves. Tremors began to shake Cous, but they immediately stopped before any damage could be done.

The Maker knew what had happened. He changed back into a dark spirit – a whiff of smoke. God appeared before him in the same form.

"It's been a while since we last disagreed on anything, Maker."

"How dare you interfere with the punishment that I have chosen for my own people?"

"Cous is close to your universe, but it is still mine. And I will defend even a grain of sand in my Universe. You cannot defeat me, and I cannot defeat you, but both of our universes will crumble. Is that what you wish?"

The Maker thought it over and grudgingly admitted, "Of course not. Cous is yours and I will cease operations in your Universe, God."

God smiled and remarked, "Wise choice, Maker. Maybe we can get together under friendlier circumstances later. Some food and drink, perhaps."

The Maker grumbled, "Don't count on it."

God then vanished to his own Universe.

After its brush with the Maker, the inhabitants of Cous settled into self-indulgence on their own world – courtesy of the Generation Device. They lost interest in anything beyond their own race. As the generations rushed by, the Cousian beings began to change through evolution. Because the Generation Device looked after the wishes of all the people on Cous, they became sedentary. Everything they wanted was brought to them instantly by the Device and it even fed them.

Due to this inactivity, they gradually lost all four limbs. Because they never went anywhere and slept most of the time, the eye lids became permanently closed. The last to go was the sense of smell and their nose. The mouth remained through which the machine fed them, and their auditory channel remained so they could hear the entertainment.

The last duty for the Leader occurred when he proclaimed through the thought process, "As we are unable to take prisoners any longer, the Generation Device will destroy anything it perceives as a threat to our planet on its own. Cousians will no longer control the Device. As a result, all leadership positions have been cancelled. Please excuse me. This speech has worn me out and I must take a nap."

***

The other two ancient planets to form early civilizations were far behind Cous in every respect but were close to each other. Very close. One was called Obliiv and the other was Uutoooln. These two planets, near the centre of God's Universe, were far removed from Cous.

Obliiv was a large world, the fifth planet orbiting its large star. One gas giant was beyond Obliiv. This world was divided into five main independent countries. They were all dictatorships except for the largest country which was a democracy. At times, these countries fought wars with each other. But the democracy was the strongest and it was the only one to have a space program. It had a fleet of 106 space vehicles that were armed. Each one had a circular shape, about twenty feet high and one hundred feet in diameter. It appeared to have a dull-metallic finish.

The world of Uutoooln was smaller than Obliiv and was in the same galaxy. It was the closest planet to its small star with two other rocky planets and two gas giants beyond it. This world was united under one emperor. He ruled his world with an iron fist, but his people were very happy. They had an enormous economy that traded with other nearby primitive planets. No one on the planet wanted for anything.

Uutoooln had a fleet of over two hundred commercial space craft that carried out a booming trade. They were privately owned and were all of different sizes and shapes. Uutoooln also had a fleet of heavily armed space war craft. There were different models, but most of them looked like a pipe two hundred feet long and fifty feet in diameter, black in colour. Each one was armed with weapons ranging from small fire to one that could destroy a small town.

On Uutoooln, the emperor met with his war minister in a lavish palace just outside the capital city. They met in the throne room – a large chamber about ten thousand square feet. The throne was in the middle on a pedestal. Paintings decorated the white walls. Statues were everywhere, including those of past emperors. A working fountain, with fish and water plants in the pond, stood to one side. The noise of the water tended to calm the entire room. The ceiling, two hundred feet up, concealed the source of dazzling white lights.

The beings from Uutoooln looked very much like the people that would eventually occupy Earth. Maybe these traders had left their seed behind in a visit to Earth. On average, they were white, about six feet tall, 150 pounds, and had hair ranging from blonde to black. But mainly blonde.

The emperor asked, "How's the porthole coming?"

"It's a slow project, but we have our best people working on it," the minister replied.

The minister carried on, "But the real reason I'm here is that Obliiv is planning to cut into our trade with the other uncivilized planets. We have intelligence that they are building fifty commercial space vessels."

The emperor pondered, "I don't get it. We have a united planet, but we're getting trouble from one that is divided. We should be able to just sweep into there and destroy their world."

The minister replied, "They are the only advanced world that we have to deal with. If we could take over Obliiv, the universe known to us would be ours. I suggest we send an invasion force to Obliiv and force the issue."

The emperor remarked, "Go ahead, but make sure our force

is large enough to beat them. I don't want to lose because you underestimated them."

"That will never happen, my Lord." He bowed and left the room.

The beings on Uutoooln hated the Obliivians, not only because they were their only competitor, but also because of their appearance. They were literally disgusted by their rivals. The Obliivians were much smaller than the Uutooolnians. They had bald heads, large eyes, no lips, and two holes where the nose should have been. The heads appeared to be normal in comparison to their bodies, but would evolve over the next generations to become very large. The skin was ash-grey in colour, with two short legs and two short arms.

A few solar cycles after the meeting on Uutoooln, the Obliivians held an urgent meeting of their own. The Minister of the Defence Forces was meeting with his staff, just fresh off the campaign trail trying to win another term in office for his party.

"Are you sure about this?" the Minister asked, still astounded at the arrogance of the Uutooolnians.

"It's true, Minister. There are one hundred war craft from the Uutoooln world headed toward us. They are being followed by fifty commercial craft, that, we think, are filled with troops," his aide replied.

The Minister looked at the Chief of the Military. "Can you handle this, Chief?"

"Their craft are bigger and more powerful than ours, but we can easily out manoeuvre them in a tight battle, the Chief responded. "My staff has been going over plans for an invasion such as we have today. We can do it, Minister."

The Minister remarked, "Very well, carry on with your plans. I have to advise the Premiere."

They would not have long to get their plans underway. The war fleet was getting close.

As the war fleet finally approached Obliiv, the Fleet Commander on the lead space craft was surprised. "We're getting close to their atmosphere, yet their is no opposition from the Obliivians. Something is very wrong here."

The control area was small and dark. There were only four people manning the instruments. The Leader's chair stood in the middle where the commands originated. It was occupied, however, not by the craft's Leader, but by the Fleet Commander.

The Commander turned to the craft's Leader and quizzed, "Do you detect any hostile movement from the surface? The launch of missiles or space crafts?"

The leader curtly answered, "No, sir." He was angry that the commander had taken his command away from his own space craft.

But the Commander's caution turned out to be well founded. As the Uutoolnians were focused on the planet, one hundred Obliivian war craft, which had been hidden behind one of the moons on the other side of their planet, silently circled around from two different directions toward the enemy.

A member in the Uutooolnian control area shouted, "Enemy craft are quickly closing in on us from both sides."

But their detection came too late. The Uutooolnian war craft were targeted first. Missiles from the surface and from the Obliivian space vehicles hit the enemy craft in rapid succession. The Uutooolnians tried to turn their craft to get into a position to return fire, but they were too big and too slow. The smaller Obliivian craft were able to easily outmanoeuvre them. The Uutooooln craft were caught in a trap with little room to manoeuvre. The atmosphere was ahead of them. And the Obliivian vehicles were behind them and on both sides. It was turning into a slaughter. The enemy could not even retreat.

The commercial craft saw the battle rage ahead of them. They also saw that their side was losing. Each one of the craft made wide turns, because of their size, to retreat. But they were in close formation and ran into each other causing huge fireballs, which quickly disappeared leaving debris floating in space.

The few commercial vehicles that were able to safely turn were pursued by the faster Obliivian craft. It took just one missile to destroy each one. Each of the commercial craft carried ten thousand troops. All gone without even entering combat.

When the battle had ended, all that was left of the entire Uutoolnian war fleet was a wide area of debris floating in space. Not one of their craft survived. The Obliivians, however, lost only two of their vehicles.

There was much joy on the Obliiv world, but only anger and revenge on the Uutoolnian world.

The emperor sat on his throne with two men standing in front of him.

He lashed out at the war minister, "How could you fall into such a primitive trap? You made us look like helpless fools! The Obliivians right now are celebrating the loss of half of our war fleet and a quarter of our troops."

The emperor pulled out a small device no bigger than his hand, pointed it at the minister and squeezed it. A beam of light hit him, and he just disintegrated.

The emperor turned to the other man. "You are now the war minister. I WANT REVENGE!"

The new minister calmly replied, "And you will have it, my Lord. I will rebuild the fleet and our army. It will take time, but we will defeat the hideous Obliivians. I have a plan that will not fail."

The war minister bowed and left the room.

But the emperor died without his revenge. And his successor lived a long life without seeing vengeance. The third emperor, however, was different.

The seventh war minister since their humiliating defeat at the hands of the Obliivians attended at the throne room in the emperor's palace. The chamber had changed very little over the generations.

The emperor was late in his life. An old fragile man who wore a thick purple robe to keep warm. But his will was as strong and as dangerous as it was sixty years ago. No one dared to cross him.

The emperor asked, "To what do I owe for the pleasure of your company?"

"Good news, my Lord," the minister replied. "We are ready to invade Obliiv. We have assembled three hundred smaller space craft that are still powerfully armed. They can manoeuvre much better than the old models. And we have fifty space carriers that can carry fifteen thousand troops each. Each one is also armed."

"There won't be a repeat of the fiasco we had the last time?"

"No, my Lord. We have corrected the problems we had the last time. Plus, the element of surprise will be ours in this invasion."

"Very well."

The minister bowed as he backed away.

Life on Obliiv had been good since their defeat of the Uutooolnians. In the absence of the military power of the Uutoooln world, Obliiv had increased trade with the primitive planets. The economy grew to levels never seen before. And all the countries benefited, reducing the chance for wars. They were a happy people and they never saw it coming.

A few miles above the Obliivian atmosphere, a huge porthole opened. It was square with an area of one thousand square feet. The entire surface was a shimmering black. Uutooolnian war craft flooded out ten at a time and sped at high speed into the atmosphere.

Each craft was shaped like a tube, thirty feet long and ten feet in diameter. As they sped through the air, the craft were in a vacuum that allowed each one to go anywhere at any speed. The first targets were military bases. The Uutooolnian vessels swept down destroying missile sites and Obliivian space craft sitting in the open. They spread out over the entire world causing death and destruction. Some Obliivian craft did manage to get off the ground, but they were swarmed and destroyed by the invaders.

The Uutooolnians used missiles, but had also developed a new weapon that disintegrated its target. As the craft continued to level cities and towns, the military vessels carrying the troops crossed over from the porthole. They slowly made their way into the atmosphere, each one going to a pre-selected target to kill any Obliivians that they could find. The troops expected to be there at least a full generation to make sure that this disgusting race was wiped out.

The war craft returned to space. To guard against any surprises, one hundred remained in orbit around Obliiv. The rest returned home through the porthole.

The minister happily informed the emperor, "My Lord, we are victorious. Vengeance is finally yours. Our troops, at this moment, are combing through the rubble looking for any survivors to kill."

The old emperor could not restrain himself. He jumped to his feet and shouted, "The emperors before me have now received their reward!"

The emperor sat back down and added, "I have a better plan for the Obliivians. Killing them is too easy and they won't suffer. I want this race to feel agony for eternity.

"You will round up every Obliivian that you can find and put them in concentration camps around their world. I mean our world. They must be fed, but only enough to keep them alive. They will live in cold huts with nothing else where they can find comfort. They will truly know hell.

"Some can be brought here as slaves. Every Uutooolnian can have as many slaves as they wish, but the only stipulation is that the slaves must be mistreated. The Obliivians will wish that they had never become civilized."

The minister replied, "As you wish, my Lord. I will immediately carry out your orders."

He bowed as he backed away. He didn't know why, but the minister felt uncomfortable letting this race live. The minister's instincts were right on target.

* * *

With their only rival out of the way, the beings on Uutoooln prospered. The planet became rich beyond imagination. And so did their greed. They traded with planets that were far-less advanced than their own, using the porthole to trade with worlds half of God's Universe away. It certainly did not match God's portholes, but other races over the next few thousands of generations would try to match the power and reach of the Uutoooln porthole. None would succeed.

Most of their wealth came from trade. But if a race would not trade or demanded too much in return, the Uutooolnian military would just invade that world and take what they wanted. They were the most powerful world in God's Universe and the most technologically advanced. Or so they thought.

The war minister met in his office with a very powerful Uutooolnian trader. His office was the size of a kitchen, with a metal desk and two metal chairs. The white walls contained no decorations. The minister wore a plain-black one-piece suit, while the trader wore red trousers, a green and yellow top, orange shoes and an orange hat. He was carrying a blue coat. All his clothes were made from the finest materials from across the Universe. So much for the rewards of public service.

The trader revealed, "I have just returned from a trading mission through the porthole to a quaint little planet on the other side of the Universe. They had much to offer and really wanted to please us."

The minister interrupted, "That all fine and good, but what does a successful trading mission have to do with me?"

The trader warned, "I am not use to people cutting me off, except for the emperor, of course. I am very good friends with the emperor and have been to his palace for banquets several times. Do you understand me?"

The minister back tracked. "Of course. I apologize."

The trader continued, "The race I was trading with mentioned a planet where the beings do not have to work. They just think and what they think of will appear. Whether it be food, entertainment or whatever. They apparently created a machine that carries out their every wish."

The minister smiled and remarked, "I didn't think there was anyone with technology beyond ours. I was wrong. We must have that machine."

The trader added, "There are rumours that these people do not have any legs, arms or eyes. They just sit in one spot and do not move. An easy target."

"I don't want to invade right away. Send one of your assistants to this planet and see if they will give up the plans for their machine peacefully. I will advise the emperor."

The trader nodded and left. He went straight to his company office in a large building he had built. The different rooms were multicoloured, decorated with paintings, statues, and other works of art from many different worlds. He met with his chief assistant.

"Ro, you are about to earn the big salary I pay you," the trader declared. "You will leave for the world that we had heard about on our last trade. The war minister wants you to trade for the plans to their thought machine."

"Those were just rumours. It might take me a while to find it," Ro cautioned. "But I can't even remember its name."

"Cous."

Ro was given special clearance by the war minister to use the porthole so soon after their last mission. He was piloting a small vessel that was not designed to carry goods. Instead, it was used to scout various planets for future trade. And it was armed with the disintegrator weapon. It had a crew of three in a darkened control room. It was about thirty feet long and ten feet in diameter, with a shiny-metallic

finish. It was not meant for long trips and so there were few comforts inside.

After going through the porthole, Ro checked at various planets and was only able to find out where Cous was from a world that had just begun to explore space. He entered the atmosphere and was attacked by a primitive air vessel. It was disintegrated in seconds by Ro.

He contacted the beings below using a translator, "We mean you no harm. We are explorers and traders."

Ro heard a reply from a very strange voice, "Please do not harm us. We are no match for you."

"We are looking for a planet called Cous."

"Ah, yes, Cous. I will send you a text message for its location."

Ro turned to his friend and asked, "A text message?"

"I have an idea what it is," his friend, Egnnu, replied.

Egnnu then asked the alien, "Do you mean that you will send us words."

"Yes, of course," the alien replied.

Egnnu turned to Ro. "I have been on many more missions than you and we have the means to gather primitive technology. We will get his words and then use the translator to get the directions. Going to primitive planets to trade allows us to go beyond any obstacle."

"That's why I'm glad to have a person of your experience with me," Ro admitted.

The alien's voice returned, "Just a word of caution. These beings on Cous are said to be able to destroy enemy craft with just a thought."

The Uutooolnians just laughed at that idea.

After receiving the location of the planet, they headed toward it at the highest speed possible. They decelerated and slowly advanced toward the atmosphere of Cous. The Generation Device detected the craft approaching. It could not identify the vessel and so it automatically became an enemy. The Generation Device powered up. The Uutooolnian space craft blew up in a brief fireball.

The trader and the war minister attended at the emperor's throne room on Uutoooln.

The trader disclosed, "My craft and three members were destroyed on their peaceful mission to a world called Cous, my Lord."

The emperor quizzed the minister, "Do we have confirmation of its destruction?"

"Yes, my Lord," the minister replied. "The porthole picked up the destruction of the craft and relayed the information to the military headquarters."

"Do we know if our craft was destroyed with just a thought from these people?" the emperor asked.

The minister responded, "We have no data to prove that one way or another."

The emperor ordered, "The war minister has briefed me on this planet. Send as many war vessels as you need through the porthole and take their thought technology. Then destroy ever being on that world. Having no sight or limbs will make them useless as slaves."

The porthole opened just outside of the Cous atmosphere. War vessels went through the porthole, ten at a time. The vessels, as they approached the planet, were destroyed. But a few were getting through. And there seemed to be no end of them coming through the porthole.

The Generation Device was busy destroying what craft it could, but it was being overwhelmed by numbers. The Device, however, had no limitations and it decided to destroy the home world of these invaders. The Generation Device will do what it takes to protect the Cousian race.

As it thought of destruction, the Generation Device stopped destroying enemy space craft. It powered up to levels it had never attained. It sent a shock wave of unimaginable terms through the porthole, which was instantly devastated.

The shock wave carried on to the Uutooolnian planet and hit it full force. Uutoooln was knocked off its axis. Earthquakes simultaneously occurred around the world. Old volcanoes erupted. The shock wave created high waves in the oceans that drowned coastal cities. Power plants and fuel depots blew up, setting entire cities on fire. The palace was reduced to rubble and the emperor was killed. Military bases, where fuel for their space craft was made, went up in smoke. The military head-quarters was razed to the ground. People fled onto the streets, but there was no where to go. All the air and space craft were gone.

Satellites above Uutoooln, before they blinked out, recorded the carnage below them. Fires and explosions were visible even from space. Entire cities were shattered.

With the destruction of the Uutooolnian world, the last of the invaders were easily eliminated by the Generation Device. The Cousians, who had just seen enemy craft enter their at-mosphere for the first time in thousands of generations, settled back to their normal life. They gave no thought to what their Device had just done.

* * *

Meanwhile on Obliiv, the Uutooolnian guards were receiv-ing reports of the destruction on their home world. The com-mander ordered them to abandon their posts around the planet and wait for orders from headquarters in their barracks. He ex-pected to be called back home and wanted to be ready.

The Obliivian prisoners took this opportunity to break out of the concentration camps by the thousands. There was no real leader, just the will of each Obliivian to survive and to crush their enemies. They were a disciplined race.

On the Uutooolnian world, the war minister found himself as the most senior government survivor. He was meeting with a few junior military officers. The senior ones died when the headquarters was razed to the ground. They were all filthy with torn uniforms.

The minister revealed, "Seeing that I'm the most experienced among us, I am declaring myself the emperor of Uutoooln. Does everyone here support me?"

He had his hand on a small disintegrator in his pocket.

All the officers, wisely, bowed to acknowledge their new leader.

At that moment, a powerful aftershock ripped through a nearby city. They were overlooking it as a large building came crashing to the ground to complete the total destruction of that city.

The new emperor ordered, "I want you men to find a safe piece of ground that hasn't been ravaged by earthquakes. And nothing close to water. Then round up as many soldiers as you can, and we'll set up camp to plan our next move."

One officer asked, "My Lord, what do we do about the civilian survivors?"

The emperor replied, "Admit them to our camp if they are unhurt. If they have suffered any injuries, execute them on the spot.

The officers were not surprised and had been used to carrying out such orders in the past regime. And they would carefully follow the emperor's instructions this time as well.

Over on Obliiv, the fleet of Uutooolnian war vessels left the planet and headed straight toward Uutoooln at high speed. They did not slow down as the fleet entered the atmosphere where they broke off into groups travelling in different directions.

As the emperor was talking to the officers, one of them pointed to the distant horizon. "Look over there. It looks like air vessels coming our way."

The entire group peered at the coming vessels. There weren't any instruments to detect who they were.

Then the emperor finally recognized them. He smiled and shouted, "They're our own war craft that were stationed on Obliiv!"

His smile disappeared, however, when the vessels fired on the group. They were all disintegrated. The craft carried on chasing and killing any being they found on the surface. They also disintegrated any buildings left standing. If they found any city or town still intact, bombs would be dropped to set the buildings on fire. These war craft carried out a mission of total annihilation on the planet's surface for several days until there was no sign of life left on Uutoooln. There probably would be a few scattered survivors, but the Uutoooln civilization was now dead. The war craft then returned to Obliiv.

* * *

When the Uutooolnian guards had abandoned their posts, the Obliivian prisoners had escaped and had stormed the different barracks. All the guards had been slaughtered, except for a few pilots. Before their death, they had taught Obliivian pilots how to fly their craft.

When a strong leader had finally emerged that the people had accepted, he had directed the fleet of war vessels to destroy what was left of Uutoooln.

What had really helped the Obliivians, after the destruction of their enemy, was the fact that the Uutooolnians had not completely destroyed their world. In the initial invasion, they had massacred millions and had reduced some cities to rubble. All the military bases had disappeared. Some cities and towns, however, had been spared. Essential services, such as hospitals, in some places still functioned, although deserted.

* * *

Now the leader of Obliiv was keeping a promise. "My

brothers and sisters of Obliiv," he began. "We have defeated the Uutooolnians. Rebuilding our world should be easy because we have our own technology still intact and have captured some Uutooolnian technology. As I had promised all of you, I will now re-establish each nation that existed before the invasion."

True to the leader's word, each nation was reborn – even the democracy. But a big change in the spirituality of the Obliivian people was just around the corner.

God was distressed to see these wars inside his own Universe, but he had decided at the very beginning to never interfere in the lives of beings inside his realm. Of course, there were the books, but that was the work of his angels who were allowed to intervene in the lives of these life forms. God, however, would defend his Universe from outside threats for eternity.

CHAPTER TEN

A Plot Against Heaven

A young woman laid in her bed holding three babies – two boys and a girl. Her name was Diane. At this moment, because she had just given birth, her long brown hair was unkempt. The sweat still glistened on her light-brown face.

A midwife and her husband stood beside her bed. His name was John. He was white with short brown hair. He stood about six feet and had a slim build.

The midwife was a plump middle-aged lady. Her grey hair was tied in a bun on her head. She was smiling. Another successful natural birth, although she had never delivered triplets before. But it would not be the last.

John took a seat beside the king-size bed. They were in the master bedroom of their mansion outside of Erie, Pennsylvania. The bedroom was bigger than most people's homes. There were two walk-in closets, two huge dressers made from solid oak, two matching night tables with lamps, and three original oil paintings on the powder-blue walls.

He caressed the babies with a kind fatherly smile. "You were right, Diane. A year and a half ago, you predicted that you would give birth to triplets."

She remarked, "Don't forget that I see that there will be nine more."

"How could I forget that?"

"I could never doubt the word of the best clairvoyant in the world," John added.

"I wouldn't say I was the best," Diane modestly said.

"Most of the main-stream media around the world say you are. You've been on T.V. World leaders consult you. If you aren't the very best, then you have fooled everyone on the face our planet."

Diane revealed, "This is only the beginning, John. Eleven of our twelve children have been with us before in another life. I can feel that. And they will be returned to us for a purpose."

"What's the purpose?" John asked.

"Our family will change the world forever. We will bring peace and unite all the people on Earth. I can see that happening around 2090 or so," she replied.

"And it all started right here in Erie."

That made Sette snap out of her vision. The Obliivian clairvoyant had seen enough. She remembered what Diane had said in Sette's vision of future events, "Eleven of our twelve children have been with us in another life."

Sette looked like most Obliivians. A large bald head, large eyes, a slit for a mouth. Her stature was short as were her arms and legs. Plain grey and white clothes covered her ash-grey skin.

Sette must find that family and stop them before they can start their new family in Erie. The security of Obliiv depends on stopping them. She closed her eyes and went into a trance.

* * *

Sette's spirit temporarily left her body and was replaced by her spirit guide. She had a dangerous plan in mind, but before she could carry it out, her soul was pulled into God's Place. Her arrival was unexpected. If the angels had known, they would have set up a parade – Sette's spirit was in the top twenty in God's Place. But God had sent for her.

His voice thundered, "What are you up to, Sette? You used to be my trusted servant on Obliiv, but now you have chosen to abandon me."

She could not see him, but she could feel his presence. "I am still your servant, my Lord, but my planet is in danger from Earth. I must stop them."

God replied, "What danger? Obliiv is much more powerful."

Sette explained, "A family will soon unite the humans. As a unified race, they will overtake us in strength. They are violent beings and will no doubt attack us. My people cannot attack them because you have forbidden us to do so."

God roared, "You have angered me, Sette. I do not interfere with the worlds in my Universe. It was my angels who came to Obliiv and told you not to destroy the human race. It was also one of my angels that set up the family and the books that may unite the humans on Earth."

God added, "Have you forgotten, Sette that one of my angels did exactly the same thing for the Obliivians so many of your generations ago? Your people are united and strong because of that."

"I have not forgotten, my Lord."

"But now you want to stop the humans from receiving the same gift. How dare you interfere with the business of my angels!"

"Go now, Sette," God angrily told her. "I know what your plan is to find this family. Carry it out."

God added, "Be warned. The angel who is in charge of this project will not sit by while your people try to destroy this human family. Your people are no match for my angels."

* * *

Sette found herself back on Obliiv in her sleeping chambers. Her body was still sleeping, and she appeared as a white whiff of smoke. To carry out her plan, her spirit flew to a nearby military base where huge portholes operated. Her first task was to enter the base without being detected. If she was caught, her spirit would be captured, and her body executed because she is a clairvoyant. Because of her position with the Great One, however, she had inside knowledge that the security system had one small hole in it. She followed the perimeter to the kitchen which backed onto the boundary.

It was a large square building, grey in colour, that worked around the clock to feed thousands of hungry workers. The food was made in that structure and then sent to the eating areas. There were no windows, but several sliding doors. Exhaust pipes protruded straight up from the roof. One pipe, however, was at an angle and permanently pierced the force field. Only the Great One and a few top officers knew about it. Even the Ministers had no idea. It was agreed not to fix it because the system would have to be shut down for several days to repair it. And then it would take weeks to restart it. As a result, the base would have to be closed. And that would be costly. Anyway, what danger was a four-inch pipe?

But that's all Sette needed. She scrunched herself down and entered the pipe. It came out over a huge stove. Workers rushed around in the brightness of the kitchen. They all wore white clothes, white hats, and white gloves. She bolted to the nearest wall and walked through it. Once outside, she could see the gigantic pothole building.

It was about five miles long, two miles wide, and two thousand feet tall. It was black, made from different material than any other building. There were no widows. Six, small doors that a person could enter were set along each side. Two large doors were visible at each end. They measured about two thousand feet wide and five hundred feet tall.

The inside was well-lit from the white ceiling and walls. In the middle was the porthole. It measured the same as the end doors and could be used from both sides. It's bottom rested on the black floor, with a smooth black velvet-like material extending in the porthole toward the ceiling and walls. It was always left operating, using energy from a nearby tower. If it was turned off, it would take weeks to restart it.

Sette flew up, but was careful not to hit the force field. She could see ten other porthole buildings, and several dozen hangers. She would have to check the hangers for a space vehicle that was scheduled to journey to Earth. That should not be that hard of a task, however. Commercial vehicles were not allowed to go there – only military craft were permitted to travel to that world.

* * *

While Sette was looking for a space craft to take her to Earth, God summonsed his angel, Joyce to his chambers. Joyce had been to his great white hall many times. She approached God's mahogany throne on the white marble floor. She passed the golden pillars, the artwork from other worlds, jewels embedded in the walls. She stopped before the ten-foot-high platform, upon which the throne stood. Angels from different planets were standing at the base of the platform. She silently bowed before God.

Joyce had the typical white wings and white flowing gown of all angels. But because her spirit had many physical lives on Earth, she appeared as a human with long blonde hair.

God sat on a white cushion on the seat of his throne. He had chosen to keep his original appearance – a white whiff of smoke.

God asked, "Do you know a spirit by the name of Sette?"

Joyce relied, "I do, my Lord. She is one of the most experienced and knowledgeable spirits in your Place."

He revealed, "She has strayed from being my servant to a servant for her people on Obliiv, although that in itself is a noble pursuit. The problem here is that she wants to interfere with your project on Earth."

"How, my Lord?"

"She wants the family destroyed. If she is successful, the second book will never be published, and the family will not be together in the next life to unite all humans. I will not interfere."

"I am capable of stopping her, my Lord."

"You have great powers, but remember that you must show forgiveness and mercy as I do."

"My Lord, I am your faithful servant, and I will use my power to carry out your will. And nothing more."

God remarked, "It is my will that the family on Earth be allowed to grow and to prosper so that they can bring peace to Earth."

Joyce bowed and disappeared.

* * *

Sette had found a space craft that was scheduled to leave for Earth that afternoon. It was a small military craft shaped like a disc. The vessel was about only about one hundred feet in diameter and ten feet high. Although it was heavily armed and very manoeuvrable, there was only a three-person crew. There was no space for passengers. Its mission was to check on military bases around Earth and keep an eye on the advancement of human weapon-making capabilities

Sette walked inside the empty space craft. There were only three rooms – the control centre, an eating area, and a sleeping area. She chose to hide in the sleeping area, hoping that anyone coming in to sleep would be too tired to sense her.

A few hours later, the three-member crew arrived. Wearing grey military uniforms of the Air and Space Section, they all entered the control room. They looked like the typical Obliivian – large heads, large eyes, a slit for a mouth, short stature, and ash-grey skin. The Leader took his seat of command in the middle of the room. The other two took up their positions, standing at the consoles. There were very few instruments – the craft's Brain did most of the work at the Leader's command.

The Leader ordered, "Take us to porthole number three."

The space vehicle lifted off the ground about five feet and then followed a designated route to the porthole building. As it approached, the huge doors slid open. The craft went inside the building and stopped at the porthole.

A voice told the crew, "You may enter the instrument. Destination Earth."

"Enter the instrument," the Leader barked.

The craft went inside the darkness and immediately emerged in high orbit over the Earth.

The vessel's Brain warned, "We have been detected by several stations."

The Leader asked, "Have they taken any action?"

The brain replied, "No. This is standard-operating procedure for humans. They will not attack us unless we get close to their military bases where new weapons are being developed or stored."

A junior officer asked, "May I go to the eating area and get a brew? It's been a long day."

The Leader replied, "You may and bring back two more for us. We have a lot of work to do."

The officer left the control centre through a sliding door. She entered a short hallway. There were two doors: one on the left side and one on the right side. As she approached the eating-area door on the right side, its door automatically slid open. Because the sleeping-area door was right across the hall, it also opened. The officer stopped in her tracks and peered into the sleeping area. She immediately went back to the control centre and reported to the Leader.

"There's a presence in the sleeping area. From my training, I believe it's a spirit."

The Leader looked startled. He softly enquired, "Brain, do you know anything about a spirit with us?"

The Brain responded, "Yes, I do. The spirit is from the still-functioning body of a high-ranking citizen connected to the Great One. Her name is Sette."

"Why didn't you inform us?"

"When I was created, I was instructed to never question the Great One or any of his acquaintances."

The Leader commanded, "You two stay here."

He got up and went to the sleeping area alone. As he entered the room, the lights came on. There were just two beds and a smaller room where they were able to relieve themselves of bodily waste products.

He announced, "Come forward, Sette. We have found you."

Just a whiff of smoke, she came out of a corner and approached the Leader.

"I'm going to cancel this trip. We're heading back to Obliiv where you will be arrested."

He started to leave when Sette cautioned, "I would think twice about taking that action."

The Leader stopped and turned back to her. "What do you mean?"

Sette revealed, "If you turn me in to the military, I will be punished. However, I am close to the Great One. He will not be able to help me, but he will remember what you did. You can expect your career and, eventually, your life to end."

"But if you keep quiet and help me to accomplish my task," she continued, "you can be sure that the Great One will reward you and your two officers."

The Leader sat down on the bed and thought over the offer. "Death or reward. Nothing to really consider."

He stood up said, "I accept your offer. My two officers will go along with it – I know them well."

Sette was pleased. "Drop me off anywhere on Earth. I can find my way around. Pick me up at the same spot one Earth-day later. I'll stay in here until you set down."

The Leader nodded in agreement and joined his officers in the control room. As he entered, both looked questioningly at him. He understood that they were waiting for his order to notify headquarters about the illegal spirit.

He announced, "I have decided to help this spirit accomplish her goal on Earth and then return her safely to Obliiv. The authorities will not be advised."

The two officers stared at him in stunned silence.

Finally, the female officer pointed out, "Our superiors must be notified, sir."

The Leader shot back, "How dare you question me!"

The officer bowed her head.

The Leader revealed, "As you heard from the Brain, this spirit is a close associate of the Great One. He would not be pleased if we caused her to be punished. But he would reward us if we were able to save her."

"We are going to carry out my orders and you are free to report my actions when we get back. But I will tell them that you were a party to it from the beginning. You know what they're like at headquarters. To be on the safe side, they'll execute all three of us."

He sat in his chair and ordered the Brain, "Land on Earth in a remote area in darkness. And travel as fast as you can."

The space craft enter the atmosphere at a high rate of speed. A normal object like a meteor would have burned up. But Oblivian space craft were protected by a vacuum that surrounded the craft. The Brain selected the Sahara Desert at 2:30 A.M. It silently landed. Sette walked through the wall into the desert and the space vessel quickly left the scene.

A family with eleven spirit children on Earth would have been a target of the Dark Side. As a spirit, Sette knew that the Dark Side on Earth was the among the strongest in God's Universe. She had never met an evil spirit, but she had heard much about them. They usually went after child spirits during the night in prosperous countries. She decided to travel to Europe while it was still dark to find these wicked souls.

Sette was flying over London, England at night, when she noticed two spirits peering through a window. They were not white like her; they were black. Then they rushed inside through the window and left in a matter of seconds, laughing all the way. There was a child soul inside one of the foul souls, screaming in horror. Sette followed them. They were so delighted with their catch that they did not sense her.

They flew to an area that was covered with rock. There was no life here at all. Not even a blade of grass. They flew between two cliffs and then into an open area that smelled of sulphur. The rock below was bubbling. She almost lost them in the steam that was rising from the rocky surface. The evil spirits went up a sharply rising hill strewn with boulders. When they reached the top, they entered a small hole into darkness. The group went down a narrow steep passageway until they reached a huge hall made out of rock. The sides rose high above and disappeared into the darkness.

The two spirits were greeted by a huge crowd of dark souls who laughed at the sight of the crying child. Two of the spirits took the little girl into a hole in the wall. Then another spirit appeared in front of Sette.

"What are you?" Chamberlain asked. He appeared to be the leader. Like the others, he was a whiff of black smoke.

"I'm a spirit from Obliiv," Sette replied.

"Where?"

"It's another planet."

"I can see you're a spirit, but you seem so strange. I can sense your physical appearance and you look like a freak. Are you evil and you want to join us? We don't discriminate here."

"I'm not evil and I do not wish to join your little group. I'm looking for a family of eleven spirit children who stay here on Earth."

Chamberlain laughed and quizzed, "Does this family have a spirit mother and a human father?"

"Yes, it does."

"We know this family quite well and we will not go near them. They are very dangerous to our kind. Why do you want to find them?"

"I want to destroy the family."

"Well, lots of luck. They are very well protected."

"I have very capable associates. Where is the family located?"

"They reside in a townhouse in a city called London. It's in southern Canada in an area called Ontario."

With that information, Sette flew out of the cave and crossed the Atlantic to North America. The night followed her.

Sette quickly found the city in southern Ontario, nestled in the lower Great Lakes. The house of the spirit family was easy to find. They were the only such family in town. It was a brown-brick townhouse with light-brown siding. She carefully peered through the windows and found them in the upstairs bedrooms. The human father and spirit mother were in a queen-size bed and the eleven spirit children were in two twin beds in another bedroom. She had found them, and it was now up to the Great One to dispose of them.

* * *

Blotios, also called the Great One, was the absolute dictator of a very advanced planet called Obliiv. Since he had broken with God over the decision in Heaven to unite the people on Earth, Blotios had grown old and bitter over the prospect of Earth eventually becoming a rival.

Like all Obliivians, he was shorter than humans with a large bald head. His skin was ash-grey in colour. The eyes were large, the mouth was just a slit with no lips, and two holes where the nose should have been. His arms and legs were short. All his people had sunken cheeks, but the Great One's had sunk even more due to old age.

His clothes were very colourful. Yellow pants, a green long-sleeve shirt, and orange shoes. These clothes represented the style of the Obliivians before the first Great One, Seil, took over. Since then, all other beings on Obliiv wore grey, white, and black clothes.

He was in his office in a city that he had built for his regime. He named it Blotios, after himself. It was a heavily guarded city that housed government offices, offices from individual Obliiv-ian states, and embassies from other worlds. There were a dozen buildings that were taller than the old World Trade Center. There were no windows that could be seen from the outside. And there appeared to be no doors, but they would materialize and slide open when someone wanted in or out. These were the government offices. There were hundreds of smaller buildings that offered support services. Finally, the res-idential area grew on the outskirts of the city. The only trans-portation were long extremely high-speed vehicles that snaked through the streets.

He was standing in a large office especially constructed for him. It was a very large square room with an arched ceiling that he had seen on another world. The walls were covered with pic-tures, paintings, and drawings from other planets – taken through trade or invasion. There were statues of different sizes on the floor. There was absolutely no furniture, however. The Great One felt that people in his office, including himself, could concentrate better on their feet if they were able to pace around the room. However, he did have adjoining quarters where he could relax on comfortable furniture between appointments. And drink his favourite green wine.

The Great One's Chief of Security had just entered the office carrying a box. He looked like most Obliivians with the short stature, big head, and eyes. But he wore the black uniform of the Security Ministry. He bowed before his leader and then looked at a figure standing in a corner.

Blotios followed his gaze and revealed, "That's Sette, my personal clairvoyant."

Rovcyt, the Security Chief was stunned. "My Lord, clairvoy-ants have been outlawed for hundreds of generations."

The Great One replied, "Well, Rovcyt, I'm above the law."

Then he added, "And I'm sure that you will keep my little se-cret."

"I do as you command, my Lord." He set on box down on

the floor.

"That's as it should be. Now down to business. Sette has found out where the human spirits are. The ones that will unite Earth in their next life together. Tell him Sette."

She walked forward to where the two men were standing and disclosed, "These spirits live together as a family in a place called Canada near large bodies of water. It's a city called London. They live in a residence that is physically attached to other residences. It is very small and crowded."

Sette continued, "The family consists of eleven spirit children, one spirit mother, and one human father. Once the father dies, they will all start their new lives together as one-human family in a place called Erie. These will be very special beings and will manage to unite the entire race as one. A united Earth will mean trouble for us."

Rovcyt asked, "So, these spirits don't live in God's World?"

"Fortunately, no. If they did, it would be impossible to get to them. They only go there every morning for a couple of hours each day."

The Great One nodded and Sette returned to the corner.

He asked, "Do you have the special weapon?"

Rovcyt replied, "I do, my Lord."

He bent down and pulled a device out of the box. It was a black tube about two feet long and six inches in diameter. There were two buttons on the bottom – an orange one and a white one.

"Our...uh...your engineers have just developed this instrument from the design of the larger one," Rovcyt explained. "It can capture and release spirits."

The Great One smiled at Rovcyt's mistake and how he managed to wiggle out of it.

Blotios wanted to know, "Is there a limit to the number of spirits that can be taken?"

"The large device has no limit. This smaller one has a one-thousand-spirit limit."

"Is there a place for the spirits to go once they have been

captured?"

"No, my Lord."

"Are more being manufactured."

"We have almost one-million on order, my Lord."

"Show me how it works," the Great One ordered.

Rovcyt pressed the white button. A great flash of white light appeared and disappeared from the front of the device in seconds. A white whiff of smoke stood before them.

The spirit begged, "Please allow me to go to God's Place. Inside that thing is just pure darkness with no one to talk to."

Rovcyt was surprised. "There are other spirits in there. Haven't you made contact with them?"

"No, sir."

"Oh, well."

Rovcyt pointed the device at the spirit and pressed the orange button. Blackness appeared at the front of the weapon, with coloured sparks dancing around. The spirit was pulled back in.

The Great One questioned, "Do you have a plan to get this family out of the way before they can start their new life?"

The Chief of Security responded, "I do, my Lord. But this is a risky business and the less you know about it the better."

Blotios nodded in agreement.

* * *

The next day Sette ushered into the Great One's office the three military officers who had helped her complete her mission on Earth.

She announced, "My Lord, these are the crew of the space vessel that saved my life. They could have reported me, but they did not. And they helped me to finish my task of finding the spirit family."

The Great One smiled and walked up to the trio. "I am very pleased that you were able to save Sette. Her spirit would have been confiscated and her body killed. I owe all three of you and you will receive a just reward."

The officers smiled. They were already counting a great fortune.

But those smiles quickly vanished when the Great One changed his welcoming demeanour in a split second to one of pure hate.

"Can you keep this whole affair a secret? I think not," Blotios harshly judged. "And I do not like officers who cannot follow simple orders."

He pulled out a small weapon. It was shiny and shaped like a tube. Everyone in the room knew what it was. The junior officers loudly pleaded for their lives. The Great One was disgusted by their cowardly behaviour and disintegrated them first. Then he pointed the device at the senior officer, who did not move. He just silently stared at his murderer.

"It's always hard to kill a brave man." He fired the weapon and the senior officer was gone.

Sette smiled during the entire incident.

* * *

Rovcyt met with an officer from the Air and Space Section in a small office in the Internal Security Building. It was a plain room for the Security Chief with just two chairs and a metal desk. Because he was not on the Minister's direct payroll, he was considered low-ranking and given an office that matched. With the secret work he has done for the Great One, that's the way he liked it. Out of sight and out of mind.

The officer's name was Gelywc. Because he was visiting a Ministry building different from his own, he was dressed as a civilian in grey and white clothes. He told the building security that he was a trader. His cover story was never questioned because he was visiting a second-rate member of the Ministry.

The officer's cheeks had sunken more than normal because

of his advanced age. Despite the fact that he could still pilot a space craft better than any other officer and despite the fact he had enormous experience, his superiors were about to send him to a Retreat for Senior Officers where the state would look after his needs for the rest of his life. That thought made him cringe.

Gelywc remarked, "I appreciate this chance to personally serve the Great One."

The Security Chief revealed, "The Great One values your loyalty and silence. You are on a path that could save Obliiv from a great future threat." The part about the Great One was just a little white lie.

"You will never get any public credit if this mission turns out to be a success," Rovcyt added.

"In my line of work," the officer replied, "I have never got credit for anything I did. So, that does not bother me one little bit."

Rovcyt asked, "You do understand that this mission could result in the termination of your body and the release of your soul?"

Gelywc pointed out, "I have been in dangerous situations many times in the past. The passing of my body means nothing to me. As a matter of fact, I would enjoy my physical end much more than the Retreat they have planned for me."

The officer then asked, "The Great One will look after my safety if I make it back alive?"

The Chief responded, "The Great One will give you a just reward, just as he has done for many loyal officers in the past."

Rovcyt quizzed the officer, "You know the about the objective we have in mind?"

Gelywc disclosed, "Yes, I do. And I have a surprise for any angel that may confront me."

"What about a space craft?"

"I had to pull a lot of strings, but I got a one-person moon-class craft. It has very powerful weapons and is meant for one-way missions. I told my superior that I just wanted one-last trip into space by myself before I went to the Retreat. I just about had her in tears because she also despises the Retreat.

"And get this. She suggested three targets for me. One of them was Earth."

They both laughed.

* * *

A few days later, Gelywc was alone in the moon-class craft. It was shaped like a dull-silver disc twenty feet in diameter. The control centre was the only space on the vessel. The ceiling was five feet from the floor, giving the outside of the vessel a height of only eight feet. There were no consoles in the room, only the Leader's chair in the centre. He had to completely depend on the Brain in this craft.

The space vessel emerged from the porthole in high-Earth orbit.

The vessel's Brain warned, "We have been detected by several Earth stations."

Gelywc had been to Earth several times and he knew that this was just standard-operating procedure for humans. He was not in any danger of attack unless he got too close to one of their military bases where weapons were being developed. That wasn't going to happen, but human aircraft would intercept him when he landed in a populated area.

"I want you to land in London," the Leader ordered.

"Do you mean the city in Europe. There are several Londons in North America. And there are New Lon..."

"London, Ontario, Canada," Gelywc interrupted.

"That city lies in a densely populated section in North America. We will be seen by civilian humans. Plus, the military will quickly arrive in full force from both countries if we land in that area."

"I thought that would happen, but I need time to complete

my mission. This is my final order. You will rapidly descend to my objective. Once I have left, you will fly away to a far-off remote section and crash. But don't travel too fast. I want their aircraft to keep in contact with you."

"Your order is understood, but I am programmed to offer alternatives if the Leader is going into a situation where death of the Leader may result. I could fight off the military until..."

"No, I don't want any of that. One human will die tonight. I don't want to take any more with him. Anyway, going into battle with humans would probably breach the directive against starting hostilities on Earth."

"That directive would not be breached if they attacked us, but I understand your feelings. I will follow your order that will result in the destruction of both of us."

Gelwyc asked, "What time is it in London?"

The Brain replied, "Two A.M. local time."

"Good. It's dark. Take us in."

The Obliivian space craft entered the atmosphere faster than any human jet fighter.

The Brain revealed, "We are coming close to several American military bases. They are launching fighters to intercept us, but they are too slow."

As the space craft slowed for its landing, the Brain saw that trouble was close at hand. "I am surprised by their improving advancements. Three jet fighters will be here in six-Earth minutes and ten heavy helicopters will be here in twenty minutes."

The Leader got up and grabbed a bag. He looked inside and then approached the door.

The space craft did not land, but hovered three feet above the ground. The door slid open and Gelywc jumped off as the military jets were approaching. The vessel then silently took off and took up a position in front of the jets, being careful not to go too fast. The jets and radar followed the space craft on a wild-goose chase.

Gelywc brushed the dirt off his uniform as he watched them disappear in the distance. He took out a black weapon with orange and white buttons on it. He tossed the bag aside. He was in an unlit park, but it was surrounded by bright lights. There was green grass, lot of trees, and a river flowing through. And he was very close to a large pollution-control plant.

He took a small monitor off his belt and ordered, "Directions to the target family."

But he immediately turned it off – a motor vehicle was approaching down a black-top lane. He squatted down behind a tree. The monitor was replaced with a disintegrator.

The blue Ford sedan stopped only twenty feet away from Gelywc. Two teenage boys got out. It was a warm summer's night and they were dressed for the heat. All wore shorts and T-shirts with sock-less running shoes.

The driver was white with short blonde hair. He stood over six feet tall and had a thin build. "Are you sure that thing landed here, Mac?"

Mac was black with short black hair in tight curls He had a muscular build and was close to seven feet. "Hey man, I ain't blind. It landed right here."

The third young man remain in the car passed out from too much beer.

The driver's nickname was Spook because he like to watch ghost stories on T.V. "Okay, let's look around."

Mac was walking in Gelywc's direction. Gelwyc was in a difficult situation that he had never anticipated. He was forced to reveal himself and maybe talk his way out of it. He jumped out confronting a human that was easily twice his size.

Pointing the disintegrator at him, Gelywe demanded, "Stop or I'll kill you. I just want to leave here in peace."

Mac, however, could not speak Obliivian and just said, "Uh?"

Then he shouted, "Hey Spook, come over here. There's a weird little guy here pointing something at me."

Spook casually wandered over, but Mac was gone.

He looked at the alien and wanted to know, "What the hell are you and where's Mac?"

Gelywc didn't understand a word he said and he also didn't like the tone of his voice. So, he pointed the weapon at him and fired. Spook disappeared.

Gelywc put away the disintegrator and pulled the monitor off his belt.

"Directions to the target family," he ordered.

The monitor revealed, "There is only one way out of this park. Follow the lane way to the traffic lights and turn left. Then turn right at the next two traffic lights. Follow this road to the traffic lights where there is a McDonalds on the corner. Turn left. Follow this road to the first curve. Turn right at the lane way here and look for Unit 80."

The monitor added, "You will not reach your target on foot before sunrise and this route is very active among humans."

Gelywc asked, "Is there public transportation that I could use?"

"There are vehicles called buses and taxis, but they are full of humans. Your arrest would be imminent."

"Is there a safer route that I could follow?"

"You could go through the backyards, but these are protected by dogs."

"What are dogs?"

"They are vicious animals that humans use to guard their property."

"Just two more things. What are traffic lights? And what is a McDonalds?"

"Traffic lights are devices that humans use to control traffic. Just remember to stop on the red light and proceed on the green. McDonald's is a well-lit building where humans eat food. You can identify it by twin yellow arches standing in front of the building."

Gelywc put away the monitor on his belt and began to walk

down the black-top road. But he stopped at the Ford which was still running. He looked inside and saw a short white male sleeping in the back seat. He had short black hair and a face marked with acne. He was only a foot or so taller than Gelywc.

Gelywc opened the rear door and roughly pulled the human outside. He fell into a heap on the ground.

Looking groggily at the alien, he queried, "Hey, what's up man?"

Holding the denigrator at the man's head, Gelywc motioned to the man like he was holding a steering wheel.

The human laughed and remarked, "You want me to drive the car? Fuck you, man."

Gelywc did not understand him, but he gathered from the tone of his voice that his request had just been denied. So, he figured a demonstration of his power would change the teen's mind. He fired the denigration at a nearby tree that was caught in the car's headlights. The tree vanished.

That sobered up the young man right away. He silently went into the driver's seat and the alien sat in the front passenger seat. Pointing the weapon at his captive, Gelywc directed him by pointing left, right, or straight ahead. It was close to 4:00 A.M. when they finally arrived at the target address. A soft-white light from the rising sun could be seen on the eastern horizon.

Gelywc climbed out and closed the door. The driver looked questioningly at him. Gelywc understood. He lowered his weapon, smiled, and waved at him. The driver exhaled a sigh of relief and pulled into a nearby driveway to turn around.

At this moment, Gelywc levelled the disintegrator and fired at the car. The car and its lone occupant disappeared. He was afraid that the human would tell the military. They would send soldiers and spoil his plans.

The Obliivian then turned and looked at the unit with the Number 80 over its door. It was a brown-brick townhouse with light-brown siding. There were two floors and a basement. His intelligence revealed that the entire family should be on the second floor sleeping.

He tried the front door, and unexpectedly found it to be unlocked. Research had shown that most humans lock their doors at night, but he found out why this human did not lock his door. As he entered the house, he was confronted by three snarling and growling dogs. One was a purebred Rottweiler, one was a black Labrador Retriever mix, and the third was a brown Shepard mix. He was now doubly surprised. Dogs were kept by humans to protect the backyards. Gelywc's last mission was turning into a disaster. He quickly pulled out his weapon and disintegrated all three dogs.

But things were starting to brighten up. Gary, the human father of the spirit children came walking down the stairs. He fit the description – six feet tall, overweight, short grey hair and a grey mustache.

Gelywc pointed the weapon at him and questioned, "Where is the rest of your family?"

If he killed Gary first, all of the spirits would be gone to God's Place in a second. He had to dispose of the spirits before killing Gary.

Gary could not understand the Obliivian, but he had learned that he could talk to child spirits of different nationalities through the thought process.

"Who are you and what do you want?" Gary thought.

A surprised Gelywc could hear and understand the thoughts.

He replied through his thoughts, "I'm from the planet Obliiv. I have been sent here on a mission to talk to you and your family to determine how we could get in touch with the spirits on my world."

"Why are you pointing that thing at me?"

"It allows me to hear your thoughts."

"Where are my dogs?" Gary asked.

Gelywc responded, "I accidentally let them outside when I

opened the door."

Gary knew that the Rottweiler would tear the Obliivian to pieces if he had the chance.

Gary declared, "You're lying."

At that moment, Joyce the angel appeared between Gary and Gelywc.

"I will not allow you to hurt this family, Obliivian," she declared in his language.

Gelywc quizzed, "Is God interfering in this matter?"

"He is not."

"That's all I needed to know."

He pointed the disintegrator at the angel and divulged, "You are in the human form and as a result you will be destroyed by my weapon."

Joyce disclosed, "The moment of strength becomes a weakness."

Gelywc was so confident of killing the angel that he had briefly hesitated to savour the moment. That was the opening that the angel needed. She silently thought of pain. The Obliivian was then overcome by sharp stabbing agony all over his body. He dropped his weapon and fell to his knees. Showing God's mercy and forgiveness, however, she stopped short of killing him.

She looked at the disintegrator and it disappeared. Then she saw weapon that captures spirits on his belt. Six souls appeared from it and it too disappeared.

One soul said, "Thank you for releasing us from that Obliivian prison. It was dark, lonely and I knew time. We couldn't even contact each other."

Joyce revealed, "There's a porthole behind you. Cross over into God's Place now."

All six did as she had instructed them.

"Are you going to kill me, angel?" Gelywc asked after the pain stopped.

She replied, "Of course not. And by the same token, I will

not allow you to be taken prisoner by the humans. I will send you safe and sound back to Obliiv in a twinkle of an eye."

"Can you send me back to the office of the Chief of Security? He's not going to enjoy my story, but at least he will protect me."

"Done."

Gelywc hurriedly interrupted, "One other thing. Would my weapon have killed you?"

Joyce just smiled and Gelywc was instantly back on Obliiv safe and sound in front of a startled Rovcyt.

Joyce turned to Gary.

"When you came down the stairs, what were you going to do?" the angel asked.

Gary disclosed, "I was going to send the evil spirit away."

"He is not a spirit. He is a real being and he would have killed you!"

She added, "He told you that he was from another planet."

"He lied about my dogs and I thought that he was lying about that, too."

"By the way, where are my dogs?" Gary questioned.

Joyce responded, "The Obliivian killed them, but I made sure that their spirits had crossed over into Heaven right away."

"Thank you. So, you've been here for a while?"

"I was here before the Obliivian arrived."

"Why didn't you stop him from killing my dogs?"

"I was here to protect you and your family, and nothing more. I can't veer off all over the place. I must stay focused and carry out God's will."

Then the angel was gone.

CHAPTER ELEVEN

Our Children: A Prophetic View

Writing this book was a difficult task, both physically and mentally, for sixty-three-year-old Gary, especially with a new condition that was imposed from Heaven.

One night, while Gary and Yvonne were in their bed, the angel Joyce appeared. This angel, because she had spent several millennia as a spirit in human bodies, she looked like a solid being from Earth. She had long blonde hair, blue eyes, and the typical angelic large white wings and flowing white gown. God loved light and the colour white because he had at first become aware in the darkness.

The bedroom was on the second floor of their London, Ontario townhouse. The room was painted in an off-white colour and a picture of a thunderstorm over the Arizona desert hung on the wall over the head of the bed. The bed was a queen-size with a soft-white cover over it.

Gary had just awakened because he needed to urinate. He was about six feet tall with a round face and brown eyes. His short hair and moustache were grey. Back in the late 1960s, when Gary first became a police constable, hair had to be kept in a short-militaristic style and he just never changed it.

Yvonne, however, did not sleep because she was a spirit. But, as former humans, Yvonne and her eleven spirit children needed to go through the comforting routines of their former lives while staying on Earth. She even had to change the diaper of her five-month-old son, Christopher.

Yvonne had a grey-ghostly appearance of her former body. She was on the short side with a pleasingly plump body. Her premature-grey hair was long. Looking at her face, one would see a natural beauty that had been untouched by makeup. She had never even plucked her eyebrows. The most striking part of her face, however, were her beautiful and haunting green eyes which stood out from the otherwise greyness of her body.

Gary could not see or hear Yvonne and his children, but he could sense the presence of any spirit and could see a picture of them in his mind. He could also hear spirits talking to him as thoughts in his head and was able to reply in the same fashion.

When the publisher of this book, Colleen Cook, had shown Yvonne and Gary the cover for this novel, Gary had looked into the green eyes pictured there. He had been hypnotized. He had looked deeply into them and he could almost see Heaven.

Joyce told both of them, "We have decided that second book you are now writing must be finished before Christmas. Keeping that deadline in mind, you will no longer take in any more spirit children. The angel Rishmond, who was sent here to help you with new children, has already been withdrawn. "

Gary asked, "Why? Is something going to happen to me? Am I going to die by then?"

Joyce replied, "The reason for our decision is not your concern. Your only problem is to finish the book on time. And Gary, no more three-hour snoozes during the day. If you feel tired, take a fifteen-minute power nap."

The angel then disappeared.

In the semi-darkness, Gary quizzed, "Do you know anything about this, Yvonne?"

She responded, "I had no idea."

"I wonder if it's because I'm going to die after Christmas. Remember that my spirit guides told me I was going to die in the summer of 2011."

"Yeah, but they later told you they were wrong. Do you fear death?"

"Of course not. I'm looking forward to it so that myself and you and our children can start our new life. The only problem I have is setting up a fund for your new hospital. I'm going to make millions from the books and movie rights, and I just want to be sure it's going to be spent properly."

Yvonne cautioned, "You better get to sleep. You're going to need it. That gives us less than two months to finish the book."

As Gary fell asleep and started to snore so loud that it seemed like the walls would shake, Yvonne tenderly looked at him. She was worried that his elderly body would not be able to take the stress of writing every day, without breaks, until Christmas.

The next day, the writing started in earnest. They wrote the book in a small bedroom on the second floor that Gary called his office. There was a small widow, a computer desk, and a shredder. He sat on a chair that Yvonne had picked up from her work while she was still alive. They were going to throw it out. On the desk was a computer tower and a monitor where Gary typed the book with just one finger.

From 8:00 A.M. to 3:00 P.M. was devoted to the book each and everyday. No days off. Gary was allowed to take the dogs out once during this time and do chores like shopping, but that was it. No more long naps. He found himself falling asleep in his chair. He took up drinks and chewed gum to stay awake. He even started to take Super B vitamins.

Writing this book was a different experience. The first was joint venture only between Yvonne and Gary. This book, however, was written from Heaven through Yvonne's eyes. Sometimes it was her own experiences, but other times the words came from angels and top spirits.

So, Gary was transfixed in front of the monitor typing as quickly as he could with just one finger. At times, he didn't even know what he was typing. It seemed like energy was coming from Heaven through Yvonne into Gary's ageing body. But it all came to a head near the end of November.

While taking the dogs for a walk around 5:00 A.M., Gary's condition at that time alarmed Yvonne. It was dark, clear, and around 30 degrees Fahrenheit. Gary was not his usual chipper self and talked very little. He normally had questions for her.

Yvonne asked, "Are you okay, Gary?'

He sluggishly replied, "Uh, uh."

"I can feel that something is wrong. Do you feel depressed?"

He had been diagnosed with clinical depression years ago and she knew that depression could be deadly for him.

"No."

"I think you are. When we get home, I want you to take one extra depression pill."

She wished that she could cure Gary of everything, but her healing powers were just not that potent. Not yet anyway. Her next life, however, would be far different.

When they arrived home, JoJo knew something was wrong. He was one of their spirit children. He was fifteen-years old, short, a bit overweight, and had his brown cut in a style that looked like the Beatles. He was a real jokester, but he was also a very caring boy.

"Are you okay, Dad?" he wondered.

"I'm fine," Gary answered.

But Gary knew something was not quite right. His head was spinning in a cloud and he was coming close to tears.

JoJo could sense something was wrong. "Are you going to cry, Dad? Maybe you should go to the hospital."

Gary defiantly said, "I am not going to the hospital."

Yvonne ordered, "This is ridiculous. Gary, you get something to eat and then go straight to bed. You stay there until I get back."

"Where are you going?" Gary questioned.

"I'm going to cross over into Heaven and tell them that they're pushing you too hard," Yvonne revealed.

Gary could feel her anger and said, "Take it easy, Yvonne. Stay out of trouble."

She did not answer. A porthole appeared and she stepped into it. She now found herself in the peaceful confines of Heaven, but that did not calm her. Oddly enough, although she had taken on the form of a spirit – just a whiff of smoke – her anger still consumed her. For a spirit in Heaven, that should never happen. Or maybe it was a very deep concern for Gary.

Heaven was white in colour and brightly lit, just the way God had created it.

Yvonne called out, "Joyce. We need to talk."

The angel materialized in front of her with the same human appearance that she had displayed on Earth.

"I know why you're here, Yvonne. Come with me to meet someone who is very familiar with the awakening on Earth."

They reappeared in a small white room. The lights were bright, but there was no door. Then again, spirits don't need doors.

Waiting for them was the newest angel, Rouj, adorned with white wings and a white gown. She was smiling, looking like an Obliivian. The ash-grey skin, the large head and eyes, and the short stature.

Yvonne had taken on the appearance of her former body, except it appeared to be solid.

Rouj walked up to Yvonne and took both of her hands into hers. She momentarily lost her smile as she looked into Yvonne's green eyes. A single tear trickled down her cheek and then the smile reappeared.

Rouj confided, "As a spirit, the awakening on Earth was my idea. After God's approval, I took the steps to allow you and Gary to write three books. But due to my carelessness, your soul and Gary's soul ceased to be kindred spirits. Joyce was forced to cancel the last two books and the awakening was finished. Thanks to the grace of God, however, the second book will now be completed. In my mind, the second one is the most important book of the three. Well, the most important of the two, now. Its publication will allow the awakening on Earth to begin."

Rouj let go of Yvonne's hands and stepped back.

Joyce then added, "Part of the fault of the terrible tragedy that you and Gary had faced, also lies with me."

Joyce continued, "We know that writing the second book is a very hard task, especially for an older human. And we recognize this, but the book must be published. There's no getting around that, even if it means the incapacitation or even the death of Gary. We have good reason why the book must be completed before Christmas 2010, but our reasoning will not be shared with you. It is the stuff of angels and not spirits."

She carried on, "I see that Gary has been given from nine months to ten years to live. Things keep changing for him in the Universe. I don't know why. I had once tried to predict his death, but I was wrong to do so. Gary will die when he dies, but the books will be done and his great fortune will build the Yvonne Betts Hospital for Children. All these things will happen and he must not be concerned."

Yvonne pointed out, "That maybe true, but Gary is suffering from the workload. He was going through depression this morning and he was in bad shape."

Joyce laughed. "Yvonne, you are such a minor spirit and you have much to learn."

Yvonne looked questioningly at Rouj who simply nodded her approval.

Joyce revealed, "Gary is stronger than you think. He just has a minor case of the flu and he will be better tomorrow. Let him rest today and not even think about the book. But this will be his last day off until it's done."

"But we have also decided to give you two a little breathing room," Rouj concluded. "The wall at Christmas has been changed from brick to jelly."

Yvonne asked, "What does that..."

Rouj declared, "Enough has been said. Go to your husband."

Yvonne was transported directly back to the bedroom where Gary was restlessly sleeping. She lovingly looked at him thinking that Joyce was going to treat Gary more gently. Boy, was she ever wrong.

When Gary got up the next morning, he was still tired. "Do you think Joyce would mind if I took a nap on my own time?"

Yvonne was intrigued and asked, "What do you mean, your own time?"

Gary explained, "When I get up every morning, I always go one-line, read e-mail, play games. Would it be okay if I just had a nap instead of going on-line?"

"I don't see why not. It is your own time," Yvonne agreed.

So, Gary had a two-hour nap that morning and they did manage to write twelve new pages. But he had a visitor that afternoon.

He could hear a voice in his head calling, "Gary."

He questioned Yvonne, "Are you calling me?"

She responded, "That's not me."

"Gary."

"Who is this?" Gary enquired through his thoughts.

The voice stated, "You know who this is. I'm Joyce."

The angel continued, "I told you that you were not to have anymore long naps until the book is done. Yet, you had a two-hour sleep this morning."

Gary suggested, "Yvonne and myself agreed that the early morning was my own time that I could..."

Joyce angrily interrupted, "No more long naps after you wake up until the book is finished!"

Joyce added, "And Yvonne, please stop covering up for him. You're just encouraging him to slack off."

Thinking she was gone, Gary thought of an old Three Stooges line, "I resemble that remark."

Joyce said, "What?"

Gary replied, "Nothing."

When they got back to writing the book the next day in the upstairs office, Yvonne announced, "I want to put an extra chapter at the end. It has nothing to do with Heaven, but it will give humans a hint at what is in store for them when our family returns for our next life on Earth."

Gary was concerned. "That was supposed to be what the third book was about. God told me himself that there will be no third book."

"I know he did, but this is not a book. And it won't tell them what's really going happen. It will just be a hint by describing how each member of our spirit family will turn out in our next life. The children themselves seem to know what's in store for them. You heard Shirley say this morning that she's going to be a priest."

How could Gary say no. With both books, he has not been the author. Just the writer. A big difference in his mind. "Okay, but if Joyce shows up to give us shit for doing this, it's all your idea."

Yvonne smiled and stated, "Damn right it's my idea. I think we'll start with me, then we'll get the kids up here to give their take on the future."

Leigh shouted from the living room, "We are not baby goats, Mom!"

"I mean children," Yvonne corrected herself. "She's really sensitive about that, isn't she?"

"No kidding," Gary agreed.

* * *

Yvonne had died in hospital from liver cancer at forty-seven. As a spirit, she now sees her next life beginning when she was born as Diane in the American Midwest, west of the Great Lakes. She was born to a string of female clairvoyants on her mother's side. As a result, her mother watched Diane very closely.

When Diane was only two, her mother heard her talking when she should have been sleeping. Diane was a typical little girl with dark skin and long black hair, and a flawless complexion.

Her mother had come from a mixed marriage and her skin

was close to tan in colour. She was a tall handsome woman with short back hair and red lips.

Diane's bedroom was small with a twin bed and a nightstand with a lamp. There was a single window and a closet with a folding door. The pink walls were decorated with images from educational children's cartoons.

She went inside her daughter's room and asked, "Who are you talking to?"

Diane responded, "Grandpa. He is standing by the window."

Her mother looked and could see her father in the semi darkness. He had passed away a year ago. As a clairvoyant, she was not surprised. She had seen so much more over the years. He had the ghostly appearance of a thin white man with a bald head. He smiled at his daughter.

"Hi Dad. Nice to see you, but you have to let Diane get some sleep. If you want to drop by, the evening would be better."

He disappeared. She tucked Diane into her bed and left herself.

When Diane was ten years old, the family moved to a house in Erie, Pennsylvania on the south shore of Lake Erie. It was a small city directly across the lake from Port Dover, Ontario. A fishing village.

One evening, the family was watching T.V. in the basement family room. The room had imitation wood on the walls and a soft-purple carpet. There was a sand-coloured matching chair and sofa, both with soft cushions. Diane's mother and father were sitting on the sofa and her younger brother was on the chair. Diane was on the floor.

She turned to her mother and asked, "Mom, I've been dreaming about a village across the lake from us. There are fishing boats in its harbour. Do you know its name?"

Her mother replied, "You mean in Canada? I'm sorry sweetie, I don't. What did you dream?"

"It's like I'm there with another family. We parked our truck and then walk down a very long pier that goes way out into the lake. The water was very calm. At the very end of the pier, we stop and the man with us points at the lake and says, 'Erie is just across the lake. That's our future home.' Then one of the children takes my hand. I'm their mother!"

"Sounds like you were dreaming about a past life that you had once lived. What's tomorrow? Friday. We'll talk about that on Saturday."

"Okay, Mom. Will we still have my lessons about the spirits?"

"Of course, honey. I want to develop your special gifts properly."

When Diane was just eighteen, her clairvoyant powers had surpassed that of her mother. She had matured into a lovely woman of six feet, a sexy figure, shoulder-length black hair, and a beautiful brown face.

At such a young age, she was the host of an hour-long live program on WQLN-TV where she talked to guests about the future, the after life, and the spirit world. It was a top-rated show watched in the states of Ohio, Pennsylvania, and New York. But it was also widely watched in Canada just across Lake Erie in the lucrative London market on cable. The show had no problem attracting high-profile guests. And the calibre of the guests just kept getting higher.

After finishing a recent show in the Erie studios, her publicists sat down with her over a cup of coffee.

His name was Jack. He had a slim build, was under six feet tall, with short brown hair. He wore a dark tailor-made suit and a tie.

He produced a large notepad and revealed, "NBC is offering you a nightly show in prime time again. The pay is beyond your imagination."

Diane responded, "This is what...their third offer?"

"Fourth."

"The answer is the same. No. I want to keep my roots here in Erie. And what am I going to do with more money? I'm already a multimillionaire and I live very comfortably. I charge $1,000 an hour for readings and people come from all over the world. It can't get any better than that."

"Will you still consider the odd guest spot on T.V. shows?"

"Yeah, sure. They give me a high profile."

"I've also got feelers from Europe and Asia."

"Well, it depends on what they're offering, but I've got an open mind."

At twenty-three, Diane got married to a man named John. He was a chemical engineer who lived in Erie, but travelled in the tri-state area on business trips. He was over six feet tall and slightly overweight. He had blonde hair and blue eyes.

About six months after their marriage, while John was packing for a business trip to Philadelphia, Diane walked up to him. They were in the master bedroom of their mansion outside of Erie. The bedroom was enormous, bigger than a two-bedroom apartment. There were two walk-in closets, two huge dressers made from solid oak, a king-size bed, two matching night tables with lamps, and three original oil paintings on the powder-blue walls. The bathroom was as large as most people's master bedrooms. There was a walk-in shower, a bathtub with air jets, a sink with a mirror surrounded by lights, and a sauna.

"Did you see me on the cover of Time Magazine again?" Diane asked.

"How could I miss it? You left it in my suitcase," John laughingly replied.

"How do I know you don't cheat on me on your trips?"

He smiled, "I'm married to the best clairvoyant in the world and I'm going to cheat on you? I think you would find out about that in five minutes flat."

"Do you remember me telling you that we were married in London in our last lives?"

"Yeah, I do. And I seem to be having flash backs. Usually

looking over a body of water and pointing."

"And about the twelve children we're going to have?"

"How could I forget that. In an age where the population of the world is actually dropping, having twelve kids would make headlines."

"And?"

"And these children were with us in our last life together as spirits."

'Well, I've got...'

John interrupted, "The only part about your prediction that I don't like is that you and the twelve children are going to change the world, but I won't be a part of it."

"Well, shit happens."

Diane then smiled and shouted, "Well, baby, it's all going to start now. I'm pregnant with triplets!"

John just stood there with a dumb look on his face and then laughed out loud. Diane and John tightly hugged each other as he thought to himself, "I'm going to be the best father in the world to all of my kids. I just know I am."

* * *

Shirley had been killed by her drunken father at age seventeen. As a spirit, she now sees her next life beginning as a baby in Diane's first set of triplets. She was named Maria and turned out to be very intelligent.

When Maria was only twelve-years-of-age, her parents were invited to her school to discuss their child. She attended a private school on East Lake Road. It was an exclusive school that took in very few pupils. It took a hefty contribution from her family to get Maria in as a student.

By this time, Maria was starting to develop into a woman. A figure like her mother's was taking shape on her tall frame. She had long black hair that curled down her back. No make up ever touched her face. Her skin colour appeared to be a white girl with a tan.

When Maria and her parents arrived at the school, they were surprised to find, not only the teacher, but also the Bishop of the Roman Catholic Diocese of Erie.

The teacher was a lady in her fifties. She was short and on the heavy side with her long grey hair tied in a bun on her head.

The bishop wore a black suit with a white collar. He was bald with white hair around the edges. He was thin and seemed to be in great shape, despite his advanced age.

After the usual formalities, they got down to business.

The teacher revealed, "As you know, Maria is a very intelligent girl. She has outgrown what we can offer her at this school. Or any other high school, for that matter. She needs the intellectual stimulus that only can be provided with post-secondary education."

Her parents knew this day was coming and were prepared for it, but they weren't prepared for what came next.

Maria revealed, "Mom, Dad, I've been going over several opportunities in various colleges and universities. I've decided that I want to attend St Peter's Seminary in London, Ontario. I want to become a Roman Catholic Priest."

Before her parents could digest what they had just heard, the bishop added, "I know them quite well at the Seminary. I went to London and talked to them about Maria. The fact that we now allow women to become priests, has increased the number of women applications. But they recognized Maria's superior intellect and will allow her to become a student there. And the youngest student ever."

Her parents were overwhelmed and just looked at each other. Her father finally remarked, "Well, I guess you're off to London, Maria."

Maria got up and hugged both parents.

After becoming a priest, Maria moved up the ladder fast. By the age of forty, she became the youngest and the only woman to ever become a cardinal. Then the current Pope died. In a big surprise that shook the world, Maria was elected as the new Pope. She took the name Pope Jeanne d'Arc.

For the last ten years, Father Timothy had been her right-hand man. Someone she could trust with her life. And that just may be the case in the Vatican.

Father Timothy was a thin man of just over five feet. He had a full head of short black hair. The white skin on his face showed a few scars from the acne in the distant past. But despite his petite appearance, he was a strong person who was active in the martial arts. He had been a priest for over thirty years and, despite the fact he was never promoted, he was extremely well-connected and held in high regard.

The Pope called Timothy to her quarters inside the Vatican. It was only one of several rooms that were hers for the rest of her life. Her quarters were centuries-old with equally old furniture inside a place that many past Popes have called home over the centuries.

The Pope was sitting in a chair when Timothy was escorted in. He knelt in front of her and kissed a ring on her finger. She nodded and the servant left, closing the door. She pointed at an old CD player.

Timothy walked over. He looked at it, trying to remember how it worked. It's been decades. Ah, yes. He picked up a CD and put it in a slot on the front. A choir singing hymns filled the room. After turning it up even higher, he sat close to the Pope. Their faces were six inches apart.

"Tim, with everything I'm about to do," the Pope explained, "I think my life will be in danger. It wouldn't surprise me that all my rooms were bugged. I think that's how they found out about Pope John Paul's plans concerning the Vatican Bank and poisoned him. There's never an autopsy, so it's a perfect crime."

Timothy asked, "Who are they?"

"I don't have any names, but these people are the establishment in the Vatican. They are the real power and they will take out any Pope they conceive as a threat."

The Pope carried on, "I want you to be close to me at all times. Bring me food and drink that I don't have to worry about. Secretly, if possible."

"I understand. What are you going to do that will upset the establishment of the church?"

Timothy's eyes widened as she replied, "I'm going to declare tomorrow in a speech broadcast around the world that the faiths of Judaism, Christianity, and Islam are the same faith that worships the same God with Abraham as the founder of all three. Then I'm going to announce a summit of leaders from all three faiths, including Protestants, and try to find common ground to form just one religion under God."

The Pope made her speech and there was wide acceptance around the world. The summit at the Vatican with the Pope as the host was a huge success. Another summit was scheduled six months down the road in Washington DC. But then tragedy struck.

The Pope and Timothy were in the Pope's quarters when the door flung open. Five men, dressed as priests, entered. The man in the lead had a steel baton. He was a short and dumpy man with a head full of short grey hair.

The Pope jumped to her feet and shouted, "How dare you..."

The priest in the lead, pointed his baton at her and interrupted, "How dare you come in here with your devilish ideas? We are just as close to the Jews and Muslims as we are to Satan. We thought that because you were young and a woman, you would be easier to control. That was our mistake and you will have to die for it."

Two men spread a large plastic sheet over the floor as the priest continued, "Our choice of death is usually poison and then blame it on a heart attack. But questions would be raised because of your young age. Therefore, you are going to have a nasty fall down those stairs. You will be dead when the servants find you in the morning. Just an accident with no investigation.

And Father Timothy, you will just disappear."

The Pope and Timothy were pushed into the centre of the plastic sheet. The priest walked up to Timothy as he was praying and hit him in the head several times. He continued to pound him as Timothy lay on the floor. Blood flew everywhere including on the priests.

Then he walked over to Pope Jeanne d'Arc, covered in blood. They looked each other in the eye. Then he raised the bloody baton and hit her on the head once. She fell to floor.

One of the priests had a stethoscope and checked her vital signs.

"She's dead," he announced.

He looked at the battered head of Timothy and remarked, "With his brains hanging out like, I'm sure he's dead."

Two men placed Timothy's body in a green garbage and dragged it down the stairs. Bump, bump, bump echoed throughout the halls.

Three men hauled the plastic sheet to the top of the stairs with the Pope still on it. Two men then picked up her body and pushed her down the stairs. She ended up in a crumpled heap on the next landing. One man then put the plastic sheet in another garbage bag, while the other two cleaned up what little blood there was in the room.

The death of Pope Jeanne d'Arc, or just plain Maria, did not stop the attempt to unify three of the world's great religions. The summit was carried out in Washington DC and another was planned. Before a new Pope was selected, all the Cardinals approved of the idea. It would take years, and its ultimate success was far from assured, but at least the ball was now rolling.

* * *

Stephen had been murdered by his father at the age of seventeen. As a spirit, he now sees his next life beginning as a baby in Diane's first set of triplets. He was named Henry.

He attended the same private school as his sister Maria, but he did not excel academically like she did. He was nothing more than an average student, but outstanding in public-speaking classes. He often gave speeches without even looking at his notes. And no. The school did not have teleprompters. Henry was over six feet tall and had a muscular build from playing football and hockey. He had short black hair and was clean-shaven.

Henry, who liked to be called Hank, was a restless teenager, but he had close ties with his father who stopped him from drifting away. His father did not have any special skills or powers like the rest of his family, but he was the one person who acted like glue to keep his family together.

Hank had no idea what his future had in store for him. But then one night, while watching a speech by a presidential hopeful with his father, he noticed something about that man. He was giving a speech without looking at his notes, just like Hank could.

Hank announced, "Dad, I'm going into politics. I can give a speech without looking at my notes like that guy can."

His father revealed, "Hank, let's think this over. That man was reading from a teleprompter."

Hank ignored the comment and set out to find a college course that would help. And, because both of his parents were registered Democrats, he joined the Young Democrats of America. He enrolled at Penn State Erie, The Behrend, which is affiliated with Pennsylvania State University. He graduated with a Bachelor of Arts degree, majoring in Political Science.

While working for the re-election of a Democratic state senator, Hank met with the campaign chairman in a back room. The room was filled with phones, T.V.s, empty coffee cups, and people wearing clothes that were wrinkled. But no one was smoking. There were very few smokers in the U.S. at this time.

The chairman was a man in his fifties, bald, and wearing a white shirt with a stain on it, and a loosened tie. Hank, however, appeared in a well-pressed black suit, a spotless white shirt, and a blue tie. When Hank entered into the room, the chairman saw him and walked over. He shook Hank's hand and lead him over to a small table in the corner.

They sat down and the chairman said, "I've had my eye on you, Hank, for a couple of years. You're a hard worker, ambitious, and you want a future in the Party. Well, I'm moving over to Washington to help in the re-election President MacDonald. If you've seen his numbers, you know that he doesn't have a chance. But that gets me into the crowd that calls the shots in the Party. And I want you to come with me. It's a great chance for you to rub shoulders with the Party elite."

Hank smiled and replied, "Where do I sign up?"

Both men laughed.

A few years later, Hank sat in the large office of the Democratic Party Chairman, Joe Johnson. Both were dressed in tailor-made dark suits, pressed white shirts, and blue ties. A dark-wooden desk stood to one side, with a well-padded chair behind it. Hank sat on a chair in front of the desk. A comfortable sofa stood against a far wall.

Johnson, sitting behind the desk, revealed, "We haven't been in the Whitehouse for twelve years. It looks like Randy Bell is going to win the nomination for us, but he's got big problems. He's old, he can't give a speech to a grade-one class without a teleprompter, and he's a lousy debater. But the Republican President is also all of those things. I think that the winner will be the ticket that has the best vice-presidential candidate."

He looked at Hank for a few seconds, pointed at him, and said, "I think you're our man. You're young, good looking, you can give a speech from memory, and you can think fast on your feet. Opportunities like this don't come along very often. What do you say?"

"Will Mr. Bell go along with this?" Hank asked.

"He knows who puts the butter on his bread. He'll do anything we tell him."

"In that case, you just got yourself a great-looking vice-presidential candidate."

Both men smiled, stood up, and shook hands.

A year after the election, Hank was awakened by his aide at Number One Observatory Circle in Washington DC. His aide knocked on his bedroom door and entered without waiting for a reply. Having never married, Hank was alone in a large nineteenth century bed. The dresser, the pictures on the white walls were all from the late nineteenth century.

Hank turned on a lamp. His aide, Amy Bright, was immaculately dressed in a dark-blue dress, blue high-heel shoes, with her long blonde hair tied in a bun on the back of her head.

"What is it, Amy?" Hank asked.

She replied, "The President has just died, sir. An apparent heart attack. A car is waiting to take you over to the Whitehouse to be sworn in. The Chief Justice of the Supreme Court is being contacted."

Hank gleefully thought to himself, 'This is the chance I've been waiting for. I can be president for eleven years.'

But he kept that to himself. He solemnly bowed his head in silence.

Then he ordered, "I won't shave or shower. Our country cannot be without a president. Time is of the essence. Just get me some casual clothes and we're gone."

On the way out the door, he disclosed, "I want live T.V. cameras at the swearing-in ceremony. Look after it, Amy. If the media looks after me, I'll look after them."

"Yes, sir. Anything else?"

"Not right now."

A few months after he was re-elected as President of the United States, Hank was having a conversation alone with Amy in the Oval Office.

Amy pointed out, "I'm going to be blunt, Mr. President. You have everything going for you. Great numbers, the economy is growing, the national debt is almost gone, and there are no wars. Now you want to throw all that away."

"I've always liked the way you speak you mind, but this is something I have to do. Those two books were written by my parents and I..."

"That's impossible. Your parents would have to be..."

"They were my parents back then and they're my parents now. It's a difficult concept to grasp."

"If you talk like that in public, you'll never win another election. Not even as a dog catcher."

The President smiled. That's why he liked Amy so much. She always spoke her mind behind closed doors, but quietly worked behind the scenes in public.

"So, you're a member of the family that's going to unite the world?"

"Exactly. Look at what my sister did, look at what..."

"Forgive me for interrupting you, Mr. President, but you're talking about our defence here."

"I know I am. Are you with me, Amy?"

"You know I am."

"Thank you. I want you to go out and twist some arms at the Pentagon. Here's the plan."

Amy took out her note pad and started to write in pencil.

The President instructed, "I want all U.S. military bases around the world to be closed this year. All navy vessels will dock in American harbours on American soil. Military aircraft will fly only in American airspace."

Hank continued, "Then I'll give a nationally televised speech in prime time from the Oval Office. I will explain the significance of those two books written by the Betts family decades ago. I will tell the world that we are all a single race called humans. And we should be united as such."

He carried on, "I will tell the world that the American military is in the process of standing down. I will offer the entire world peace and I will host a conference in Washington DC of all nations to discuss the unification of the human race."

"I think the fact that we all know now that aliens are in fact visiting Earth will help the unification process," the President added.

Amy got up to leave and looked at Hank. "I'll twist a lot of arms and I'll kick some ass. I'll even call in some favours. I'll get the military to back you. But getting the whole world to back you, that is going to be a hard sell."

* * *

JoJo, or Joseph, had been murdered by his father at the age of fourteen. As a spirit, he now sees his life beginning as a single birth after Diane's first set of triplets. They named him John Jr. after his father. Because of his size, everyone called him Junior. He was born at over thirteen pounds and gained weight up to his late teens where he tipped the scales at 320 pounds.

But he wasn't fat. Junior worked out everyday and was very muscular. At well over six feet tall, he was a natural for football. He kept his brown hair cut extremely short because it felt better inside his helmet.

He was a football standout in high school, and received a scholarship from Pennsylvania State University as a defensive lineman. He graduated with a Bachelor of Arts degree, majoring in Law and Society from the University Park campus. Junior was also drafted in the first round by the Green Bay Packers.

Junior was talking with his father on evening, in his small basement office. Whenever Junior needed to make a big decision, he always spoke with his father. His mother was busy either having babies or talking to world leaders about their future and the future of Earth.

His father's office was very small with a desk and a single chair. On the desk was an old monitor that also housed the computer. He could have easily afforded a newer and faster model, but he liked his old one. It was like an old friend. Junior was standing.

John, whose hair was now a salt-and-pepper mix, was so happy. "Well, Junior, you are almost a millionaire. All you have to do is sign on the dotted line."

Junior replied, "I'm not sure I want to play football, Dad."

John could see that Junior was troubled and asked, "What's going on, Junior?"

"I got really interested in law at Penn State and I think I may want to go to law school."

"We'll support you in any decision you make, but just keep in mind the millions that you'll be losing."

"I realize that, but it doesn't seem that important, anymore. It's almost like I'm being called from beyond to be a lawyer. Almost like a religious experience."

"I'm not surprised. Your mother has never been wrong and she always said that all of you kids would be very special. Just look at brother and sister. I think that you are also special and maybe being a lawyer will help you to somehow change the world. Who knows?"

Junior smiled and shook his father's hand. "Thanks, Dad. And by the way, we are not baby goats."

His father looked at Junior, puzzled.

Junior attended the law school at University Park. He loved law, and not being involved with football anymore, Junior excelled. He graduated near the very top of his class. There were several offers from prestigious law firms, but he chose to become a street lawyer – helping the unfortunate for whatever money they could pay. Most times it was nothing.

He had a small bachelor apartment in a run-down area of Brooklyn. It was just one room that acted as the kitchen, the living room, the bedroom, and the dining room. And there was a small bathroom that did have a shower stall. There was one small window that had a great view of an abandoned factory. His door had four separate locks and a peephole. He had a metal table and two metal chairs, a very small cupboard, a hotplate, an ironing board, and a bar fridge. The apartment was surprisingly expensive, but his parents sent him a monthly cheque by Western Union.

His apartment also served as his office where he would meet his clients. He always met his clientele with a clean well-pressed suit, a crisp white shirt, and a red-print tie. Junior only had one appointment the afternoon before Christmas. It was a 2:00 P.M. appointment with a man named Todd.

When Todd knocked at the door, Junior checked the peep-hole to make sure he was alone. Then he opened all the locks and let him in.

Junior smiled, extended his hand and said, "My name is Junior. Come in and have a seat."

Todd shook Junior's hand. Then he removed his tattered overcoat and his snow-covered boots. He took a seat at the table across from Junior.

Junior asked, "What can I do for you today?"

Todd was a young man just under thirty. He was close to six feet tall, had an unkempt black beard and wind-blown black hair. He was extremely thin, with sunken cheeks.

Todd replied, "I've fallen on hard times and I don't know where to start."

"How about the..."

"I know – the beginning."

Todd carried on, "I was a child prodigy. I had five university degrees before most people could get one. The world was at my feet. I wrote a lot, but research was what I really liked to do the best. I made some startling discoveries in my own research facilities that I never made public. Then I got in with the wrong crowd who were much older than me. They lead me around by the nose, giving me sex, drugs, and alcohol. We travelled around the country. When my money ran out, they dumped me here in New York. I've sobered up, mainly because I have no money to buy anything."

Junior revealed, "I'm sorry for you, but I'm a lawyer not the Salvation Army."

"Here's how a lawyer can help. After I sobered up, I remembered several of my research breakthroughs. But there was one idea that will change the world. I need a lawyer to put a patent on it and then to legally protect my interests when I reveal it to the world."

Junior was intrigued. "Tell me about your idea."

* * *

Gary, who was writing JoJo's tale of the future, was concerned when JoJo went silent.

He asked, "Are you here, JoJo?"

No response.

"Is JoJo here, Yvonne?" Gary questioned.

She replied, "Yes, he is."

JoJo then disclosed, "I can't see what happens next. I'm sorry, Dad."

Gary remarked, "You have nothing to be sorry for. You did really well to see into your future as far as you did. Thanks, JoJo."

JoJo smiled and left the room.

Gary enquired, "Who's next?"

Yvonne responded, "No one."

Gary was surprised, "What? We have eight more children to go."

Yvonne observed, "Gary, just look at their ages. When they were murdered; Anthony and Leigh were only seven, Oliver was five, Jason was four, Julie and Deborah were three, Gabriel was one, and Christopher was five months. Now, if JoJo is having problems at fourteen, what can these kids tell us?"

Leigh shouted, "Mom, we're not..."

"I know – baby goats," Yvonne interrupted.

Gary agreed, "Yeah, I guess you're right."

CHAPTER TWELVE

The Spirit Children

The angel Joyce had come to Yvonne and Gary one night and had told them, "We have decided that the second book you are now writing must be finished before Christmas. Keeping that deadline in mind, you will no longer take in any more spirit children. The angel Rishmond, who was sent here to help you with the new children, has already been withdrawn."

* * *

A couple of weeks after those words were spoken, while Gary and Yvonne were sleeping in their queen-size bed, Gary woke up with a funny feeling.

Their townhouse bedroom was dark. Gary was sleeping on top of the white-satin blanket and Yvonne was beside him, but she was not sleeping. Spirits do not sleep. The glow from the outdoor lights revealed a room painted in an off-white colour. A picture of a thunderstorm in the Arizona desert hung over the bed.

Gary was sixty-three years old with short grey hair and a grey moustache. He was six feet tall and weighed about 240 pounds. He only slept in his underwear.

Yvonne was forty-seven when she had died of liver cancer and was a ghostly image of her former physical self, with a little colour here and there. She was under six feet tall and had a full figure. Her long hair was premature grey. Penetrating green eyes dominated her fresh and clean face.

But Gary was unable to see her or any of the spirit children. He could, however, sense them and get a picture in his mind of what they looked like.

The feeling Gary now had was a tightness in his stomach like something was about to happen. He rolled over to the edge of the bed so that he was facing the far wall. Then he saw her in his mind. He couldn't see her with his eyes, but he knew she was standing on the floor facing him.

It was the spirit of a six-year-old white girl who was murdered by her father. She had short brown hair that was just long enough to cover the ears. The girl was under four feet tall with a thin build.

"What's your name?" Gary asked.

The girl replied, "I'm Allison. I don't know what happened, but I'm alone and scared. Some things brought me here to you. They said you would help me."

Gary could hear the sobs in her voice and could feel her body tremble with fear.

Gary promised, "We'll protect you. Nothing will happen to you here. And we have other children just like you."

Yvonne sat up and reminded Gary, "Have you forgotten what Joyce told us?"

Gary responded, "No, I haven't, and I'll probably get a visit from her for doing this. Why don't you take her to your special place?"

When Yvonne and Allison disappeared, the angel Joyce arrived. She was in the form of a solid human with long blonde hair and blue eyes. White wings had grown out of her back and she wore a long flowing white gown.

She accused Gary, "You have deliberately disobeyed me by taking in this spirit girl."

Gary declared, "I wasn't going to send her away to probably be taken to the dark side by those evil spirits. I promise you that the book will be done on time, but we will take in any spirit child that comes to us."

"I greatly admire you that you have the courage to stand up to a powerful angel so that you can save spirit children. That is a noble cause and I will not interfere with it."

"With Rishmond gone, who will take the girl to Heaven?"

"I'm just making matters worse by helping you," Joyce sighed. "Call me when she's ready and I'll take her myself."

Two days later, Yvonne and Gary decided it was time for Allison to cross over and called the angel. Joyce showed up, smiled, and took the little girl to Heaven.

* * *

A few days later, while the entire family was watching T.V. in the basement, two spirit boys arrived.

Gary and three of his youngest spirit children were sitting on a sofa against one wall watching the T.V. at the far wall. Behind the T.V. was a window that showed the wooded ravine behind the house. Beside the window was a door that led to the patio. The other spirit children were on the floor, except for five-month-old Christopher. Yvonne, sitting in a chair, was holding him.

Yvonne revealed, "Two boys just appeared. They're in front of you, Gary."

Gary could not see them, but he could sense them and see them in his mind. They were brothers who had been murdered in the United States. One appeared to be five and the other was just a year younger. They were both around three feet tall with a slender build. Their brown hair was cut short. They were standing very close to each other out of fear.

"What are your names?" Gary asked.

The oldest boy told him, but Gary could not quite make him out. This has happened in the past.

Gary assured them, "You boys can stay with us and we'll protect you. As you can see, we have children just like you."

Yvonne took the boys to her special place. Two days later, they decided that the boys were ready to go to Heaven. After calling her, Joyce appeared and gently took the boys in her arms.

Just before they left, Joyce turned to Yvonne and Gary and suggested, "You should put another chapter in this book showing how generous you two have been to the spirit children."

Then they disappeared to the other side.

* * *

While Gary was sleeping in his bed, he felt a presence and woke up.

Yvonne, who was laying beside him, revealed, "Gary, there's a boy standing on the floor on your side of the bed."

Gary could not see him, but he got a picture of him in his mind.

The boy was over four feet tall with a slim build. He had long brown hair that cascaded down his neck, stopping at his collar. His hair hid both of his ears and there were long bangs down the forehead to his brown eyes.

Gary asked, "What's your name?"

The boy, who struggled to remain calm but Gary could still hear the fear in his voice, replied, "I'm John. Some ghosts told me to come here. They said you would protect me."

"How old are you?"

"Twelve."

Gary assured him, "We will protect you. You're safe here. Do you know what happened?"

"Yeah. I was on the balcony when I got into a fight with my mother over my MP3 Player. She just spazzed out and pushed me off the balcony."

"How far down?"

"Twelve floors. I remember getting off the ground and looking at the blood all over the pavement. Seven ghosts appeared and they were worried about something. They rushed me here and said I would be safe."

Gary said, "We'll look after you. We have other children just like you. Yvonne will take you to her special place for a talk."

After they were gone, Julie appeared at his bedside. She was only three-years old when her father murdered her with a knife. She had short blonde hair, blue eyes, about three feet tall, and a chubby build. When she smiled, Gary's heart would melt. Gary hated to admit it, but, of all the eleven spirit children they had, she was his favourite. She could wrap him around her little finger.

"Dad, can I sleep with you tonight?" she asked.

He picked her up and put her on the other side of the bed.

As Gary closed his eyes, Julie enquired, "Is that boy going to be part of our family?"

Gary replied, "No. When he's ready, an angle will take him to Heaven."

"Will he watch cartoons with us?"

"Yes, he will. Now please be quiet. I need to get some sleep."

Yvonne returned later that morning and met Gary in the computer room on the second floor. It was actually a small bedroom with a desk and a chair, a tower, and a monitor. A shredder stood to one side.

She told Gary, "John is a remarkable boy. He knows what happened, he accepted it, and he's ready to cross over."

Gary was surprised. "That's really fast."

"Like I said, he's a remarkable boy."

Gary called out, "Joyce."

Joyce appeared and questioned, "Yes, Gary?"

"John is ready to be taken into Heaven," Gary disclosed.

Then he called for John who was watching cartoons with the other children downstairs. He immediately came up.

Gary pointed out, "This is an angel. Her name is Joyce and she's going to take you into Heaven. It's a good place and you'll probably meet some of your family there."

John simply said, "Thank you."

In his mind, Gary could see John hugging Yvonne. Then he could feel a tug at the back of his neck as John hugged him.

Then they disappeared.

* * *

Following Joyce's recommendation, Yvonne and myself have written this short chapter. But we did not do it to honour ourselves. This chapter is dedicated to Joyce, one of God's angels.

CHAPTER THIRTEEN

Eternal Love

Gary was in the laundry room folding clothes when Yvonne came to him. He could not see her, but he sensed her presence. He could hear her in his mind.

She said, "I don't care what the angels have said that our love is lost. I don't care what God himself has said that we will never be kindred spirits again. Gary, we are kindred spirits that can't be so easily broken. I can feel it. We will love each other for eternity."

Gary agreed, "I was thinking the same thing myself. I love you now as much as I did a hundred years ago. I've got the same feeling as you. We will be together forever."

The angel, Joyce heard this conversation and went to God. She entered his chambers and bowed before God who was sitting on his throne.

She revealed, "My Lord, I just heard Yvonne and Gary speak of their eternal love. Are they still kindred spirits?"

God disclosed, "I also heard them. And yes, they are still kindred spirits. I am pleased that the bond which holds kindred spirits together is stronger than what I had thought. Their love for each other will survive for eternity."

Joyce smiled.

CHAPTER FOURTEEN

Alice

On December 20, Gary had phoned Colleen Cook. She had been the publisher of Never Ending Publications which had agreed to publish the two books Yvonne and Gary had written. The first book already had been in the hands of her editor.

Gary was a sixty-three-year-old white man with short grey hair and a grey moustache. He stood about six feet tall and weighed in at 236 pounds. He had lost close to forty pounds since Yvonne's death by following a strict diet she had set up after passing away. He was a retired police constable. He had only come to understand and embrace the spirit world through Colleen's tutoring

Colleen was in her mid-fifties with shoulder-length hair that she had coloured blonde. She was full-figured, but had lost weight due to cancer. The doctors, however, think that the cancer is now gone. She has five university degrees and has written several books. None of the books, however, were in her own name. That's because she had shunned the spotlight. But her most amazing attribute is the gift of clairvoyance. After her death, Yvonne's spirit had said that Colleen was the best clair-voyant in the world.

"Hi Colleen," Gary had said, "The second book is now fin-ished."

"Wow, that was quick," Colleen had replied.

"Yep. Just four months for this one."

"I thought we would take time off for Christmas," Colleen suggested, "but we'll get together in the new year to discuss any changes to the first book. You and I will sit down with my Ed-itor. You can drop off the second book then."

Things, however, took an unexpected turn soon after that phone call.

*** *** ***

Gary was alone in the basement T.V. room watching *Ghost Hunters* three days before Christmas. Its walls were painted white. The T.V. was in front of the only window with a sofa and a chair at the opposite wall. A door led to the patio with a view of the wooded ravine running behind the townhouses. He was only able to watch *Ghost Hunters* when Julie was not around. She was afraid to watch it. Gary figured that Julie, only three-years-old at the time of her death, probably thought that the *Ghost Hunters* were actually hunting spirits like a hunter would hunt a deer.

Gary's spirit wife, Yvonne and his eleven spirit children were upstairs in the living room enjoying the decorations that Gary had put up for the 2010 Christmas season. He bought a white artificial tree with hundreds of white lights. He also put up decorations that Yvonne had used at her work before her death last March. And she wanted the lights tuned on in the China cabinet and the curio cabinet. And finally, there was the Santa Clause that played different Christmas tunes. Gary did not join them because Christmas was not his favourite time of year.

Gary could not see them or hear them, but he could sense spirits and see them in his mind. He was also able to converse with spirits through thoughts.

Gary could sense a different spirit standing in front of him in the basement. She was a white girl who appeared to be around twelve years old. She had stringy shoulder-length brown hair. She was thin and tall for her age. There were a few small blemishes on her cheeks.

"What's your name, honey?" Gary asked.

The child spirit replied, "I'm Alice, and I'm eleven, not twelve."

"Do you know what happened?"

"Not really. Things happened so fast. There was a lot of noise and screaming. Some ghosts brought me here. They said I would be safe."

Gary called out, "Yvonne, help me here."

Yvonne revealed, "I'm already here, Gary."

"Do you notice a difference with yourself?" Gary questioned the little girl.

"Yes. What's going on?" Alice wanted to know.

"You will be safe here," Gary assured her. "We have other children just like you upstairs celebrating Christmas. Go upstairs and join them."

After Alice went upstairs, Gary asked, "What do you think?"

"She's going to be a tough nut to crack. She might be with us until after Christmas," Yvonne replied.

"Are you going to take her to your special place and talk to her?"

"No. Maybe tomorrow. I want her to enjoy Christmas with us."

When Yvonne went upstairs to the spirit children, Gary got a partial vision of Alice's death. He saw a man in a very dark room. He could only see the man's face. It was white with a black beard. The man was holding a gun similar to the one Gary carried early in his police career. A .38 calibre revolver.

As with the other visions of murder that Gary has seen, he blocked this one, too. But he knew he could only block it so long until it flooded into his head in full colour.

When Gary went upstairs to get more beer, he could see that Alice was sitting on the sofa beside Yvonne and Julie. And Julie? Jealous Julie?

"Is something wrong, Dad?" Julie asked.

Gary responded with a smile, "No. I'm just surprised to see you sharing Mom with Alice. And I'm very pleased with you, Julie."

Julie smiled.

Alice then enquired, "Can I stay with you and Mom, Dad?"

"She's already calling us mom and dad?" Gary incredulously thought.

Yvonne jumped in. "I wouldn't mind keeping her, Gary."

Gary remarked, "You know that's impossible, Yvonne. When she's ready, Rishmond will take her to Heaven." Rishmond was an angel assigned to the Betts family to take spirit children to Heaven.

Gary got his beer and went back into the basement."

The angel Joyce, well known to the family, appeared in front of Gary. She had the solid form of a white human with long blonde hair and blue eyes. She had white wings that had grown out of her back and wore a long flowing white gown.

She declared, "Gary, Alice is very special. You will keep her and she will be part of your family in the next life."

Gary was surprised and just nodded his agreement. When Joyce disappeared, Gary went upstairs.

He disclosed, "Joyce says that Alice will stay with us and you will give birth to thirteen children in our next life, Yvonne."

Alice was so happy and Yvonne was grinning from ear to ear.

* * *

Much later, Gary saw a vision of murder. Yvonne had warned all the children not to read Gary's mind. This was a vision of the final moments of Alice's life.

A forty-two-year-old drunken man had been in a dark bedroom, lying across his double bed on his stomach. He had been wearing a white undershirt and black pants. Only grey socks had covered his feet. His long black hair had covered his ears and a full black beard had covered his face. He had been over six feet tall and had weighed over two hundred pounds. In his right hand, he had been holding a fully loaded .38 calibre revolver. It could fire six deadly bullets.

This man had just lost his job as a railroad engineer for drinking on duty. Instead of going home, he went to a bar and got even more drunk. When he finally arrived at home, he went straight to his bedroom without saying a word. Now he had made his decision.

He entered the dining room and found his family already eating supper. They were seated around a large oval table made out of solid oak. Six matching chairs stood around it. A small chandelier was centred above the table. The walls were decorated in blue gold-trimmed wallpaper. They stopped eating when he entered.

His forty-year-old wife sat at the head of the table. She was a white woman with long brown hair done up in a bun on her head. She wore tan slacks and a white blouse. She was thin on a five-foot, six-inch frame.

His son was seventeen years old and was seated at the side of the table. He had short brown hair and a muscular build. He was wearing blue shorts and a blue T-shirt.

His only other child was Alice who sat across the table from her brother. She was wearing very tight white shorts and a tight white shirt that revealed her small breasts.

"Why didn't you call me for supper?" the man growled.

They all noticed that he was drunk and that he was holding a gun.

His wife softly replied, "I just wanted you to get some rest."

"You mean to sleep it off," he shot back.

The man continued, "I just lost my job. I'm into debt up to my eyeballs. I've had it!"

He put the gun to his own head when his son unwisely jumped his father. The two females started to scream. The man threw his son unto the table, knocking plates and silverware all over the place. As the boy landed hard on the table, his left shoe hit his sister in the head. Alice fell semi-consciously to the floor.

She could hear her mother's screams, but she could not move.

Then two shots had rang out. The mother had screamed at the death of her son and then in terror as the gun had been pointed at her. Two more shots had stopped her screams. The man had then walked over to Alice and killed her with a single bullet into her foggy mind. Then the man had ended his own life with a single shot inside his mouth.

* * *

Yvonne, Gary, and their twelve spirit children had a great Christmas. The younger children got toys. The three older children and their parents, however, got nothing. Gary cooked up a great turkey dinner. The lights on the Christmas tree and carols from the Santa Claus figure played well into the night. And they watched only Christmas shows on T.V.

Gary had bought some whisky and wine at Yvonne's insistence. She wanted to experience Christmas as she had remembered it. He drank some of the wine at dinner. Then he mixed some whisky and water, the way Yvonne had drunk it during her life. He took a drink and grimaced at the taste. But he managed to finish the bottle the way she wanted.

Shirley and JoJo wanted some of Gary's drink. Yvonne agreed that the three older children could have a sip, but Stephen refused.

Then Yvonne took a sip and commented, "I use to drink mine a lot stronger than that."

Before he had too much to drink, Gary even danced for everyone while they were watching the Nutcracker ballet in the living room. He danced to the "Waltz of the Flowers" on the floor in front of them. He couldn't help himself. He had to dance every time he had heard that music. Everyone was sitting on the sofa and the love seat while he performed for about six minutes or so. They were all laughing and clapping their hands. They loved the unexpected entertainment.

Then disaster struck on Boxing Day. Early in the morning while everyone was in the living room of their townhouse, Gary could sense that Alice was missing.

He asked, "Where's Alice?"

Shirley, his older black spirit daughter replied, "She's gone, Dad."

Gary was shocked. "Gone where?"

"Rishmond took her to Heaven."

Gary called out to the Angel, "Rishmond!" There was no response.

Gary later tearfully phoned Colleen, "Rishmond took Alice to Heaven. I didn't tell him to do that and now he won't answer me. I think she's gone."

Colleen tried to reassure Gary, "They just took her so she could learn a few lessons she missed because of her death. She'll be back."

When Yvonne and the children returned from their daily trip to Heaven, Yvonne revealed, "I saw Alice up there. She's a very special girl, and the angels are just preparing her for her next life with us. She'll be back soon."

Two days later, Gary was watching *Ghost Hunters* alone in the basement T.V. room. The rest of the family were up in the living room enjoying the Christmas lights and music, when a spirit appeared in front of Gary. He was very happy to see that it was Alice.

Gary said, "It's nice to have you back, Alice."

Alice replied, "It's nice to be back, Dad. I missed all of you."

"We all missed you. Especially me."

"I know."

"Why did Rishmond take you to Heaven?"

"I'm not sure. It was sort of like going back to school."

"Can I stay with you, Dad?" Alice asked.

"No. I'm watching *Ghost Hunters*. You know how this program scares Julie. I don't want you to be frightened. Go up stairs with the rest of the family."

When she left, Gary called out, "Rishmond."

The angel replied, "Yes, Gary."

"Thanks for bringing Alice back home. But why did you just take her without letting us know?"

"I was just obeying a command. Alice is more special than you can now imagine, but it will become abundantly clear with your family in the next life. You're going to have a remarkable family in remarkable times."

Then Gary remembered something that the angel Joyce had told Yvonne's spirit when Yvonne had recently gone to Heaven with concerns about Gary's health.

Joyce had said, "Things keep changing for him in the Universe. I don't know why."

Gary then questioned, "As an angel, Rishmond can you control the changes in the Universe?"

Rishmond replied, "No angel can."

"Can God control the changes in the Universe?"

"No."

"Thank you, Rishmond."

When Rishmond vanished, Alice reappeared. "I want to stay with you, Dad. I'm older and it won't scare me like Julie."

"Okay. Have a seat," Gary agreed.

As she sat beside him on the sofa, Gary said, "You let me know if the show frightens you. Okay?"

"Okay."

Then Julie called down, "Is Alice sitting beside you, Dad? That's my spot."

She was a three-year-old girl who got so jealous when her father was concerned.

Gary patiently answered, "When you come down, Julie, you can have your spot back."

"I'm coming down now."

"I'm not turning off *Ghost Hunters*. Just wait until it's over."

"Okay," Julie grudgingly agreed.

Afterword

There you have it. Heaven as seen through the eyes of a spirit named Yvonne Betts, who crossed over into Heaven on March 2, 2010. This book not only gives you her own experiences in Heaven, but also those of an angel named Joyce and a spirit/angel named Rouj. These two shared their own personal knowledge as well as revealing secrets. All of this was made possible with the approval of God himself.

Keep in mind that Heaven is the true and only home for all of our spirits. One day, your soul will return to that magical place to maybe begin a new life. And there is nothing to fear. When a physical body dies, we should all rejoice and not cry at their good fortune in returning to Heaven. And rest assured that God will not judge your soul based on your last life. All spirits who choose to do so will be admitted into Heaven without question. And contrary to what several religions preach, there is no hell and there is no devil.

I feel privileged to be able to write the foreword and the afterword to this book. Although the cover lists me as a co-author, I had nothing to do with this book except to actually type the words. Yvonne, with the help of angels and spirits in Heaven, is the real author. But I had to be recorded as a co-author because Yvonne is ineligible to collect the royalties. Something about having a living body.

You also have been given the opportunity to get a quick look at Earth's future in Chapter 11. This chapter was not even part of the thought process that conceived this novel. It came at the last minute when Yvonne decided to share with our loyal readers a brief picture of what lies ahead through the eyes of three of our spirit children.

And finally, and I only hope it is finally, Yvonne and myself have unexpectedly added Chapter 14 to announce a new addition to our spirit children. Alice is her name and she will be a welcome addition to our huge family in our next life together. As always, however, having visions of murder always makes me physically and mentally tired.

Yvonne and I thank all of those who have read this book. Whether you believe in it or not, it is just a matter of faith. But mark my words that everything you have read here is true. It gives you an accurate picture of Heaven and its occupants that will be confirmed the day your physical body dies and your spirit crosses over into that eternal place we call Heaven.

Gary Betts